BREAKING WITH TRADITION

Sidestone Press

BREAKING WITH TRADITION

Cultural influences for the decline of the Circum-Alpine region lake-dwellings

BENJAMIN JENNINGS

Published by Sidestone Press, Leiden
www.sidestone.com

ISBN 978-90-8890-275-8

Lay-out & cover design: Sidestone Press
Photograph cover: Mountain Panorama Photo: Dachstein, Austria, © Jakubcejpek | Dreamstime.com; Drawing based on reconstruced pile dwelling from Pfahbau Museum Unteruhldingen/Bodensee, Germany

Preface and Acknowledgements

The research presented here forms part of a doctoral thesis submitted to the University of Basel, Switzerland in September 2013. Under the Swiss National Science Foundation project "The end of the lake-dwelling phenomenon; cultural vs. environmental change" led by Professor Francesco Menotti at the University of Basel (2009-2013), a multi-disciplinary research team began to address the issue of cultural influences in the abandonment of the lakeshore and decline of the tradition of establishing lake-dwellings in the northern Circum-Alpine region during the final stages of the Late Bronze Age and beginning of the Iron Age. As part of this research, an extensive assessment of material culture as indicators for exchange and communication routes flowing through the northern Alpine region during the Late Bronze Age was undertaken. Results of this analysis have been published elsewhere, and a summary is provided here, while the contributions from other members of the project have been summarily presented in the book *The end of the lake-dwellings in the Circum-Alpine region* (ed. F Menotti). The main focus of this volume is in linking the material indicators of exchange networks to social changes within the lake-dwelling settlements, and the construction of narratives linking such cultural developments to the decision to abandon a tradition of settlement construction which had endured for over 3500 years. Previous interpretations have focussed on the role of climatic fluctuation as a driving factor in the abandonment of the lake-dwellings, but one of the key elements highlighted by present day research on human induced climatic change is that cultures and societies are resilient and do not lightly abandon traditions or settlements.

There are many people and bodies who facilitated the production of this volume. Firstly I must thank Karsten Wentink and Corné van Woerdekom of Sidestone Press, for their patience and guidance in the preparation of this manuscript and the images. The financial support of the Swiss National Science Foundation is gratefully acknowledged, and without this it would not have been possible to undertake the research.

Francesco Menotti was an extremely supportive, encouraging and insightful supervisor for my PhD, and I am eternally in his debt for the advice and guidance which he provided, and not least for his suggestions and corrections on several draft manuscripts for this volume. Philipp Wiemann proved a sounding board for many of the principles discussed throughout the volume, and provided many a mind-relieving coffee break.

All of the maps presented in this volume were created using ArcGIS 10 with SRTM (© NASA, NGA, USGS EROS, ESRI) and GTOPO30 (© USGS EROS, ESRI) background data and River, Lake, and Country Border overlays (© ArcWorld). All data is available on the ESRI® Data & Maps 9.3 Media Kit, and SRTM and GTOPO30 data are freely available for download on the internet.

Some of the images used in the volume have been kindly supplied by the Historisches Museum Basel, Swiss National Museum in Zurich, Amt für Archäologie Thurgau, the department of Unterwasserarchäologie Zürich - Amt für

Städtebau, and the Eidgenössisches Archiv für Denkmalpflege – Swiss National Library. I am very grateful for their permission to reproduce the images here.

Without listing individuals, because I am likely to forget someone, I would like to extend a thank you to all of those people, they know who they are, who have engaged with me in inspiring discussions, or facilitated in some way the completion of the research contained herewith: thank you! Members of the Institute for Prehistoric and Archaeological Science at the University of Basel provided useful conversations, and made me aware of numerous sites to be included in the study, as did the Archaeological service of the Canton of Bern. I wholeheartedly thank Katrina Jennings for her patience, support, and willingness to relocate (again …) so that I could undertake my PhD research. Your support is truly appreciated, and I hope you think it was worth it. I am also very grateful to my parents for their continued and unstinting support.

Ben Jennings, June 2014

Contents

List of figures

List of tables

Chapter 1

Introduction

The prehistoric lake-settlements of the Circum-Alpine region are well discussed in archaeological literature, and well known to the general public. In fact, the recent ascription of UNESCO World Heritage Status to a collection of lake-settlements in Austria, France, Germany, Italy, Slovenia and Switzerland (Suter and Schlichtherle 2009) has introduced these sites to a new audience and led to the embracement of new technologies in the presentation of cultural heritage (e.g. the creation of a "Palafittes Guide" App: Palafittes 2011; Texetera 2011). These lake-dwellings typically have excellent levels of organic preservation, not only for structural timber elements, but also for macrobotanical and archaeozoological remains, in addition to various small finds including worked timber, bark containers, textiles and remains of fishing nets and equipment (e.g. Médard 2011; Menotti 2012: Chapter 4) (Figure 1.1, Figure 4.7). Although lacustrine villages have received a considerable level of academic interest, they are not the only form of settlement or archaeological site to be encountered in Circum-Alpine region; hoards, burials, cemeteries, lowland, hilltop, and fortified settlements are, as with other areas of Europe, present throughout the region. However, such sites rarely match their wetland contemporaries in terms of quantities of finds or quality of preservation. There has, to some extent, been a relative over representation of lake-dwellings compared to other sites in some regions – particularly Switzerland – which can be seen as a result of the explosion of interest in lake-dwelling research during the 19th century (the *Pfahlbaufieber*, see Kaeser 2013; Menotti 2012: 3-4).

Considerable levels of research have been conducted on individual lake-dwellings, including highly accurate dendrochronological studies, which has permitted the establishment of relatively secure phases of lakeshore occupation (e.g. Benkert and Egger 1986; Billamboz 2009; Bleicher 2009; Leuzinger 2000; cf. Menotti 2012: 260-63). Such individual studies, and site bridging comparisons, have demonstrated that far from being a continuous form of settlement, several periods of lakeshore abandonment occurred. These periods of abandonment are typically seen as the result of climatic decline, but it is notable that following a return to more favourable climate the lakeshore was re-occupied and the lake-dwelling tradition continued. However, following a climatic decline during the Late Bronze Age, the lakeshore was abandoned and not re-occupied in the form of lake-dwelling construction. This volume presents an alternative hypothesis to the climatically deterministic – or prioritized – model of abandonment, instead focussing on the role of indigenous cultural change drawing influence from communities' participation in inter-regional exchange routes.

Figure 1.1: Waterlogged conditions at the lake-settlements create excellent preservation conditions. Even though many of the Late Bronze Age settlements have suffered erosion of the upper layers, remarkable organic materials have been well preserved, for instance this in-situ wicker basket from Zurich-Alpenquai (broadly 1050-800 BC, see Künzler Wagner 2005). (Photograph © and courtesy of Unterwasserarchäologie Zürich, Amt für Städtebau).

The remainder of this chapter will provide an introductory overview to the region of study from a geographical, archaeological, cultural and chronological perspective, and also detail the issue of intermittent lake-dwelling hiatuses and final abandonment at the Late Bronze Age and early Iron Age transition. Chapter Two provides a background to the theoretical principles used in the research and development of the cultural change model, before Chapters Three and Four address trans-European exchange routes during prehistory, and specifically the position of the lake-dwelling communities of the northern Alpine region in those exchange routes and the identification of changing cultural practices and attitudes from material remains. Chapter Five addresses the settlement dynamics in the northern Alpine forelands, before Chapter Six draws upon burial and artefact deposition evidence as a method of interpreting changing cultural and ritualistic practices between the Bronze and Iron Age. Chapters Seven and Eight then combine all of the evidence to produce a narrative leading to the demise of the lake-dwelling tradition in the early Iron Age and a consideration of future research prospects.

1.1 The Circum-Alpine region

The Circum-Alpine region, with the Alpine mountain range forming its spine, covers a strip of central Europe extending from south-eastern France to Slovenia (Figure 1.2). Constrained by the valleys of the rivers Po, Rhône, Rhine and Danube, the Circum-Alpine region covers a variety of different landscapes and environments in Austria, France, Germany, Italy, Slovenia and Switzerland. This study is primarily focussed on the northern Circum-Alpine region – namely eastern France, southern Germany, and, primarily in this study, Switzerland – and ranges from the Central Alps to the northern Plateau and French Jura (Figure 1.2). Reaching heights of over 4800 metres, and with an average height of c. 2000 metres, the Alps superficially appear to have posed a formidable barrier between the regions to the north and south. However, it is well known from archaeological evidence that interaction was occurring across the Alpine passes throughout prehistory (e.g. Köninger and Schlichtherle 2001; Spindler 2001). Likely routes of interaction and traversal points include the Val d'Adige and Valle d'Aosta (Bietti Sestieri 1997) and the San Bernardino, St. Gotthard and Simplon passes (Della Casa 2007; Pearce 1995).

Although lakes do occur in the central (mountainous) Alpine area, these are primarily small in surface area and were not selected for occupation by the lake-dwelling communities – possibly due to climatic considerations related to their high

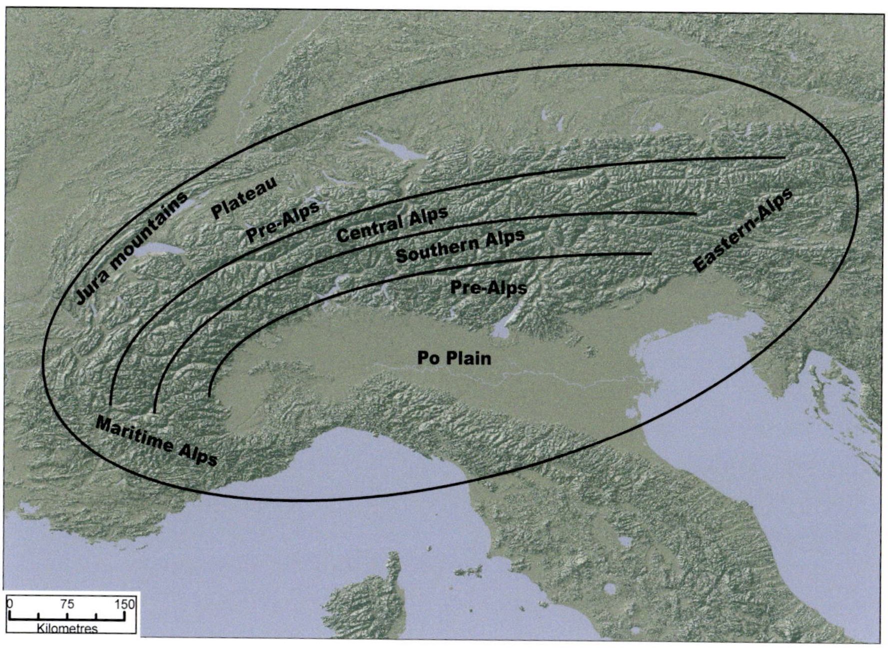

Figure 1.2: Definition of areas in the Circum-Alpine region. The Alpine region is not only about mountains; the Pre-Alps area covers broad swathes of foothills and plateau flatlands.

altitude limiting agricultural production and freezing during the winter months. The larger lakes of the Swiss plateau, and the pre-alps in France, Germany, and Switzerland were, however, intensively used for settlement (see maps in Suter and Schlichtherle 2009). Water levels in these lakes are related to both the prevailing climate, with generally increased levels during the spring and summer months as water is released from snow and ice fields in the mountains, and the balance between the lake inflow and outflow (Magny 1992; Menotti 2001a: 121-22). Indeed, several of the lakes are directly connected to major riverine systems, such as Lake Constance to the Rhine and Lake Geneva to the Rhône, while others form water basins in tributaries of the larger river systems, such as Lake Zurich and Lake Neuchâtel. Connection, either direct or tributary, to larger river systems was not a precondition for the establishment of a lake-settlement, as can be seen by those on Lake Feder (Federsee Moor, Southern Germany), Lake Nussbaum and Lake Greifen (both in Switzerland), which are not only comparatively small lakes, but lack significant in- or out-lets.

The modern climate system of the Circum-Alpine region is primarily temperate, but can be furthered refined into broad prevailing schemes for specific regions, for instance "dry" in the "Inner Alpine Valleys" and "cold and wet" in the "External Northern Alps" (Aeschimann and Guisan 1995). Palaeoclimatic indicators suggest that the prehistoric climate of the Circum-Alpine region should be seen against a background of rapid climate fluctuations throughout the Holocene, with a particularly significant period of cooling between 3500 and 2500 cal. BP (Mayewski *et al.* 2004). Palaeoclimatic reconstruction in the Alps can be traced back to the 1960s and 1970s with researchers such as Patzel (1977), Schindler (1971), and Zoller (1977), and has continued in recent years, particularly through the work of Magny (e.g. 1992, 2004a; 2013b). Such reconstructions have addressed the past 10,000 years, but the most relevant period for this study is that covering the Subboreal and Subatlantic (respectively 4700-2700 cal. BP and 2700 cal. BP-present, Magny 1995: 48). It has been argued that the Subboreal began with a relatively mild climate, with favourable conditions between c. 4400 and 3600 cal. BP, but ended with the coldest phase of the post glacial era, featuring glacial advance, increased precipitation, and lowering treelines through the Circum-Alpine region (e.g. Burga 1988, 1991; Gamper 1981; Magny 2004b; Magny *et al.* 1998; Renner 1982; Van Geel and Magny 2002). The beginning of the Subatlantic was marked by a brief period of climatic improvement, but dendrochronology suggests that this was relatively brief and followed by further cold phases, glacial advance, and depressed treelines from c. 2700 to 2490 cal. BP, with a brief warm phase between 2640 and 2570 cal. BP (Holzhauser *et al.* 2005; Van Geel *et al.* 1996). From 2490 cal. BP the prevailing climatic system has been dominated by fluctuations, but tended towards cooler conditions than those of the Subboreal (e.g. Leemann and Niessen 1994). Dendroclimatology has provided further indications of climatic fluctuation during the Late Bronze Age, particularly a prolonged decline during the early Iron Age (c. 800-750 BC) with a return to more favourable conditions from the final quarter of the 8th century BC (Billamboz 2003), a model which finds further support from peat profiles and glacial retreat markers (Hormes *et al.* 2001; Roos-Barraclough *et al.* 2004).

One of the effects of these periods of climatic fluctuation was to influence the water level of lakes throughout the Alpine region, with colder/wetter and warmer/drier periods increasing and decreasing water levels (Magny 2004b; Magny *et al.* 2009; Maise 1999). The influence of present day climate and weather systems on northern Alpine lakes can be seen through the annual records maintained by regional authorities (Menotti 2001a: 131). Such studies have highlighted that the lake volume relies upon a complex system, including precipitation levels, and is also dependent upon the "sensitivity" of the specific lake in question (Magny 1992). Amongst other factors, it is the sensitivity of lakes to variations in water input which makes broad – Alpine wide – schemes of lake-level heightening or depression difficult to establish and correlate (cf. Bleicher 2013; Magny 2013a).

1.1.1 Archaeology

As mentioned previously, there is a wide range of prehistoric sites present in the northern Circum-Alpine region, but a quick review of the data presented in overviews of Bronze Age archaeology in Switzerland (e.g. Hochuli *et al.* 1998) demonstrates the high representation of lake-dwellings compared to other forms of sites. The first investigation of a lake-dwelling on Lake Zurich, conducted by Ferdinand Keller (Keller 1854), began a period of intense interest in lake-settlements within Switzerland, and across Europe as a whole (see Menotti 2004c). Unfortunately this interest, in some instances, rapidly degenerated to treasure hunting and the un-systematic recovery of artefacts from the lakebed (Altorfer 2004a, b; Leuzinger 2010: 86-89; Menotti 2004c). Subsequent legislation and protection, and the development of archaeology as a scientific discipline improved the situation dramatically, and excavations began to be conducted on a methodical and investigative basis, not only of those on the lakeshore, but also in other wetland environments (e.g. Wasserburg-Buchau, Germany (Reinerth 1928)). During the latter half of the 20th century several major water level maintenance and road building projects led to the discovery of a number of lake-settlements across Switzerland (Menotti 2001a; Ruoff 2006). Discoveries are in fact still being made, with the recent construction of a new car park for the Zurich Opera House (where previous construction was also responsible for the discovery of the well-known site Zurich-Mozartstrasse during the 1980s (Gross *et al.* 1987; Schmidheiny 2006)) revealing the remains of a large multi-phase settlement (Bleicher *et al.* 2011).

The database of the recent UNESCO World Heritage Status application listed approximately 1000 lake-dwellings from the Circum-Alpine region (of which 111 were proposed for and subsequently awarded World Heritage Site status), many of which are accurately dated through dendrochronology and/or radiocarbon dating (Palafittes 2010; Suter and Schlichtherle 2009). However, the history of lake-dwelling research and application of investigative techniques is not homogenous across the entire Alpine region, and variation can be seen between different countries and areas (see Menotti 2001a; Menotti 2004c).

Archaeological evidence suggests that some lakes, such as Lake Feder, were seasonally occupied or exploited during the Mesolithic, but it is not until the Neolithic that the first 'lake-dwellings' were constructed in the northern Alpine region (e.g. Egolzwil, c. 4300 BC (CH, Vogt 1951)). A currently accepted hypothesis suggests that the establishment of lake-settlements occurred under the influence of communities from southern Europe. This proposal is connected to the occurrence of the so-called 'lake-dwelling wheat' (*triticum durum/turgidum*), which is of Mediterranean origin and in addition to a presence in the Iberian peninsula and central Italy has been found in many lake-settlements in the Alpine (northern and southern) region from the sixth Millennium BC (Menotti 2004b; Schlichtherle 1997). At the opposite end of the lake-dwelling tradition, the youngest known settlement is that of Ürschhausen-Horn, with a final occupation in the seventh century BC (Gollnisch-Moos 1999). Over 3500 years separate the first and last lake-dwellings in the northern Alpine region, but the tradition of occupying wetland environments was far from continuous. In fact, a number of hiatuses, when lake-settlements were not constructed, occurred between the Neolithic and the Late Bronze Age / Iron Age transition (Gross and Ritzmann 1990; Menotti 2001a).

1.1.1.1 Lake-dwelling hiatus

Broad lake-dwelling hiatuses occurred in the northern Circum-Alpine region in the Neolithic (N) between c.3550 and 3400 BC, during the Early Bronze Age (EBA) between c. 2400 and 2100 BC, in the Middle Bronze Age (MBA) between 1500 and 1100 BC, in addition to the final abandonment at c. 800 to 600 BC (Figure 1.3). The southern Alpine region was not exempt from these periods of lakeshore abandonment, and though the current lack of dendrochronological dating in the region makes identification of such hiatuses more difficult, it is clear that the lake-dwelling tradition there declined earlier than its counterpart in the north, culminating during the 12th century cal. BC (De Marinis 2009; Menotti 2004a).

One of the main influences proposed for the abandonment of the lakeshore, both north and south of the Alps, is that climatic change directly or indirectly affected the settlements, making continued occupation impossible, as has been proposed for

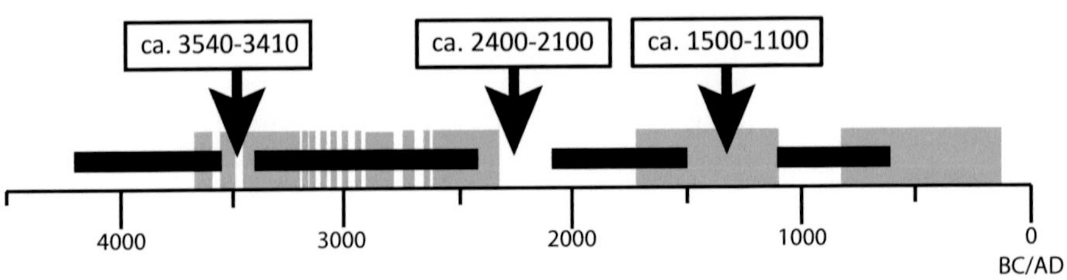

Figure 1.3: Periods of lake-dwelling occupation in the northern Circum-Alpine region. Phases of occupation (black bar) have been compared – and inferred as correlating with – periods of higher lake water level (blue bar) (data from Magny et al. 1998: Fig.46; after Menotti In Press: Fig. 1.5).

the MBA hiatus (Menotti 2001a, 2003, 2004a). Direct effects of climatic change could be the inundation of settlements located in liminal wetland locations, i.e. climatic deterioration leading to lake water level increase and settlement flooding. Conversely, indirect influences may have been felt through the loss of economic sustainability, i.e. climatic decline caused flooding in the lake hinterland removing potential agricultural areas, or cooler/wetter conditions meant that sufficient crops could not be produced for the comparatively, when contemporary inland sites are considered, large and high population density settlements (see Arbogast *et al.* 2006). The effects of indirect climatically induced stresses can occasionally be observed in the material culture of lake-dwelling communities (e.g. Gross-Klee and Schibler 1995; Schibler and Chaix 1995: 117-18). It is also possible that cultural factors influenced the decline of lake-dwelling occupation, as has been suggested for the 2500 – 2000 BC hiatus (Magny 1995, 2004b; Menotti 2001a: 118). In spite of the high quantity and standard of environmental reconstruction undertaken in the northern Alpine region, it is imperative that climatically deterministic models are not adopted uncritically and without thorough interrogation of the available data (cf. Bleicher 2013) at the expense of attempting the identification of cultural factors in the social choice to occupy specific environmental locales (cf. De Marinis 2009; Leary 2009). It is however, essential to remember that any form of determinism is an over simplification, and many factors combined to influence past social dynamics (Walsh 2014: 4), and it is not the intention to suggest that climate did not play a role in the abandonment of lake-dwellings, but rather to introduce other factors to the mix instead of following a primarily mono-causal explanation.

Direct and indirect effects of climatic fluctuation may not have been significant enough to cause the abandonment of the lake-dwelling tradition across the entire Circum-Alpine region, particularly given the varying sensitivity of lakes to varying levels of precipitation (see above) and uncertain synchronicity of lake-level changes across the region (cf. Bleicher 2013). The widespread abandonment may also have required some cultural influence, with the effects felt by a small minority of sites communicated through local and interregional exchange networks attaching a stigma to the occupation of wetland locations and ultimately leading to the abandonment of sites unaffected by the climatic fluctuations. Such a scenario has been proposed by Menotti for the Middle Bronze Age hiatus (Menotti 2001a). The influence of 'negative' attitudes and perceptions of an area in the face of climatic and environmental change have recently been illustrated by Leary (2009) through discussion of the early 20th century abandonment of Holland Island (Chesapeake Bay, Maryland, USA) as a result of sea level rise, which created negative attitudes towards the future of the island, despite the fact that the island remained habitable for significantly longer (see also Arenstam Gibbons and Nicholls 2006). After the MBA hiatus (i.e. from 1200 BC onwards) lakes were re-occupied across the Circum-Alpine region, although the number of lake-dwellings never reached the level of the earlier occupations, and they began to disappear at the very end of the Bronze Age (9th – 8th century BC).

Smaller, localized hiatuses also occurred, such as between 3540 and 3410 BC in the northern Alpine region, representing the abandonment of specific lakes or regions. Influences for short-term abandonment could again be climatic and/or cultural. The brevity of abandonment may suggest a greater climatic influence as opposed to cultural. For instance short term exoduses could be caused by rising lake levels, with an immediate return once the lake levels were stabilized. However, some of these short abandonments occurred during favourable climatic periods (Hafner and Suter 2000). There are also instances where wetlands were occupied during unfavourable climatic conditions, such as between 3700 and 3500 BC and – particularly in western Switzerland – during the 34th century BC (Menotti 2009: 62), suggesting that the link between a positive or negative climate and lake-dwelling occupation is not always conclusive (Magny 2004a, b; Pétrequin and Bailly 2004). The synchronicity of lake water level changes across the northern Alpine region has recently been debated (Bleicher 2013), creating further doubt as to how accurate a climatically driven abandonment model is for the whole region.

The long-term tradition of lake-dwellings in the Circum-Alpine region masks the transitory nature of individual lake-dwelling occupations. For instance, the Zurich-Mozartstrasse site shows cultural occupation over 24 centuries between the Neolithic and the Late Bronze Age, with at least 15 phases of occupation and hiatuses (Conscience 2001; Gross *et al.* 1987; Schmidheiny 2006). The site of Zurich-Kleiner Hafner (Suter *et al.* 1987), covers a period from the 4th to 2nd millennium BC, with five distinct phases of settlement and occupation. Shorter cycles of abandonment and re-occupation also occurred, for example at Bodman-Schachen 1 (Lake Constance, D (Köninger 2006)). Some settlements, for instance Unteruhldingen-Stollenwiesen (D (Schöbel 1992)), Cortaillod-Est/-Plage/-Les Esserts (CH (Arnold 1986)) and Auvernier-Nord (CH (Arnold 1983)), were re-occupied, but underwent a spatial shift, and were gradually moved with each phase of re-occupation and new building activity. This may be indicative of changing climatic conditions and the lake water level, as settlement structures were relocated to shallower areas less likely to experience inundation in the event of lake water rise. In a process similar to that described by Menotti (2001a, 2003, 2004a), when faced with rising lake water levels, communities may have relocated to safer areas of the shoreline, but without severing their ancestral and traditional links to the lake. There are also lake-dwellings which show only a single short occupation, such as Arbon-Bleiche 3 (Jacomet *et al.* 2004; Leuzinger 2000, 2001) and Greifensee-Böschen (see section 5.2.2). These settlements are interesting as they may represent a brief attempt by a community to access traditional and ancestral links or legitimization through the construction and occupation of lake-dwellings (see section 2.3).

The wide spread occurrence of the lake-dwelling tradition across the Circum-Alpine region suggests that there was cultural homogeneity throughout the region. However, the material cultural evidence does not support this; instead, the Circum-Alpine region consisted of a patchwork of many different cultural groupings and societies (see section 2.1).

1.1.1.2 The Late Bronze – Early Iron Age abandonment

While some consideration has been given to *why* lake-dwellings were *constructed* and inhabited (e.g. Coles and Coles 1992; Menotti and Pranckėnaitė 2008; Pétrequin and Bailly 2004), a more interesting question to address is *why* were the lake-dwellings *abandoned?* Both cultural and climatic factors have been argued for the abandonment of the lake-dwellings. For instance, the climatic interpretation has been favoured for the Middle Bronze Age (see also Magny *et al.* 2009; Menotti 2001a; Van Geel and Magny 2002), but, as far as the final abandonment of the lake-dwellings is concerned, at c. 800-600 BC, in the northern Circum-Alpine region and c. 1200 BC in northern Italy (De Marinis 2009), cultural factors have probably played a more significant role. In fact, although the beginning of the Iron Age was marked by a slight climatic deterioration, that period was also followed by several phases of favourable lake water levels (e.g. Härke 1979: 32, 65; Pétrequin and Bailly 2004: 40-44). Further disagreement concerning the climatically driven abandonment of the lake-dwellings is provided by the assertion that "... the Late Holocene appears to be punctuated by two major phases of higher lake level at 1550-1150 and 800-400 BC ... and two periods of pronounced lowering at 1150-800 and 250-600 BC." (Holzhauser *et al.* 2005: 795-96, Fig. 4). The exact period when lake-dwellings were being abandoned across the northern Alpine region appears to correspond to a prolonged period of prolonged higher lake levels, but the gradual decline in the occupation of such sites began during the period of lower levels up until 800 BC (but cf. Bleicher 2013).

The Bronze Age to Iron Age transition in Europe is a complex time period, which can, in many respects, be seen as the expansion of cultural systems and processes that existed during the Late Bronze Age (Thurston 2009: 351). While this is not the place to conduct an analysis of the European Bronze Age to Iron Age transition (see Ruoff 1974; Sørensen 1987; Thurston 2009), it is evident that Late Bronze Age (LBA) and early Iron Age (EIA) cultures of the Circum-Alpine region gradually rejected a tradition of lake-dwelling occupation in favour of open lowland and upland settlements, fortified hilltop sites, and later princely residences or *Fürstensitze* (Benkert *et al.* 1998; Härke 1979, 1989).

As previously mentioned, the last lake-dwelling in the Alpine region to be abandoned was Ürschhausen-Horn, with occupation during the latter half of the 9th century BC, followed by an occupational break of roughly 130 years, before being finally abandoned by 630 BC (Billamboz and Gollnisch 1998; Gollnisch-Moos 1999). Unlike the MBA hiatus (see above) the LBA/EIA abandonment process occurred over an extended period of time, with lake-dwellings gradually being abandoned and not reoccupied. In the northern Circum-Alpine region this long phase of abandonment can be seen to have begun immediately following the MBA hiatus, as many former lake-dwelling sites were never re-occupied, and the number of lake-dwellings known within the Circum-Alpine region are significantly less after the MBA hiatus than before (Magny 2004b: Fig. 4; Magny and Peyron 2008). Clearly there is a significant reduction in the number of lake-dwelling sites that were occupied during the early Iron Age, i.e. Ürschhausen-Horn (Lake Nussbaum), when compared to the number occupied during the Late

Bronze Age (see Palafittes 2010). A number of the Late Bronze Age settlements show no indication of previous site occupation such as Greifensee-Böschen (CH) and Konstanz-Raue (D), and others, such as Steckborn and Kreuzlingen (Lake Constance) and Mörigen (CH), show re-occupation from the Neolithic or Early Bronze Age.

1.2 Chronologies and cultures

Aspects of the northern Alpine cultural chronology have already been mentioned in the discussion of lake-dwelling abandonments, and indeed the construction of these chronologies have benefitted extensively from the availability of dendrochronological dates from lake-settlements. Despite the highly variable – over short periods – regional chronologies within the northern Alpine area (see

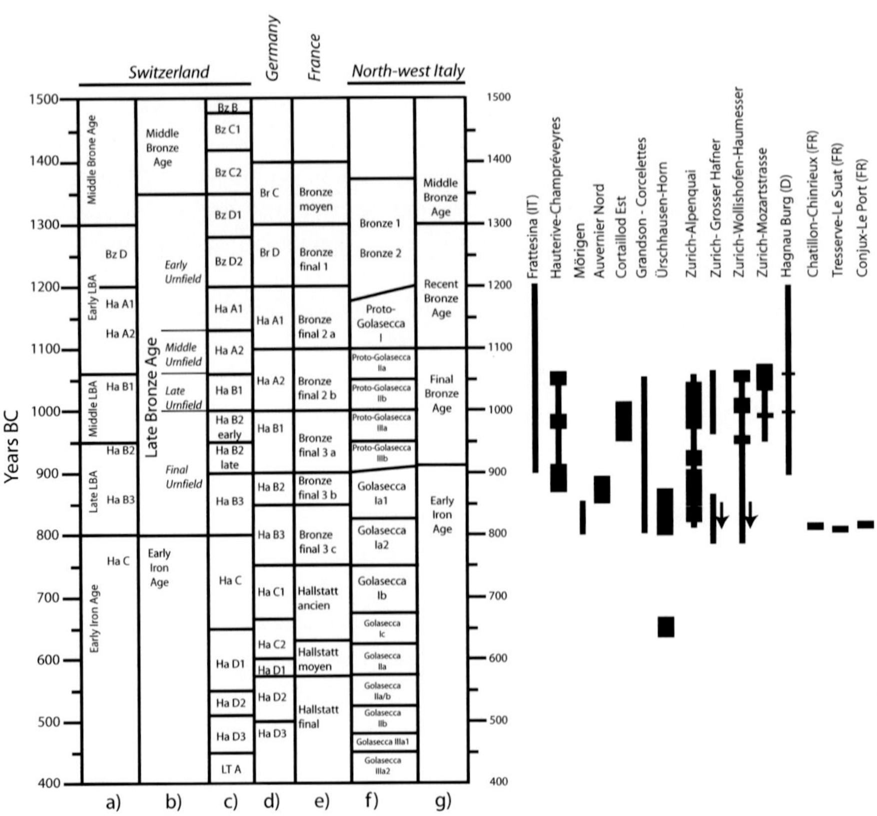

Figure 1.4: Different chronological systems used in the primary regions of study. Data from: a) Seifert 1997; b, c) Müller et al. 1999; Hochuli et al. 1998; d, e) Vital 1993; f) Rubat Borel 2009; g) De Marinis 2009, and dating for selected lake-dwellings in Switzerland unless stated (dendrochronological dates in thick line, typological narrow, data from Arnold 1983, 1990a; Benkert and Egger 1986; Bernatzky-Goetze 1987; Bietti Sestieri 1984; Billamboz and Gollnisch 1998; Billaud 2006, 2008; Billaud et al. 1992; Böhringer and Honegger in preparation; Fischer, V 2005; Hafner 2005; Künzler Wagner 2005; Mäder 2001; Palafittes 2010; Schmidheiny 2006; Schöbel 1996.

Menotti 2001a), it is possible to make general chronologies for broader areas. These are detailed and compared in Figure 1.4. As already hinted above, there are some difficulties in directly relating the regions north and south of the Alps (see also Trachsel 2004), but those countries north of the Alps are more readily reconcilable. Within Switzerland the Bronze Age–Iron Age transition is generally accepted as occurring around 800 BC, but this is largely a construct based on the disappearance of the lake-dwellings (Della Casa 2013: 713). In fact, it has previously been suggested that burial evidence could be used to argue for an early beginning of the Iron Age, around 850 BC (Seifert 1997). The perpetual archaeological problem must however be remembered: the division of time and cultures into defined blocks does not truly reflect the gradual phasing (in and out of styles over extended periods) and transition of cultural and typological chronologies (cf. Childe 2003: 43).

Just as the chronologies of the northern Alpine forelands differ from region to region, the cultural identifications are also highly variable. This is particularly evident during the Neolithic and Early Bronze Age, before becoming more homogenously "Urnfield" cultures in the Late Bronze Age (Della Casa 2013; Strahm 1997; von Freeden and von Schnurbein 2002). However, it is still possible to identify regional 'flavours' of Urnfield culture in the northern Alpine region (Figure 1.5), which can be generalized as different groups in western and central Switzerland, eastern Switzerland, and the inner Alpine region (Rychner 1998a).

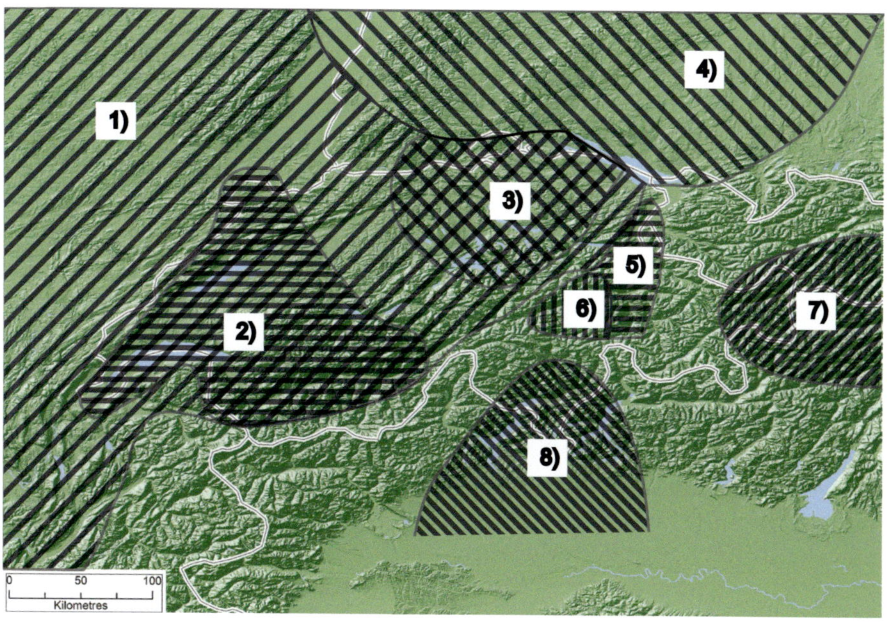

Figure 1.5: Urnfield cultural variant regions of Switzerland during the Late Bronze Age. 1: Rhine-Swiss-East France (RSFO); 2: RSFO - west Switzerland group; 3: RSFO - east and central Switzerland group; 4: Main-Schwabian group (MS); 5: mixture of RSFO and MS attributes with Laugen-Melaun elements; 6: North Alpine zone with RSFO and MS cultural attributes; 7: Laugen-Melaun Culture; 8: Proto-Golasecca culture (after Jennings 2014b; re-drawn from Rychner 1998a: Fig. 39).

Although future research will modify and confirm regional chronological schemes, there will always be materials which blur the boundaries of chronological divisions; from a material culture perspective these will be the prototype objects which start new trends or the outdated objects retained by individuals reluctant to abandon favoured and trusted items. *Cultures*, as defined by their material culture repertoire, provide an effective way to study prehistoric communities on the larger scale and across broader regions, but archaeology should also attempt to identify communities at the smaller scale (Harding 2013: 394). Therefore, the following research is conducted without excessive reference to abstract principles of 'culture' or 'cultural group' in an effort to highlight how individual communities may have utilized and modified their material culture to suit their own desires and needs, potentially individualizing themselves within the broader 'cultural group' to which they may or may not have considered themselves constituent.

1.3 Data sources

General archaeological interest in the northern Alpine region, and particularly within Switzerland, has – to some extent – resulted in a relative over representation of lake-settlements compared to other types of site, such as burials and hoards (Figure 1.6) (see also Ebersbach *et al.* 2010). However, this is not only an issue of modern research agendas, but also of prehistoric cultural practices. For instance, there is a general dearth of information relating to the burial practices of the Late Bronze Age lake-dwelling communities, with very few cemeteries or isolated burials known from the region (see section 6.1). The under representation of hoards may also be the result of 19th and early 20th century excavations, e.g. of Mörigen, which did not recognize structured deposits within the perimeter of settlements. The latter 20th century excavations have shown that hoard deposits did exist within the lake-settlements (Fischer, V 2011, 2012; Rychner 1987), as they did in contemporary hilltop sites further afield (e.g. Hagl 2008; Nebelsick 2000; Stein, F 1979).

Environmental conditions and building requirements have also influenced the excavation record for different types of archaeological site. For example, many lake-dwellings were exposed during climate induced low-water levels and institutionalized water level management (see Ruoff 2004). In contrast, the higher altitude Alpine valleys are relatively inaccessible, undeveloped, and forested environments and so have experienced relatively little archaeological investigation, but new research is showing their undoubted potential (Curdy 2007). Similarly, relatively little was known of the prehistoric occupation of the hinterland of Lake Neuchâtel and Lake Murten until large scale excavations were conducted in advance of motorway construction, revealing a higher density of occupation than previously envisaged (Boisaubert *et al.* 2008; Poncet Schmid *et al.* 2013).

The generally high levels of organic preservation at the lake-settlement sites has permitted high quality dendrochronological studies to be undertaken (e.g. Eberschweiler *et al.* 2007), allowing the identification of phases of individual building construction for the entire site, or small sections thereof, indicating

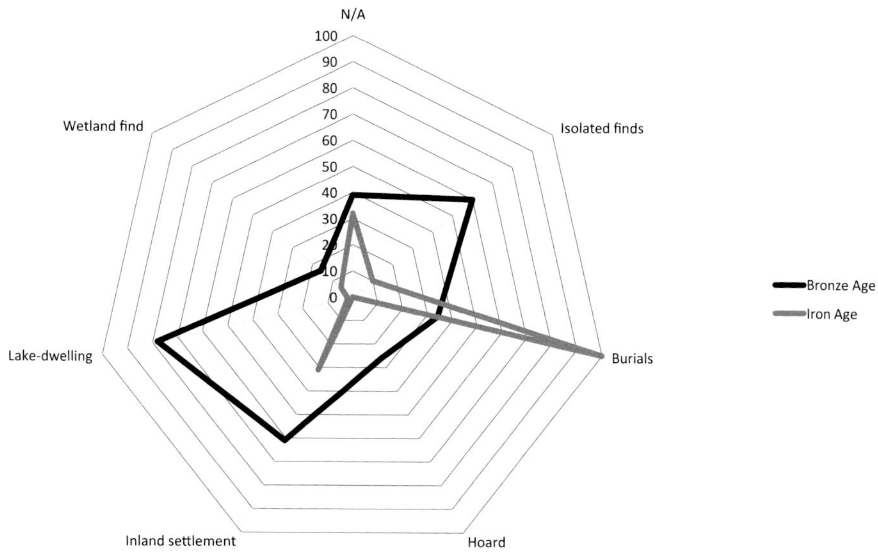

Figure 1.6: Representation of different site types in the studied assemblages from Switzerland relating to the Bronze and Iron Ages.

general phases of occupation (e.g. Billamboz 2009). For inland and hilltop sites radiocarbon dating has often been used, which is generally not as precise as the dendrochronological dating of lake-settlements. However, the many forms of bronze and inorganic artefact recovered from both lake- and inland settlements do not have the benefit of accurate absolute dating, and so are placed into typological schemes with a general resolution tied to that of the regional chronologies, resulting in periods of circulation lasting up to a century or more. Several of the forms of Late Bronze Age material culture encountered in Switzerland have been reported under the *Prähistorische Bronzefunde* series, such as sickles, swords, and ring jewellery, while others have been classified in local typological schemes (e.g. knives). Such sources were employed in the identification of trade and exchange routes flowing through Late Bronze Age lake-dwelling communities in the northern Alpine region (see Chapter 4). Subsequent research aimed at reconciling the evidence for trade and exchange with evidence of settlement and burial practices and climatic change to create a scenario of events leading to the final abandonment of the lake-dwelling tradition during the early Iron Age (see Chapter 7).

1.4 The issue of disappearance

The research objective can be simply posed as: is it possible to observe any cultural influences for the final abandonment of the lake-dwelling tradition in the northern Circum-Alpine region during the Late Bronze Age and early Iron Age? Current models for the abandonment are reliant upon proposals of climatic change influencing the lake environment, and directly affecting the lake-dwelling communities through inundation or economic degradation. However, recent studies have questioned how synchronous such changes were across the whole of the northern Circum-Alpine region (Bleicher 2013). It is well recognized that the Alpine region was incorporated in exchange and communication networks flowing between northern and southern Europe, and it may be possible that inclusion in these networks influenced cultural change in the lake-dwelling communities.

Chapter 2

Theoretical Development

In order to reconcile the varied forms of material evidence utilized in this study, a theoretical approach was developed to link objects, settlement dynamics, exchange routes and burial practices to potential cultural changes influencing the decline of a specific mode of settlement construction and landscape occupation. The basic building blocks of the theoretical approach are the principles of *relational theory* and *object biographies*. This chapter provides a detailed account of the theoretical principles developed for the research, and considers past approaches which have been taken to similar problems.

2.1 Relational theory

Relational theory stems from the anthropological work of Gell (1998) and Strathern (1988) with concern, respectively, to human/art/object agency and personhood in Melanesia. Strathern describes Melanesian personhood, contrary to Western notions of personhood and the individual, to be *dividual* and *partible*; persons are perceived to be a culmination of social relationships, inalienable possessions, and enchainments (see also Fowler 2004; Strathern 1991; Wagner 1991; Weiner 1992; Whittle 2003). Trifković (2005: 42) describes the interaction of relationships through the metaphor of the diffraction of light through a prism, whereby the prism redirects the beam of light, while also attaining new properties. In the case of persons this represents their ability to engage and transform relationships through which they attain their own defining properties (Trifković 2005: 43-45). With regard to relationships, Strathern (1988) argues that all are gendered, that all are exchange relationships, and that they are visible only through their indexes – their material manifestations. Thus, it is possible to perceive persons as indexes of the relationships between other persons; they are not only the result of relationships between their contemporaries, or their direct parents and ancestors, but also of relationships between their parents (ancestors) and other persons, which contributed to the growth of their parents (ancestors). Sahlin's (1974: 186) statement that "if friends make gifts, gifts make friends." can be rephrased as: *if people make relationships, relationships make people.*

One of the quintessential points of relational theory is that it is possible to place people and objects as equals; people can be objects and objects can be people, in what Strathern (1988: 177-79) terms "mediated relationships", and Gell states "… 'objects' merge with 'people' by virtue of the existence of social relationships between persons and things, and persons and persons *via* things." (1998: 12, original emphasis). Through the principle of dividual personhood objects can presence and symbolize people (or their attributes), and the relationships that they objectify, in locations distanced from the actual persons. Gurevich (1968: 131) provides an example of this in his study of the Scandinavian Medieval period, when it was common for persons to accept gifts from their chieftain, and they would hope to acquire good luck and success through ownership of the objects – a quality which the chieftain was seen to possess and had been absorbed by the object/gift. Similarly, Gosden and Marshall (1999: 170-72) have noted that sawn sperm whale tooth necklaces are significant for Fijian people, as once possessed and touched by chiefs they become powerful and dangerous; properties of the

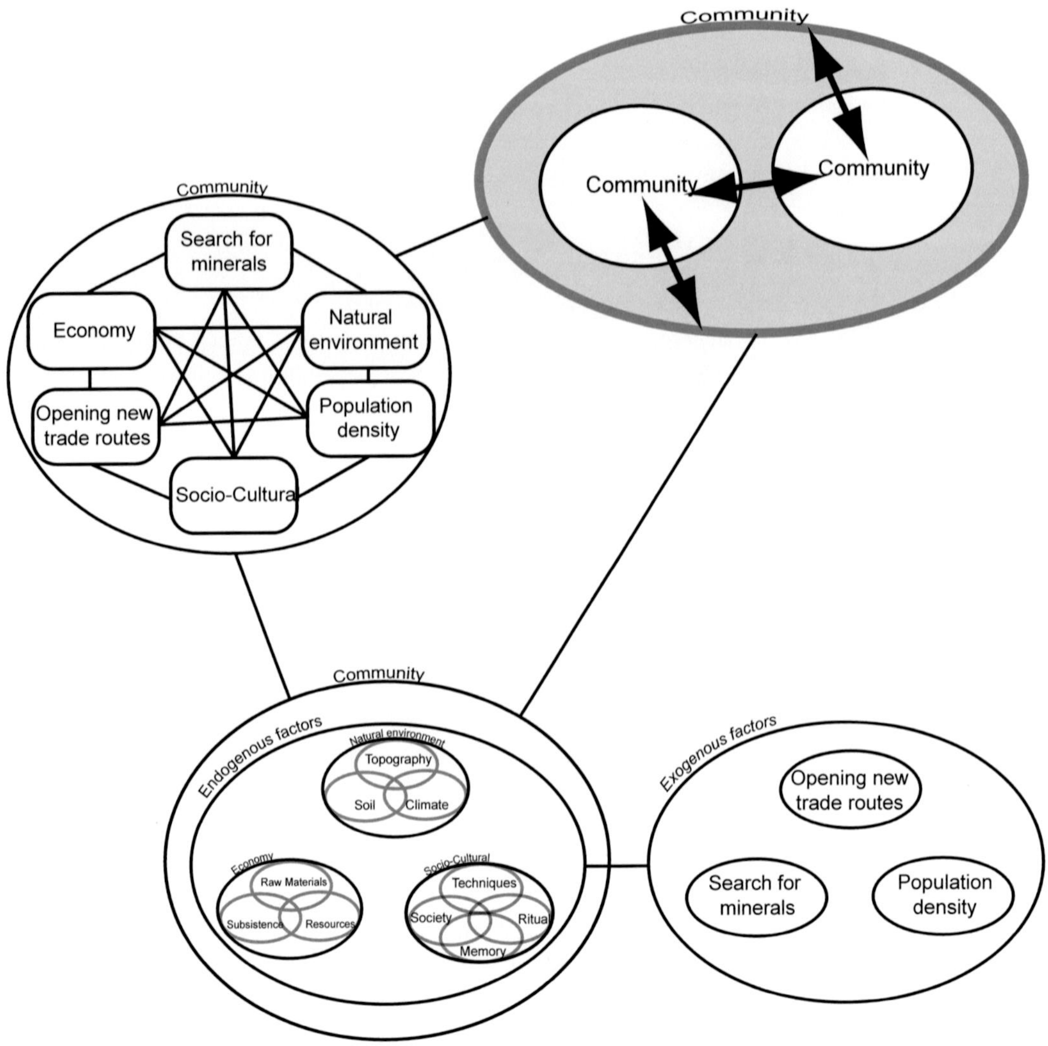

Figure 2.1: Relational model depicting the influence of various factors upon the cultural composition of communities. (After Jennings 2012b).

chief become incorporated with, and are seen to reside in, the necklace (or other such object).

A possible greater use of relational theory in this study is to utilize the theory in the macro scale instead of the micro scale. Following the assertion that persons in Melanesia are a result of connected relationships, is it possible, without drastically over-generalising, to say that *cultures* (or communities, societies) are similarly a product of interconnected relationships? This is not to enter a diffusionist stance, implying that cultural change is instigated through the migration of people and ideas into cultures from an advanced 'core', but instead to theorize that cultures would not take the form that they do, if it were not for the wider network of relationships in which individuals within that culture are incorporated. In a discussion of the Hallstatt to Early La Tène transition in Europe, Parzinger (1995) provides brief glimpses of this proposal, but does not develop them, preferring to continue with the traditional notions of object diffusion, the exchange and 'immigration' of ideas, and the 'influence' of foreign regions.

Della Casa (2001), in some ways reminiscent of 'culture systems' (Renfrew 1984a), proposes that the movement of people through, and settlement of, a landscape is dependent upon the interaction between internal and external factors. Using the broad categories which Della Casa details, (internal factors: natural environment; economy; social-cultural context / external factors: density of population; the search for metal minerals; the opening of new trade routes) and the concept of relational theory, it is proposed that 'cultures' are the composite of the relations between these internal and external factors (Figure 2.1), and their relationships with other 'cultures' (cf. Harris 2013; see also Moore, T 2007: 95-97).

With reference to Tilley's (1982: 34) statement that "... the social formation is a totality of human experience and action, the entire ensemble of the relations between individuals and groups and of their relationships with their natural and social environment." we can see that society (community, culture) is the sum of its constituent parts. Thus, a society is partly influenced by its connections to other societies; changes to those connections will produce readily apparent changes. However, this is not a suggestion of Renfrew's (1975: 32) notions of "exogenous" growth, in which societies centralized and developed due to contact with more advanced cultures and civilizations. In the proposed relational model there is no hierarchical structure or concept of transition of 'advanced' ideas, simply the proposal that contact with 'another'/'other' culture(s) will result in social changes in a given community, society, or culture. These changes may be small, or they may be large, sometimes they may be temporary and quickly forgotten, other times they may be cumulative or long lasting. In this sense the model is similar to Chapman's (2008: 340) assertion that "... exchange contexts, ... developed enchained social relations, opening the way to increased sociability, information exchange and perhaps eventually new ways of creating personhood.". Thus, changing external (and internal) networks of relationships, and access that these relations enabled to products and individuals, will cause and influence cultural change. As Andrew Jones (2007a: 84) states: "Cultural practices are components of networks of referentiality, and as such change can occur by drawing on any other component of the network.".

2.2 The biography of objects

The concept of 'object biographies' has been well discussed in recent archaeological literature, but some of its basic principles can be traced to the early 20th century. For instance, in studies of inheritance laws, Rivers (1910: 7), suggested that charting plot ownership on a genealogical tree would highlight the structuring principles of inheritance: effectively he was creating a land plot biography. Later, through studying the Kula exchange network, Malinowski (1922: 89-99) suggested that participants gained prestige by possessing famous objects or those previously owned by prominent or renowned individuals (see also Campbell 1983; Damon 1983; Munn 1986). The history of the arm-shell or necklace remained with, and formed a facet of, the item as it circulated through the Kula network. Effectively, a biography of ownership is created for, and retained by, the object, which participants in the exchange system could manipulate for their own ends, and through which object and social value could be developed (Appadurai 1986; Gosden and Marshall 1999: 170).

Kopytoff (1986: 66-67) developed the principle of biographies of ownership to address the reflective nature of the relationship between humans and objects, and suggested some interrogations which may highlight the social attitudes towards objects:

> *What, sociologically, are the biographical possibilities inherent in its 'status' and in the period and culture, and how are these possibilities realized? Where does the thing come from and who made it? What had been its career so far, and what do people consider to be an ideal career for such things? What are the recognized 'ages' or periods in the things life, and what happens to it when it reaches the end of its usefulness?*

In the same volume, Appadurai (1986: 34) further extrapolated upon the biographical principle, and suggested that the approach is particularly well suited to individual items, either as a general object category, e.g. Kopytoff's (1986: 73) Suku hut, or specific and "singularized objects", e.g. Kopytoff's (1986: 82) Picasso painting. Yet, archaeological objects can rarely be identified as such singularized items, and it is necessary to consider groups of similar objects – for instance a certain type of pottery, ring jewellery, or sword. In this case, Appadurai (1986: 34) suggests that the "social history" of objects should be considered. The social history of an object class transcends the individual object biographies to provide a generalized biography of the entire type, and is composed of the 'typical' biography of many objects; effectively this becomes an average biography in an "ideal career" (Kopytoff 1986: 66-67).

Appadurai (1986) also suggested that, particularly in Western society but also in pre-modern non-capitalist societies, the "commodity" status or "value" of an object is not fixed and can be altered throughout its social life depending upon the context in which it is placed. It is evident that the value of a specific object is highly contentious and individually perceived: one person can hold a specific object to have a higher value than another seemingly identical, and two people can perceive different values for the same object (Kopytoff 1986: 80-81). How objects are valued by individuals is an indication of their relationship not only to the object, but also to the source of the object (Appadurai 1986: 57; also Shanks 1998: 19-20).

Following the development of the biographical principle in anthropology, numerous studies have successfully reconstructed and visualized object biographies (e.g. Hoskins 1998; Miller 1998), and it is evident that the discursive nature of the biographical approach is well suited to anthropological research in which objects can be examined throughout their life-course. However, the reconstruction of object biographies from archaeological objects becomes more problematic, as there can be no direct questioning of an objects possessor, and there are few indications to show how "individualized" objects may have been.

In the reconstruction of archaeological object biographies it is desirable that not only the "use life" (Gosden and Marshall 1999) or "life cycle" (Shanks 1998) of an object is produced from the physical changes occurring to an object during its extended use – for instance pottery breakage, repair, and deposition – as detailed by "mapping" (Sullivan, A P 1978) or "object life history" (LaMotta and Schiffer 2001: 21-24; Schiffer 1996: 13-23). Instead the social reasons behind the modification and deposition of objects should be sought.

One of the problems facing the reconstruction of archaeological object biographies is related to the simple preservation of objects. Organic materials, such as wood or cloth, are – in general – rarely recovered, due to the specific environmental conditions required for their preservation. Furthermore, it is possible that objects are destroyed prior to deposition, for instance a wooden bowl may be re-worked into a new object or simply thrown into a fire and burned, leaving nothing but ash, or occasionally where burning was not complete, charred remains (e.g. Hastorf and Johannessen 1991: 144), or metalwork could be returned to the melting pot and converted into new objects (Jennings 2014a). These factors serve to reduce the quantity of material available to archaeologists to reconstruct object biographies, and may serve to make items appear rarer than they actually were. The lake-settlements of the Alpine region present exceptional preservation conditions and many organic objects have been recovered. However, few attempts have been made to reconstruct object biographies, at least in part due to the still limited corpus of material available to study due to a lack of similar objects from other contexts. At some sites it has been suggested that some structural timbers were re-used from earlier buildings, e.g. at Gachnang-Niederwil (Ebersbach 2009) and Alleshausen-Grundwiesen (Bleicher 2009: 125, Fig. 85), which raises interesting questions concerning the potential biographical associations of residential and/or activity structures.

Despite such potential issues for the archaeological construction of object biographies, a number have been undertaken (e.g. Chapman 2000; Chapman 2008; Chapman and Gaydarska 2007; Frieman 2012a; Moore, T 2007; Renfrew 1986; Sheridan and Davis 1998; Skeates 1995; Tilley 1996). The basis to constructing social biographies of objects is to consider the object in association with its context, linking the principle of object biography to 'contextual archaeology'. Hodder has suggested the "contextual archaeology" framework in the 1980s (Hodder 1986) as a method to reassert material culture as an active element in cultural expressions, and as a way to begin recognising that "the practical meaning of an item of material culture varies according to the context in which it is used" (Hodder 1985: 14). This is not to suggest that object biographies can be reconstructed through reading material culture as per "contextual archaeology" (cf. Jones, A 2007a: 76-84), but to recognise that the awareness of context is essential to the understanding of object associations and value changes. The objective of the biographical approach is to understand the myriad concepts which an object can signify during its life; perceiving contexts as 'frozen moments' in time – as single points of reference during the life of the object (Jones, A 2007a: 82) – enables the creation of biographic snapshots, which can be combined to produce the "ideal career" of an object class. The object itself is not 'read' through its context, rather the varying cultural associations and object values through spatial and temporal separation are visualized.

Drawing influence from Gell (1998), Andrew Jones (2007a: 141-61) suggests that artefacts should be considered as part of an *oeuvre* of work, and uses the principles of 'protention', 'retention', and 'citation' to interpret the wider networks in which objects participated, and to comprehend how categories of objects interconnect. *Citation* refers to the similarities between objects, and relationships between objects within separate classes, and how associations are evoked through the inclusion (or exclusion) of specific elements, while *retention* and *protention* relate to the continuation of features from the past and into the future.

Generally, archaeologically excavated objects can only ever be found in a single context, though there are exceptional cases of intentional object fragmentation (e.g. Chapman 2000: 54; Ford *et al.* 1998). To avoid a materialistic object biography (see above) it is necessary to consider, in Appadurai's (1986) terms, the "social history" of an object class, combining a number of individual object biographies from differing contexts, changing associations, and interactions. The examination of object classes or categories produces an *idealized* biography for those objects (Tilley 1996: 248), incorporating the most frequently observed associations within the object category, and reducing the impact of rarely seen occurrences.

Drawing influence from and summarising Jones (2002: Chapter 5), Fowler (2004: 65) states: "biographical approaches are only effective when the whole story is considered, from the extraction of natural substances, to the conception and construction of the object, through various stages of use and modification, repeated acts of consumption, destruction, and the reuse of fragmented components.". This applies to the construction of idealized biographies, but is too strong in suggesting that the biographical approach can only be successful if they cover an artefact (or group) from conception to final destruction. One of the benefits of a biographical approach is the multi-contextual analysis of changing culturally ascribed values, which can be achieved without necessarily considering the primary manufacture of an object (cf. Jennings 2014b: 12; Skeates 1995). For example, in a prehistoric context, it is not necessary to consider the original source location and manufacturing site of the amber beads found at some of the Swiss lake-dwellings (e.g. Hauterive-Champréveyres (Rychner-Faraggi 1993) or

Ürschhausen-Horn (Nagy 1999)), but a multi-context analysis of amber beads from many contemporary sites, will enable the changing value associations to be identified.

The entire conception to death biography of an object does not need to be conceptualized in order to observe how objects were alternately valued through time and space; biographical 'windows' are capable of doing this (Hahn and Weiss 2013; Jennings 2014a; Joy 2009: 544). A multi-contextual examination of archaeological objects can produce object biographies and "... make salient what might otherwise remain obscure" as "... what is significant about the adoption of alien objects – as of alien ideas – is not the fact that they were adopted, but the way they were culturally redefined and put to use." (Kopytoff 1986: 67).

2.3 Cultural memory

In recent years an increasing number of works concerning the role of memory in material culture and the landscape have been published (e.g. Bender 2002; Borić 2009; Bradley and Williams 1998; Chadwick and Gibson 2013; Georgiadis and Gallou 2009; Gosden and Lock 1998; Jones, A 2007a; Küchler 1993; Lillios and Tsamis 2010), and the connection between place/landscape and memory has been the subject of broader theoretical discussions (see Van Dyke and Alcock 2003: 5). A principle, which has been widely utilized in these studies, is that of "embodied" and "inscribed" memories (Connerton 1989), whereby material objects become focal points for remembrance and memories, and so it is possible to posit a connection between the concepts of object biographies and cultural memory.

The theoretical position that 'landscapes' can have 'place values' and biographies may have relevance when considering the periodic abandonment and re-occupation of lake-dwellings in the Circum-Alpine region. As detailed previously (see section 1.1.1.1), some lake-dwelling occupations were very brief, lasting only a decade or so before the site was abandoned and another dwelling established elsewhere. One obvious question here is why were the settlements abandoned? But possibly more importantly, why were sites re-occupied, or why were sites not re-occupied? The re-occupation of former lake-dwelling sites occurred both directly, where new structures are built directly above previous ones (e.g. Wasserburg-Buchau; D (Billamboz 2009)), and adjacently, where the re-occupation occurs in proximity to the original site (e.g. Sutz-Lattrigen Rütte; CH (Hafner and Suter 2000)). Other sites, for example Greifensee-Böschen (CH), were not re-occupied (see Eberschweiler *et al.* 2007). The decision whether or not to re-occupy a former lake-dwelling site is interesting given the significant visual presence that the former dwellings will have left on the lake-scape (cf. Robinson 2013). Even today it is possible to see wooden piles protruding from the lake bed, and so they must have been visible to communities who utilized the lake in the period following a pile-dwelling abandonment.

One aspect, which may have been significant in the return to, and re-occupation of, previous lake-dwelling sites, is the notion of re-settling a previously successful site (e.g. Kohl 1981: 112); the return to a location know to have been inhabited in the past through visual remnants and social memory. It is important to consider also two other factors: 1) that places can have negative properties, negative values, and negative associations (Chapman 1998: 112) that may act to prevent the re-occupation of a lake-dwelling; and 2) that memories do not have to be direct memories, they can be of other places and other times (Bender 2002: 107). The Middle Bronze Age lake-dwelling hiatus may be seen as a good example of this (see section 1.1.1.1); during a period of climatic deterioration a number of lake-dwellings were affected by rising lake levels, which triggered a negative association with lakeshore occupation and led to the wide spread abandonment of lake-dwellings in the Alpine region. Following a return to more favourable climatic conditions and more stable lake levels, communities returned to the lakeshore, re-occupying former lake-dwelling sites, possibly through social memories of settlements and the visual recognition of former pile-dwelling structures (Menotti 2001a).

Did the sight and recognition of piles in the lake bed act as a cue for remembrance of past dwellings and act as an attractive force encouraging the re-occupation of a traditional/ancestral site? Or did they act as repulsive forces in periods of social change with societies actively trying to break associations with the past? Chapman (1998: 110) suggests that societies use historical, traditional or ancestral places as a method of reproducing, or changing, cultural value and meaning:

> ... *based on the establishment of difference from the past, which constitutes itself through spatial strategies in relation to re-use of previous monuments, abandonment or continuity of occupation. By contrast, the continued use of traditional practices at the same monument will act as the ritualised context for the maintenance of habitus, the reproduction of value and meaning.*

From this perspective, we can see that the continued use, and re-occupation of lake-dwellings may have been an attempt to maintain the social status quo; to retain links to ancestral practices, beliefs and values, creating and continuing a sense of community identity. Contrastingly, the decision not to re-occupy a former lake-dwelling site may represent a break with tradition, an attempt to change social structures, an attempt to 'forget' the past (cf. Gerritsen 2008: 157-58). However, the process of forgetting is simply a different form of remembering; to forget something through relocating is to acknowledge the existence of the past and to move away from it, to actively differentiate from the previous social identities (cf. Jones, A 2007a). Furthermore, the construction of a new dwelling can still be seen as a continuation of the past as it is still built upon social memories, upon learned principles and memories of knowledge, building, and skills based in the past (Gerritsen 2008: 148-49).

The cyclic abandonment and re-occupation of lake-dwellings also suggests that they were constructed with temporal considerations in mind (cf. Gerritsen 2008: 151); they were built with an intended life span before they were abandoned, and the occupants moved to a new location. This temporal duration may have been dictated by the durability of construction materials used, by agricultural concerns, or related to the life cycle of the community (see section 5.3.3).

2.4 Theories of trade and exchange

In addition to specific principles of relational theory, object biographies, and cultural memory, there are general theories relating to trade and exchange systems which need to be addressed in order for the developed relational model (Figure 2.1) to be fully conceptualized.

Numerous studies have already addressed the differences between 'trade' and 'exchange', 'gift' and 'commodity', 'alienable' and 'inalienable' objects, and the development of a 'prestige' economy (e.g. Oka and Kusimba 2008: 340-42; Sahlins 1974; Skeates 2009; Strathern 1988; Weiner 1992), to the extent that a repetition here is not necessary and would also do the existing literature an injustice. It is instead sufficient to say that exchanges may occur through two regimes:

1. The inalienable (non-)reciprocal gift, intended to create social ties, or
2. The alienable commodity which creates no social contract or obligations.

As has been detailed above (see section 2.1), it is possible for the value of objects to cross between the two categories, and it is possible for both forms of exchange to occur concurrently within communities for different objects. Following Chapman (2008: 334), no differentiation will be made hereafter, unless explicitly stated, between the terms 'trade' and 'exchange' as methods of circulating and transferring possession of goods and objects.

A succinct history of research into trade networks, from Renfrew's (1975) ten modes of resource attainment, through Hodder's (1984) dismissal of their testing by fall off patterns, to the recent reconciliation between 'processual' and 'post-processual' perceptions of the value of trade and exchange studies to an interpretive archaeology, is provided in a recent article by Chapman (2008). In this article he suggests the role of exchange network studies in an 'interpretive archaeology' should be primarily concerned with discovering the social implications of trade and exchange. Thus, the meaning and influence of trade and exchange was more significant than the objects which were circulated, that "... communities emphasized exotic things to the neglect of comparable and adequate local sources. By travelling far, a hitherto mundane object was transformed into something special, whatever the means of movement" (Chapman 2008: 335).

The ten modes of exchange (Figure 2.2) proposed by Renfrew (1975) are still well discussed in studies of exchange systems, not least because they are detailed in each iteration of the well-known undergraduate introductory book to archaeology by Renfrew and Bahn (2012). In the original proposal it was suggested that each of the forms of exchange would leave different distribution and density signatures in the archaeological record (Renfrew 1975). Thus, charting the archaeologically recovered objects would provide an indication of objects source locations and indications of the method through which objects were circulated. However, it was demonstrated by several authors (e.g. Hodder and Lane 1982; Hodder and Orton 1976) that the different modes of exchange would produce relatively similar distribution and fall off patterns, which ultimately led to Hodder's statement that "it is simply not possible to test whether historic artefacts moved from source to

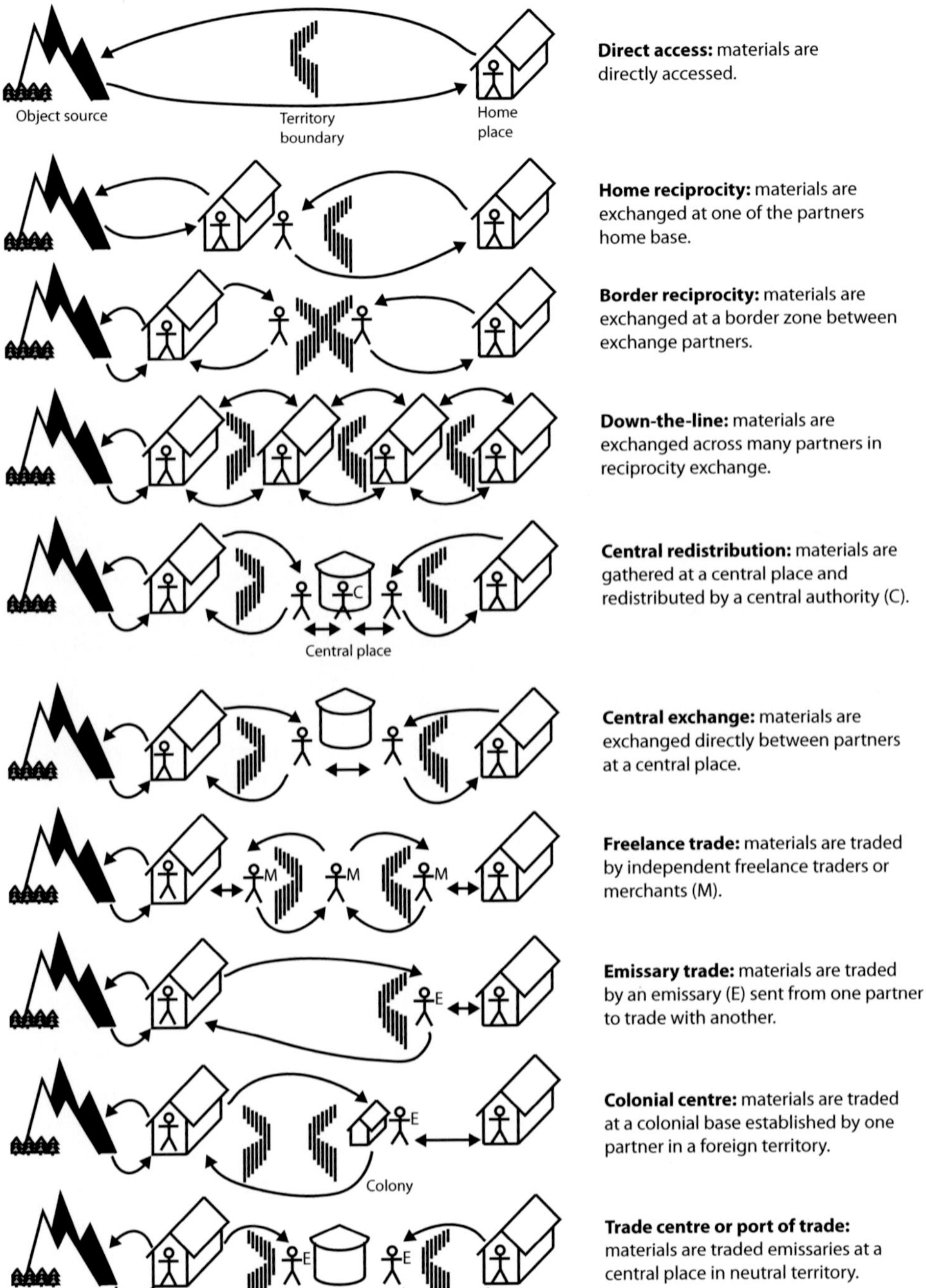

Figure 2.2: Ten possible modes of exchange and interaction used during prehistory. It is possible to discount a number of potential methods – particularly the bottom three – which may have been used during prehistory (after Jennings 2014b; re-drawn from Renfrew and Bahn 2012).

destination by exchange from person to person or whether, on the other hand, individuals went directly to the source" (Hodder 1984: 26).

Considering the Late Bronze Age communities in the Circum-Alpine region, it is possible to reduce the potential forms of exchange which would have occurred; for instance colonial enclave, port of trade, and emissary trading can be removed as likely methods of procurement. This leaves 'direct access', 'reciprocity' (home base and boundary), 'down-the-line' trade (though see Skeates 2009: 566), 'central place redistribution', 'central place market exchange', and 'freelance trading' as exchange methods (Figure 2.2). However, the mode of exchange is, to some extent, largely irrelevant in the consideration of catalysts for cultural change; more significant is the fact that exchange was occurring.

Addressing the issue of *why* objects were exchanged is problematic. Although Chapman (2008: 352) suggests that exotic objects held "... inherent value and aesthetic attractions of the things themselves", it is clear that no material possesses an 'inherent value'. All value is culturally based and ascribed to objects based on cultural requirements. Indeed, Appadurai (1986: 3-4), built upon Simmel's (1978: 73) assertion that value is a subjective judgement, and argued that value is neither an inherent property of objects, nor the cause of exchange, but rather the value of an object is created through its exchange. Similarly, Renfrew (1975: 37; also Renfrew 1993: 8) states "... interaction is possible only when the traded commodity *achieves a value* of importance in the social system, often in terms of prestige.". Value is socially constructed and dependent upon cultural setting, and can be (re)negotiated by individuals according to temporal and spatial requirements and beliefs.

As seen through the principle of object biographies, the value of objects is not constant and can increase or decrease through exchange, by crossing cultural contexts or increasing scarcity and distance from an origin (Saunders 1999). It is then a short step to suggest that individuals can gain (or lose) status through their ability to participate in exchange relationships. However, it does not only mean that individuals can participate in exchange because they have high status, they may have high status because they participate in exchange (cf. Renfrew 1986: 144).

One approach which has been taken to explain *how* objects were accepted into new cultural settings has been proposed by Chapman (2000: 32) in his discussion of "translation" and "translators" (see also Babić 2007; Monna *et al.* 2013). In some ways this is reminiscent of Latour's concept of 'translation' as "... displacement, drift, invention, mediation, *the creation of a link that did not exist before and that to some degree modifies the original two*" (Latour 1999: 179) and also Lévi-Strauss' (1989) "bricolage" and "bricoleur". In Chapman's proposal, individual 'translators' located in cultural contact zones fulfilled a similar social function to that of Helms' (1988) "long-distance specialist". The knowledge possessed by long-distance specialists of the distant 'other', 'foreign', 'alien' or 'strange' (Chapman 2008: 336; also Neustupný 1998) may have endowed them with social status and power (cf. Broodbank 1993: 326-27; Helms 1988: 263). Accordingly, the role of the 'translator' with knowledge of foreign products, and the ability to relate them to equivalents in the local cultural setting, may have generated increased social status (Chapman 2000: 32). The role of translation to the adoption of foreign goods into new cultural settings is clear; if the objects cannot be made to fit into existing social structures there will be a limited or slow uptake. Therefore, the adoption and import of objects is more likely to occur where they have contemporary parallels.

A good example of such translative acceptance can be seen in Saunders' (1999) study of the late medieval pearl trade between Amerindians and Europeans. Objects traded by the Europeans (glass, mirrors, etc.) were easily translatable to the Amerindian worldview due to their iridescence, a property already present in their social belief system, meaning that they materials required little translation – even though they may not have been used as intended in their native production zone. On the opposite side of the exchange, pearls found ready translation into Europeans' display of status, wealth and power through foreign goods, gems, and stones. Similarly, in an ethnographic study of pottery production in Dangwara, Central India, Miller (1982) effectively details the successful and unsuccessful translation of new pottery forms into local communities. Potters producing pots similar to forms already in use found open markets for their wares (Miller 1982: 93), but attempts to introduce new pottery products and forms did not succeed.

Following the successful translation of objects in to a new area, it is possible that the role of translator may shift from the importers to local manufacturers. The local craftsmen become responsible for either producing products in new materials, for instance switching from flint to bronze, or producing new forms in existing materials. It is, therefore, possible to suggest that the acceptance of new items and materials into cultures can alter social structure over both the:

- Short term (i.e. the role and status of 'translators' and craftsman in society may increase, causing hierarchical changes in the social order)

and

- Long term (i.e. the introduction of new objects and material forms may lead to significant modifications in social structures and methods of identity creation, expression, and display).

One of the remaining problems to be addressed is how imported objects are recognized in the archaeological record. For some materials it is possible to identify origins through chemical analysis (e.g. Ambrose *et al.* 2009; Angelini *et al.* 2004; Angelini and Bellintani 2005; Arletti *et al.* 2010; Balassone *et al.* 2009; Beck and Stout 2000; Frei, K M *et al.* 2009; Hodder and Lane 1982; Jackson and Nicholson 2010; Santi *et al.* 2009). Such analysis has enabled two divergent interpretations: firstly the trade of objects between distant locations (e.g. amber beads in the Mediterranean), and secondly that objects were produced in foreign styles using local materials (Biehl and Rassamakin 2008; Jones, R E *et al.* 2002; Sheridan and Davis 2002). However, not all materials can be identified to origin locations through chemical analysis, and such analysis does not address the social concept of what constitutes an 'imported item'.

Pydyn (1999: 11) addresses the issue what constitutes an 'imported' item by suggesting an import is "… a material object or idea which moved out of its original cultural 'universe', in which practical (technical) and symbolic (religious) knowledge united 'producers' and 'customers', and for a mixture of practical and ideological reasons this material object or idea was then redefined in a 'new universe'.". Yet, as already detailed above, objects do not always require 'redefinition' when imported to a new area, they can be readily translated and adopted if precedent objects are already known. Furthermore, it is unclear as to how prehistoric cultures conceived identities of 'foreignness' (the 'universe'); communities in relative proximity could have maintained separate identities and conceived of each other as 'foreign', and worldviews may have been considerably smaller than in the modern day. Whether or not communities knew of the ultimate origin or destination of objects which they were exchanging is unknown, but it would seem likely that exchange participants knew portions of the exchange route related to their direct exchange partners and not the entire network. Thus, 'foreign' objects could be imported from a distance equating to the next population centre or to a distant island, but the symbolism associated with such foreignness remained the same.

When access to foreign objects was restricted or lost, then it is possible that 'imitative' objects were produced in local communities. Such practices have been extensively discussed in *Import and Imitation in Archaeology* (Biehl and Rassamakin 2008; also Kristiansen and Larsson 2005: 16-20). Returning to the above discussion of *translation*, it is suggested that terms such as 'imitative' and 'emulative' are overly simplistic, and imply an inherent passivism in the production of objects in an imported style (Potrebica 2008: 202). Instead, the process of such production is far more complex and intended to fulfil specific social desires. Cultural translation had already occurred by the time of production, and so the new cultural values held by the local-foreign objects need bear no relation to the prototypes (cf. Kristiansen and Larsson 2005: 12-13; Stein, G J 2002; Thomas, N 1991; 2005: 96). Rather than passively replicating foreign objects, local producers were creating translated, modified, and manipulated objects to better serve their cultural purposes. The concept of object 'skeuomorphism' (e.g. Frieman 2012b; Hurcombe 2008: 102; Knappett 2002: 108-13; Monna *et al.* 2013) addresses the more social aspects of imitation and translation. For skeuomorphs to be created, the process of translation must already have occurred; skeuomorphs are not the act of translating "… a novel object so that it would fit more easily into established social or economic roles" (Frieman 2010: 42), rather, they are the product of translation. It is possible to define different forms of translation based upon the mode employed: 'importive translation' is the result of importing novel objects directly, whereas 'skeumorphic translation' can be identified as the incorporation of objects or materials through production processes.

It is often suggested that 'culture' is carried by objects, like a 'cargo' (e.g. Potrebica 2008: 199), and thereby transferred between different regions and cultural zones. This concept implies a degree of diffusion, with 'culture' being unwittingly traded and accepted by communities. The extent to which 'culture' is accepted and perceived by communities participating in exchange networks is dependent upon both the translation of the object into its new cultural locale, and the attitude of the new cultural setting towards the old. Regardless of an exchange of 'cultural' facets, Kristiansen (1998b: 338) has argued that there is significant ethnographic evidence to link long-distance exchange to cultural change in societies, whether through the ascension to power of new chiefs or the formation of new elite classes.

2.4.1 Cultural change

In the 1980s, Tilley (1982) conducted a critique of past approaches to cultural change, and criticized methods of *individualism* and *systems theory* for ascribing, respectively, too much and not enough emphasis to the potential of the individual for instigating social change. He later asserts that material culture is active, in that "It structures and is structured by the perception of actors of their social world and may be a powerful means of legitimating the existing social world. It has a dual effect, as both a creation and a creator of social practice." (Tilley 1982: 32). This is an important consideration for cultural change as it allows the possibility that material objects influence social structures and create social change. A significant point that Tilley generates through this discussion is that "... the social formation is a totality of human experience and action, the entire ensemble of the relations between individuals and groups and of their relationships with their natural and social environment." (Tilley 1982: 34). Thus, it is possible to suggest that the relations which exist between cultures/societies, through the medium of individuals, influence and generate cultural change in societies (see section 2.1).

Three broad forms of impetus for cultural change can be proposed: diffusion, evolutionary independent or autonomous innovation, and acculturation. Proposals of cultural diffusion rely upon the principles that "... the transference of cultural traits smaller than the totality of a culture occurs" (Odner 1983: 6), and that "... ideas, values, and technological innovations are being transmitted from the parent society" (Renfrew 1975: 33), or that peoples migrate to, and populate, new areas or take over older societies (cf. Kristiansen and Larsson 2005: 25-31). Renfrew's early criticism, and perhaps the most fundamental, of the diffusion approach in archaeology is that it provided little interpretative value, with the supposition of cultural change and the circulation of objects occurring through the filtering down of innovations from 'advanced' to 'primitive' societies accepted with little critical evaluation (Renfrew 1975: 21). Other criticisms of the diffusion approach (e.g. Skeates 2009) have remarked that the notion that ideas, values, and technological innovations are transmitted from a host to a new society implies a degree of autonomy and inevitability; it is known that this is certainly not the case.

There are situations where cultural contact has occurred and 'advanced' technologies have not been immediately transferred – the technology has not 'diffused' from the parent society into a new society. The manufacture of flint daggers in southern Scandinavia/Denmark during the Late Neolithic and Early Bronze age is a good example of this (Frieman 2012b); despite contact with metal using communities traditional materials were utilized in new and novel manners to fulfil a social function. The diffusion approach implies a directionality of advanced, developed, or civilized traits emanating from a developed to a less developed society, and pays little attention to the active social adoption or rejection of technologies, ideas, and values.

During the Late Bronze Age and early Iron Age of Europe, cultural connections and communication were prevalent to the extent that it is possible to remove the concept of independent or autonomous innovation as a method of cultural change. This is not to suggest that social or technological innovations did not occur, but to argue that it is not plausible to assert that innovations could have occurred in a native environment which did not in some manner draw upon influences from external contacts. An example of 'independent invention' provided by Kottak (2009: 40) is that of the development of agriculture in Mexico and the Middle East. On a large scale analysis the spatial and temporal separation is a clear indication of the independent development of agriculture in these two areas. But what about the smaller scale? Was the development of agriculture in either the Middle East or Mexico an independent innovation in the region, or was it in fact a development that took some influence from the intra-regional cultural contacts between various localized communities? It is clear that the concept of independent innovation is applicable to a broad scale analysis, but not necessarily to smaller, regional scales.

A third approach to cultural change is through the principle of 'acculturation'. In 1936, Redfield, Linton, and Herskovits issued a memorandum for the study of acculturation, and proposed the following definition:

> *Acculturation comprehends those phenomena which result when groups of individuals having different cultures come into continuous first-hand contact, with subsequent changes in the original culture patterns of either or both groups.* (Redfield *et al.* 1936: 149)

with the condition:

> *Under this definition, acculturation is to be distinguished from culture-change, of which it is but one aspect.... It is also to be differentiated from diffusion, which, while occurring in all instances of acculturation, is not only a phenomenon which frequently takes place without the occurrence of the type of contact between people specified in the definition given above, but also constitutes only one aspect of the process of acculturation.* (Redfield *et al.* 1936: 149-50).

In the proposal of Redfield *et al.*, diffusion is seen as simply a constituent part of acculturation. Clearly, under this definition there are many components to, and modes of acculturation, such as: colonization, migration, and forced or voluntary adoption. Moore (1987: 86) states that 'acculturation' is ill defined, but that it includes a number of principles including: a) inter-cultural contact between two or more different groups; b) the emulation, borrowing, adoption, or absorption of one group by the other; c) a principle of cultural hierarchy, where one cultural group is seen as inferior, or less developed than the other, and it is usually the inferior or less developed which is changed.

More recently, Kottak (2009: 39) has defined acculturation as "… the exchange of cultural features that results when groups have continuous first hand contact. The cultures of either or both groups may be changed by this contact. With acculturation parts of the cultures change, but each group remains distinct.". Kristiansen and Larsson (2005: 26) have also defined acculturation as "… the internal or local process of assimilating foreign cultural traits as a result of diffusion between cultures. In this process the new traits are re-contextualized and given meaning". Different forms of acculturation have also been proposed by some authors (e.g. Moran 2000), for example amensalism and commensalism, which involves the hindrance (or not) of one of the groups involved in exchange/contact by the other.

Unlike diffusion, contemporary (and some older) models of acculturation recognize that there is no given cultural hierarchy and direction of transmission in the process of cultural change, although Stein, G J (2002: 904) has recently argued that acculturation carries "a unidirectional bias in explaining change.". For example, Boas (1982: 631) suggested that "there is no people whose customs have developed uninfluenced by foreign culture, that has not borrowed arts and ideas which it has developed in its own way.". Using examples from the Congo and Fiji to illustrate how western tools were incorporated into local culture, Boas details how technological innovations can move from a technologically 'advanced' culture to a 'less advanced' one, but provides an example of the reverse situation with the transference of harpoon styles from Eskimo culture to British and American whalers. In this sense, acculturation can be seen as an interactive process; there is the active and selective adoption of cultural aspects by societies, dependent upon their pre-existing system of values, beliefs, and material considerations.

In 1975, Renfrew discussed some endogenous and exogenous influences for cultural change and urban development, including 'religious predominance', 'population agglomeration', 'intraregional diversity', 'imposition', 'implantation' and 'emulation' (see also Green *et al.* 1978: section 1). In this model it is possible for either one of these factors to cause dramatic social change as the result of a change to their individual weighting. For instance, population agglomeration could lead to the creation of large urban centres, as could a religious domination of the social structure. As a pre-cursor to the notion of 'translation' and 'long-distance specialist' discussed above, Renfrew also suggested that trade and exchange can be a cause of social change, but only when "… the traded commodity achieves a value of importance in the social system, often in terms of prestige."(Renfrew 1975: 37).

In a similar vein, Odner (1983: 6) suggests that one of the significant factors for cultural change and state development on Crete was the external impetus of international trade and long-distance contact and exchange. Pydyn (1998: 99) has also asserted that "… long-distance trade (where knowledge about foreign imports was limited, partial, highly symbolic and restricted to elites) always had a very important position in establishing, maintaining, and changing social, political and economic power.". Thus, it is well acknowledged that long-distance trading contacts, and the differential access to such, provides a significant impetus for social and cultural change. However, it is also important to consider inter- as well as intra- societal contact, a factor which has often been ignored or minimized in archaeological research (Stein, G J 2002: 903).

In one example of considering intra-societal dynamics, with reference to the communities of the Deh Luran plain (Iran), Hole *et al.* (1969) perceive the most important factors influencing social change as being those internal to societies (not only external contact and exchange), but also suggested that the actual form of changes was partly dependent upon their connection to external factors and other communities:

> *... each regional development must be seen in its own light, and that internal 'adaptive' change was, more often than not, the change that mattered. Each of the prehistoric regional cultures of the Near East developed its own set of behavioural patterns aimed at exploiting the grazing and farming potential of the ecological zone in which it lived. The specific adaptation depended on each group's technology, and its contacts with neighbouring groups who had different techniques to solve their own ecological problems.* (Hole *et al.* 1969: 7).

Of interest here, and particularly to the proposed model of social relations influencing cultural change, is Renfrew's (1984a, b) proposal of the "multiplier effect" (see also Wells 1989):

> *Changes or innovations occurring in one field of human activity (in one subsystem of a culture) sometimes act so as to favour changes in other fields (in other subsystems). The multiplier effect is said to operate when these induced changes in one or more subsystems themselves act so as to enhance the original changes in the first subsystem.* (Renfrew 1984a: 274).

While the "multiplier effect" is clearly linked with cultural systems theory, it is evident that it can also be applied to the relational model of cultural change. Instead of viewing the multiplier effect as a positive feedback scenario with mutual growth induction, it is preferable to interpret the multiplier effect without value. Rather, it should be perceived as simply the 'multiplication of change' where 'sub-systems' (for want of a better term) are both negatively and positively influenced by changes in one 'sub-system', the 'multiplier effect' is therefore an 'inductive effect'. Imagine a rigid box packed full with inflated balloons – at the beginning all of the balloons are the same size, but if one balloon were to be inflated to twice its original size, the remaining balloons would all be compressed and their size reduced. Similarly, if one balloon was deflated to half of its original size, then the other balloons could expand and grow in size. However, societies are not balloons, and do not respond to changes in pressure in the same manner as air particles, and so, changes in one 'sub-system' will have an inductive effect on the other 'sub-systems', though not all will experience the same level of change. To maintain, or redefine, the social structure some 'sub-systems' may expand, while others may contract, the combination of expansions and contractions will be situation and context dependant.

Particularly since the beginning of the 'post-processual' era in archaeological theory, there has been relatively little discussion concerning the explanation of cultural change, when compared to the 'processual era' (e.g. Renfrew 1973; Renfrew and Cooke 1979), although a number of publications discuss cultural change through 'evolution' (e.g. Boyd and Richerson 2005), with the use of statistical modelling (e.g. Bentley *et al.* 2004; Shennan 2009), and Cophylogeny (Tehrani *et al.* 2010). Instead, a greater emphasis has been placed on the actual changes, the influence of trade, interaction, exchange, and the role of the individual in cultural change through notions of 'agency', 'identity', and 'experience' (e.g. Barrett 2000), 'social identity' (e.g. Sherratt, S 2010), gender, and ethnicity (e.g. Stein, G J 2002), object attraction, desirability, and "thurmaticity" (Urban 2010), power (e.g. Kelly 2010), material culture studies (Buchli 2004), communication (e.g. Doonan and Bauer 2010), and the workings of the human mind (Trigger 2004). However, these notions have also been subject to heavy criticism (e.g. Dobres and Robb 2000). There has also been a recognition that cultural change has multiple influences and that cultures are complex, dynamic systems which differ from society to society, and instance to instance (Sherratt, S 2010: 138).

The notion of 'acculturation' can be seen as a general term, acknowledging many forms of influence for cultural change. Thus there seems little point in debating the relative influential weight of internal or external factors for cultural change, as they change between differing societies. As has been previously detailed, social change, and acculturation, is indeed the product of both endogenous and exogenous factors, but more accurately social/cultural change occurs due to the *interaction and relationships between* endogenous and exogenous factors.

2.5 Application of the theoretical framework

Shanks, in re-addressing his earlier study of beer can and bottle design (Shanks and Tilley 1992: 172-240), stated that "there was no object and context, simply networks of connection" (Shanks 2001: 294-95). This recognition encompasses the interaction between contextual theory, relational theory, and the biography of objects: the values placed on material culture objects by society are simply reflections of the wider network of relationships between persons, things, societies, and the environment. The preceding section has detailed how objects and people can be perceived in a similar manner, and that objects generate a biography in the same manner as persons.

It is well known that there were trade routes linking the Baltic to the Mediterranean running through the Alpine region in the prehistory of Europe (see Chapter 3). The interaction between different communities along these trading routes will undoubtedly have affected the social structures within those communities. Any changes that these links induced may be reflected in the material culture record. While the introduction of new materials and adoption of objects may have occurred at sites in the area of study, it is equally probable that social change will manifest in differing interpretations and ascriptions of the value of goods already in use and circulation in a specific region.

Appadurai (1986: 29) discusses these changes of value in terms of 'paths and diversions', where "Change in cultural construction of commodities is to be sought in the shifting relationship of paths to diversions in the lives of commodities. The diversion of commodities from their customary paths brings in the new.". Thus, if we understand the 'normal path' of an object, we can see where and how it has been 'diverted', with an associated change in symbolism or value of that object. These diversions, if observed repetitively, and not as a result of "irregular desires and novel demand" (Appadurai 1986: 29), are a physical representation of cultural change, or continuation through change.

For instance, Shennan (1982), through a comparative study of amber deposition in burials in Denmark between the middle Neolithic and Middle Bronze Age, has suggested changing notions of values for amber and bronze or copper metalwork (see also Beck and Shennan 1991). During the Neolithic amber was used extensively as decorative adornments, while at Bronze Age sites it is more commonly found in an un-worked state, e.g. at Bjerre (Bech 1997, 2003; Earle *et al.* 1998), suggesting the value of amber had changed from a social object to a trade object (du Gardin 1993; Earle 2002; Kristiansen and Larsson 2005). To use Appadurai's terms, the amber was diverted from its normal regime of value (a prestige or social item) to another (trade commodity), and replaced by bronze and/or copper metalwork.

In short, goods become more or less valued as links to external societies and communities increase, with corresponding changing notions of prestige and status, of social or community value, and ancestral or traditional importance.

A biographical study of objects and social technologies (e.g. building construction) from the Circum-Alpine region can elucidate the changing notions of value attributed to objects/technologies in these communities. The contextualization of categories of material culture and objects is essential to the creation of a biographical study, as it is important to remember that value cannot be directly observed through the archaeological remains; value can only be inferred from the context and associations of material objects (Renfrew 1993: 14). In this manner the biographical approach to reconstructing object value through time and space is similar to the 'inter-contextual' theoretical approach proposed by Kristiansen and Larsson (2005: chapter 1). The identification of 'foreign' elements in a localized material culture illustrates areas of the 'acceptance' or 'refusal' (Kristiansen 1998b) for 'foreign' objects, value, ideas, and concepts, privileging a view of localized attitudes to cultures extraneous to the locality.

Through studying these value changes, it is possible to observe the impact that the shifting long-distance trade routes had upon the Late Bronze Age Circum-Alpine lake-dwelling societies, and vice versa, while also suggesting the balance between 'local' and 'foreign' elements in regional cultures, directly representing trade, contact, and interaction induced cultural change. It is important to consider that not only the physical objects travelled between the different regions, but also their composite networks of connections, relations, and associations. Interpreting the valuation of objects, instead of attempting to understand the 'meaning' of those objects (cf. Gosden 2005: 208), will assist the assessment of social influence exerted

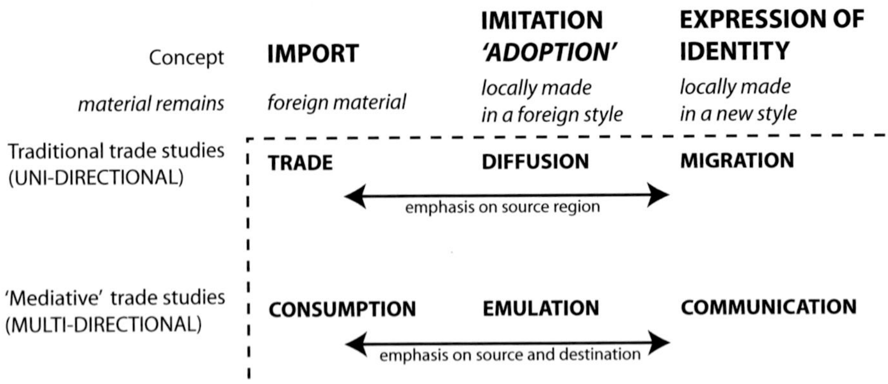

Figure 2.3: The archaeological interpretation of cultural contact through the interpretation of material culture remains. Traditional approaches to trade and exchange follow a 'uni-directional' model, tracing objects from a source area. Mediative approaches address the destination of objects, and examine the interaction between the source and destination areas (after and modified from Bauer, A A 2008: Fig. 1).

upon the Circum-Alpine lake-dwelling communities by the objects themselves and also by interaction with 'foreign' communities and materials.

In discussing trade and exchange networks with relation to the Bronze Age Black Sea region, Bauer (2008) continues Renfrew's (1993) call for trade and exchange studies to look "beyond the material" and study the "social dimensions of interaction and communication" (Bauer, A A 2008: 91), and also to examine how the 'importer' and 'exporter' roles are performed and can interact to create new cultures in a 'mediative' approach to material culture (Figure 2.3). A biographical approach to trade and exchange networks will contribute to previous studies in the Circum-Alpine region by providing such a mediative approach and permit an insight into personal and social attitudes towards value and identity.

To tackle the broader issue of cultural influences for the abandonment of the lake-dwelling tradition as a whole, it becomes necessary to take a summary approach to the intermittent periods of occupation hiatus. As Johnson eloquently states, while acknowledging "… that moment is itself the product of changing historical forces" (Johnson 1989: 205) the archaeologist "… must be prepared to describe the antecedent historical conditions in a normative way …" (Johnson 1989: 207). It is only through the viewing the lake-dwelling tradition as a normative practice – in essence the 'default' habitation system of communities inhabiting the northern Alpine forelands – that progress can be made towards the comprehension of factors inducing the rejection of this 'default' and of 3500 years of tradition.

Such a normative view also raises the issue of the hermeneutic mutual construction of the present and the past (Hodder 1991; Shanks and Tilley 1992: 107-08), and it must be noted that our contemporary cultural interpretations are in part constructed by our own cultural history. However, such hermeneutic approaches are not only relevant for researchers today; prehistoric communities perceptions of *their past* were partly created and influenced by *their present* context, and vice-versa. So, the decision to abandon lake-dwellings as a form of settlement was made with the knowledge that they were ceasing utilization of a method of settlement, and direct occupation of environmental zone, which had been utilized extensively by their ancestors and throughout their cultural history. Nevertheless, abandon it they did; clearly cultural circumstances had changed to such an extent that they required or dictated the move to new forms of settlement removed from the immediate lake-margin.

2.5.1 The problems of ethnographic analogy

It is acknowledged that some of the theoretical principles used here are developed from ethnographic studies, such as relational theory, and Spriggs (2008) has clearly detailed some issues with the use of ethnographic analogy between prehistoric Europe and the colonial Pacific regions, and particularly cites the Kula exchange ring and dividual personhood as being a product of colonial contact with the endogenous cultures in the Pacific region (see also Gosden 1985; Küchler 1993). However, the use of relational theory in this study is not a suggestion that the Late Bronze and early Iron Age societies of Europe were similar to the societies discussed in ethnographic studies from the Pacific region, or to impose notions of 'community', 'communism', 'communality', or 'plurality' on these societies (Binsbergen 2005: 19-21). Rather, it is to accept that in contemporary Western culture there is an acute sense of the individual which has developed though our scientific, political, and cultural history (e.g. Fowler 2004), and that in past societies it is possible (or even probable) that people viewed themselves more collectively, with relationships between persons assuming greater social significance than they do in the modern West.

Recently it has been shown that the relational models of people, and 'dividual', 'partible', or 'permeable' (Fowler 2004), personhood are features of spatially and temporally separated cultural locales from pre-Columbian Americas to traditional Greek society (e.g. Busby 1997; Fowler 2004; Monaghan 1998). Even in Western society there are elements (or remnants) of the notion of dividual personhood (see Jones, A 2007a: 30-31; Li Puma 1998: 56-61). For instance, when we present gifts and cards to relatives at Christmas or birthday times we are presenting them with a symbolic representation of ourselves, an object symbolising the relationship between us. Similarly, when a person moves away from home they will often be presented with a small gift, as a token of good luck but also a mode of representing the absent giver in the possessor's new home and location. Finally, through attendance of funerals and mourning people attempt to reconcile gaps which are left through the absence of people – and the absence of relationships which those people constituted. In this light, and with supporting evidence discussed earlier (e.g. Gurevich 1968), it is not a significant step to suggest that Late Bronze Age and early Iron Age European societies may have been more relational and dividual than individual in terms of personhood.

Furthermore, the fact that dividual personhood and the Kula exchange ring can be seen as a creation of colonial contact is not a significant fact in the creation of a world/object viewpoint in relational theory. It does not matter when the Kula ring or notions of dividual personhood were first conceptualized, as they have been utilized to develop a theoretical approach to objects and personhood that can be successfully applied in many different regions of the world through the archaeological notion of object biographies (see section 2.2). As this work does not attempt to suggest that European prehistoric communities were similar to those of the Pacific area, it does not incorporate the problems Spriggs (2008) suggested that other studies (e.g. Tilley 1996) encountered by creating parallels between prehistoric Europe and ethnographic studies from the Pacific area (and other parts of the world).

Chapter 3

Prehistoric European Trade Routes

Trade routes flowing through Europe during prehistory have been the focus of numerous research projects, particularly with reference to the Bronze Age Aegean and Mediterranean region (e.g. Bouzek 1997; Cline 1994; Crewe 2007; Harding 1984; Laffineur and Greco 2005; Morgenroth 1999; Sherratt, S and Sherratt 1993; Stampolidis 2003; Vianello 2005; Whittaker 2008). Occasional ship wreck finds, such as the Ulu-Burun wreck (Pulak 1998), effectively form exchange actions frozen in time and provide direct indications for the goods circulated between regions, and can be used to provide indications of maritime trade systems (e.g. Jurišić 2000). Due to the inherent variability of overland exchange routes, and unlikeness of discovering frozen exchange actions, comparatively little research has been specifically focussed on land based trade routes in northern and central Europe. Some studies have, however, considered the exchange of metalwork between northern and southern Europe (e.g. Cleland 1927; Sprockhoff 1951; Tackenberg 1971; Thrane 1975), to propose systems of long distance exchange, which have recently been re-addressed (e.g. Baron and Lasak 2007; Bietti Sestieri 1997; Della Casa 2007; Galanaki *et al.* 2007; Lang and Salač 2002; Nash Briggs 2003; Potrebica 2008; Stary 1995; Szabó and Szónóky 2002; Winter 2008).

One of the main limitations for the archaeological interpretation of prehistoric exchange routes is to identify what was actually exchanged. Preservation conditions ensure that ceramics, bone, metalwork and lithics are particularly well represented in the archaeological record, but these are not the only materials used during prehistory – as amply demonstrated by the wide range of organic materials found in the waterlogged lake-dwellings of the Circum-Alpine region. Textiles, furs, hides, people, animals, food products, and ointments may all have been exchanged over long and short distances (Artursson and Nicolis 2007: 336; Bouzek 1997: 210; Kristiansen 1998a: 180; Nash Briggs 2003; Sherratt, A 1993: 31, 38; Stary 1995), but their identification in the archaeological record is difficult, not least because many such items would have been entirely consumed. Written evidence from the Mediterranean region indicates the wide range of materials which formed "trade without a trace" (Wiener 1991: 325), and stable isotope evidence is beginning to provide indications for the circulation of organic materials in northern Europe (Bergfjord *et al.* 2012). Perhaps the most identifiable item, through both general dominance of the Baltic deposit(s) and archaeometric analysis (e.g. Angelini and Bellintani 2005), to have originated in northern Europe and circulated to the south is amber, the distribution of manufactured objects of which have often been used to suggest trade routes (Bouzek 1993; Bukowski 1988; De Navarro 1925; du Gardin 1993; Galanaki *et al.* 2007; Stahl 2006).

3.1 European long-distance trade routes

One of the more recent schematizations of long-distance exchange routes flowing through the Circum-Alpine region was produced by Sherratt, A (1998) in *The Human Geography of Europe: A Prehistoric Perspective*. Exchange between northern and southern Europe was interpreted as flowing along either an eastern "Danubian" route or a western "Alpine" route, depending upon socio-economic conditions in the driving Mediterranean region (Figure 3.1). Predominance of either the Danubian or Alpine route fluctuated over time, and during the Late Bronze Age and early Iron Age (early first millennium BC), it was the Alpine route which came to flourish (e.g. Kristiansen 1998a; Kristiansen and Larsson 2005: 116-84; Pydyn 1999; Sherratt, A 1993, 1998; Sherratt, S and Sherratt 1993). However, it must be stressed that these routes are only schematized, and objects would have in fact been exchanged over a multifarious and polythetic system culminating not only in general north-south flows, but also east to west movements (e.g. Morgenroth 1999), and that communities may have been involved in exchange partnerships leading in multiple directions (Pydyn 1999: 21, 56). Furthermore, it is unlikely that many of the goods flowing through an exchange network would travel the entire distance, through some exceptions may be amber from the Baltic reaching the Mediterranean, or so called *Pfahlbauperlen* glass beads flowing from the Po Plain to northern Germany (see Jennings 2014b: 44-54). Instead, objects most

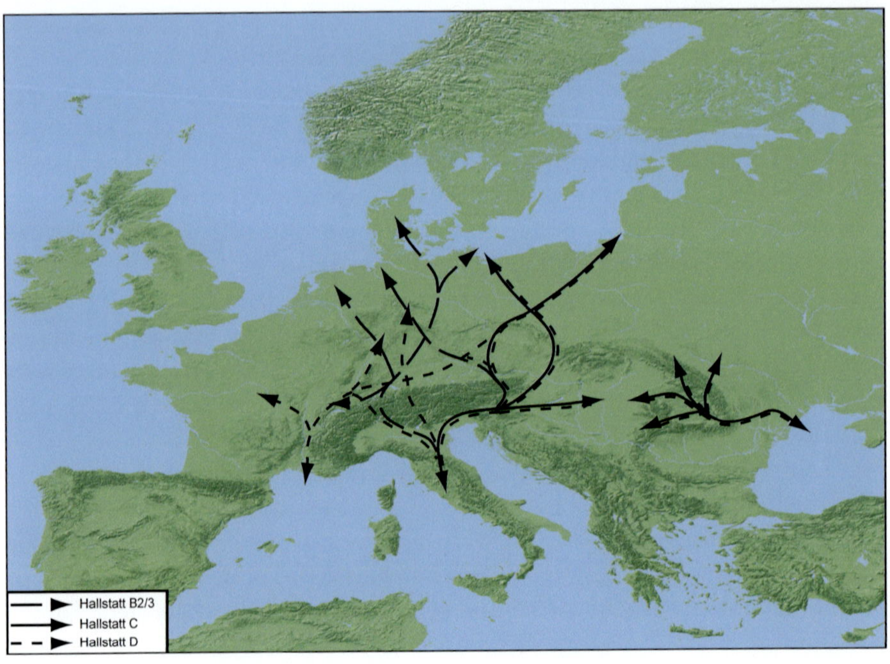

Figure 3.1: Schematic illustration of European trade routes of the Late Bronze and early Iron Ages. Mediterranean routes have been excluded from the illustration, but centres of manufacture and exchange should be envisaged in the Greek peninsula, southern Italy and in the Turkey (after Jennings 2014b; data from Sherratt, A 1998).

likely flowed in a series of regional networks between short and medium distance communities, with some objects effectively 'piggy-backing' across the boundaries of such regional networks to travel large portions of the route.

Just as objects primarily moved in regional exchange systems with few travelling the entire network, it is possible that the participants of exchange travelled primarily within the regional system and rarely reached the distant ends of a network. In this manner, it is questionable as to whether individuals knew where products they exchanged originated or were destined – even if they were only travelling short or medium distances. Knowledge of distant places would have travelled in the same manner as the objects – moving over shorter cycles and culminating in the general spread of knowledge over longer distances. However, concepts are more susceptible to corruption than objects, and just as in the English school yard game "Chinese whispers" or "gossip", knowledge of places would have mutated into myths and legends and fantastical fictions as it was communicated between individuals and communities and the distance from source location increases (Fontijn 2009: 141-42; Jennings 2014b: 20-21). The classical Greek belief that amber came from the Electridae islands near the mouth or the Eridanos river, which several authors have suggested refers to the northern Adriatic and the River Po (see Palavestra 2007: 349), provides an excellent illustration for such diffusion of knowledge. From the Greek perspective, the northern Adriatic may well have appeared as the origin of amber, with Late Bronze Age communities such as Grignano Polesine and Frattesina – prehistorically located much near the coast than today – being significant production and exchange centres which could have circulated amber into the Mediterranean world (Bellintani 1997; Salzani 2009).

The ability to participate in exchange networks, and gather knowledge of distant places may have been used as a method of creating and maintaining status and legitimacy through actively promoting and controlling the access to knowledge within communities (cf. Helms 1988; Kristiansen and Larsson 2007).

There are many forms of object found in both the Carpathian Basin / Danubian region and the Italian peninsula which support the interaction of these regions with the communities of the central Mediterranean (e.g. Bietti Sestieri 1988; Bouzek 1994; Górski and Makarowicz 2007; Jones, R E *et al.* 2005; Marazzi 2003; Vagnetti 1999). There is even a fragment of oxhide ingot from Germany which indicates the progressive circulation of forms of metal stock of Mediterranean origin to communities north of the Alps (see Jones, M R 2007b; Primas and Pernicka 1998).

Incorporation of communities into long distance exchange networks has been interpreted as having influenced cultural change, typically flowing from the advanced Mediterranean 'core' to the more primitive hinterland 'margin' or 'periphery'. For instance, with the system of Andrew Sherratt (1993), it has been argued that communities in the Carpathian Basin began a system of settlement fortification in order to control access to the material sources and trade routes linking to the Mediterranean region (see Bouzek 1994; Jockenhövel 1985; Sherratt, A 1993: 26-29). It has even been suggested that some of the fortified sites display the influence of Mediterranean cultures, directly reflecting the significance of interaction with those cultures in the construction of fortified settlements (e.g.

Kristiansen and Larsson 2005: 162). The fortified site Monkodonja on the Istrian coast also shows some indications of Mediterranean association (Hänsel 2007; Hänsel and Teržan 2000; Teržan *et al.* 1999), but the most well-known example of such influence comes from the Iron Age fortification at the Heuneburg (Germany) with a mudbrick wall (Arnold 2010; Gersbach 1995; Kimmig, W 2000b). Such sites placed in strategic locations would have been able to control the movement of people through the landscape, and centralising production practices into manufacturing centres would also have created effective trade 'magnets' attracting exchange partners due to the availability of objects in that location (Kristiansen and Larsson 2005: 125; Sherratt, A 1993: 29).

Fortified highland and hilltop sites are also known from regions north of the Alps during the Late Bronze Age and early Iron Age, and may have been positioned at strategic locations to control access to metal ore producing regions and exchange routes (e.g. Heske 2009; Jockenhövel 1974; Kuhlmann and Segschneider 2004; Winghart 1998, 2000). It has also been proposed that Early and Middle Bronze Age fortified sites in the Alps were connected to the extraction and production of copper (Artursson and Nicolis 2007; Krause 2005). Some of the Late Bronze Age fortified highland sites in the northern Alpine region, such as Montlingerberg (Figure 3.2) and Wittnauer Horn (both in Switzerland), have produced artefacts attesting to their incorporation in inter-regional exchange networks (Berger, L and

Figure 3.2: Montlingerberg in the Rhine Valley, Canton St. Gallen, Switzerland. The fortified settlement is situated on the small hill on the left of the image, and adjacent to the modern course of the Rhine. Although the settlement is situated on a small hill surrounded by higher mountains, the flat plateau enabled settlement in a position commanding the valley plain. (Image "La petite ville d'Altstatten dans la Vallée du Rhin, Canton de St. Gallen" by Johann Ludwig Bleuler (c. 1835). Image held by Eidgenössisches Archiv für Denkmalpflege (EAD): Graphische Sammlung, item no. GS-GUGE-BLEULER-2b-29).

Brogli 1980; Bersu 1945; Steinhauser-Zimmermann 1989, 2002; Steinhauser and Primas 1987).

The emergence of so-called "Princely sites" or "*Fürstensitze*" during the Iron Age continued the development of fortified hilltop sites, and represents the continuing significance of such centres in the social system across a large area of Central Europe. One of the best researched sites – the Heuneburg overlooking the Danube in Germany – indicates exchange systems reaching the central Mediterranean region (Kimmig, W 2000b). The routes by which materials travelled to central Europe from the Mediterranean were somewhat different in this period compared to the Late Bronze Age (Figure 3.1), with the founding of Massalia on the southern coast of France providing a new route which may be observed in the distribution of Attic ceramics along the Rhône valley, though trans-Alpine routes were also in contemporaneous use (Guggisberg 1991; Krause *et al.* 2008).

3.2 The lake-dwelling connection

There is abundant material evidence to indicate that the lake-settlements were connected to communities in both southern and northern Europe (Jennings 2014b), which has even led some authors to talk of a "lake-dwelling route" linking Italy to Scandinavia (e.g. Kristiansen 1993: 143; Kristiansen 1998a: 161; Sprockhoff 1951). How the Late Bronze Age lake-settlements link in to the long distance exchange systems is detailed in greater depth in Chapter 4, but it is clear that the lake-dwellings were incorporated in trans-Alpine exchange routes long before the Late Bronze Age. In fact, there is abundant evidence from the Neolithic and Early Bronze Age to suggest exchange systems linking to communities in northern Italy.

For instance, the distribution of Neolithic flint axes, clay stamps (*Pintandera*), and ceramics indicate exchange linking southern and northern Alpine regions, as do Bronze Age needles, crucibles, and ceramics (e.g. Della Casa *et al.* 1999; Köninger and Schlichtherle 2001; Leuzinger 2010: 100-01; Pétrequin 2011; Primas and Schmid-Sikimić 1997; Schnekenburger 2002; Wyss 1990). There are even significant construction similarities between Early Bronze Age pile-dwellings on Lake Constance and from Fiavé in northern Italy, suggesting that a direct – possibly personal – connection existed between the two areas (Köninger and Schlichtherle 2001: 45). It is also possible that concepts and practices of exchange circulated, as attested by a "loaf of bread idol" (*Brotlaibidol*) from Bodman-Schachen 1 (Köninger 1997; Köninger and Schlichtherle 2001: 46). These items are predominantly found in the southern Alpine forelands and Po Plain, and the Carpathian Basin (Fogel and Langer 1999), and it has been suggested that they were employed as trade counters or tokens of exchange to be broken once a partnership was completed or brought together (similar to modern friendship tokens) to show identity and right to participate after a period of separation (Bandi 1974; Cornaggia Castiglioni 1976; Fogel and Langer 1999; Zanini and Martinelli 2005).

Other than the basic requirement of human societies to interact, the reasons why lake-settlements show comparatively high rates or levels of incorporation to exchange networks when compared to inland sites is unclear. One factor may be the agglomeration of populations into comparatively large groupings forming centres of production and thereby attracting exchange partners. Alternatively, the position of many lake-dwellings on access points to riverine networks may also be a factor. Rivers would have provided an efficient means of transport – when used directly by boat – or effective navigational aids when land transport followed the river valley (Gambari 2004; Nymoen 2008; Sherratt, A 1996). Rivers are natural barriers creating obstacles in the landscape and would have formed boundaries, possibly demarcating the extent of community territory, but would also have provided locations for interaction and access between different regions (cf. Haughey 2007, 2013; Mullin 2012). The intersection between lakes and rivers would have provided excellent opportunities to control access to and from river systems, which may account for areas of high concentration of lake-dwellings, such as around the outlet of Lake Zurich (Figure 3.3, see also section 5.1.1). Many dugout canoes and paddles found in wetlands of the northern Alpine forelands suggest that lakes and rivers were being actively used (Arnold 1995; Eberschweiler

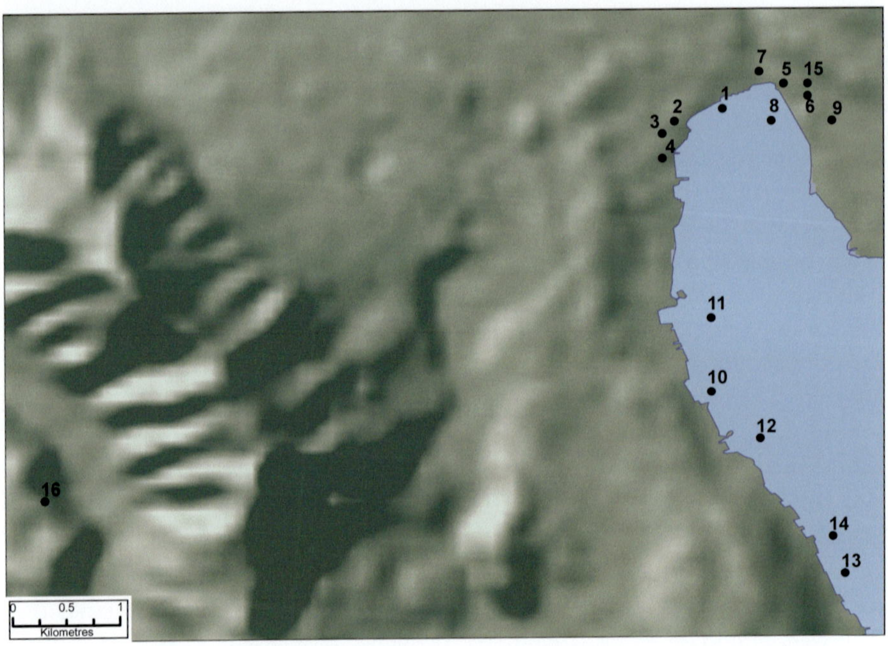

Figure 3.3: A clustering of lake-settlements around the outflow of Lake Zurich is evident compared to their more dispersed occurrence further around the lakeshore. Sites: 1) Zurich-Alpenquai. 2) – Breitingerstrasse-Rentenanstalt. 3) – Breitingerstrasse-Zürich Versicherung. 4) – Mythenschloss. 5) – Kleiner-Hafner. 6) – Mozartstrasse. 7) – Bauschanze. 8) – Grosser-Hafner. 9) – Seefeld. 10) – Wollishofen-Bad. 11) – Wollishofen-Haumesser. 12) – Wollishofen-Horn. 13) – Kilchberg-Bendlikon. 14) – Kilchberg-Mönchhof. 15) – Opéra. 16) – Üetliberg (hilltop site) (data from Bauer, I et al. 1991; Palafittes 2010).

2004), but it is unclear whether these were used for exchange purposes, fishing, or general movement and transport within the local area; it is most likely that they were used for a number of purposes.

While it would be an over simplification to suggest that lake-dwellings were established purely in order to access or control access to riverine transport routes, such aspects should be considered as contributing factors to site selection. However, it is evident that not all lake-dwellings were established with such considerations; some settlements, such as Ürschhausen-Horn (Gollnisch-Moos 1999) and Wasserburg-Buchau (Kimmig, W 1992), were constructed on minor lakes with limited access to rivers. Furthermore, when situated on the course of large river networks lake-settlements should not be considered as end points on a network, but as access points, enabling local communities within the lake and river hinterland to access exchange routes, and providing interchange points for goods between land- and waterborne means of transport. In this manner the lake-dwellings effectively fulfilled the role of fortified settlements in inland regions, by controlling access to trade routes and material sources.

Chapter 4

Exchange and Biographies of Objects in the Northern Circum-Alpine Region

Recent research has sought to address the role of northern Alpine lake-dwellings in trans-Alpine exchange routes which circulated materials between northern Europe and the Mediterranean region (Jennings 2014b). Through the study of a wide range of material culture objects, primarily different forms of bronzework, but also jewellery beads and ceramics, it has been shown that Late Bronze Age lake-dwelling communities in Switzerland were well connected to areas of central Europe and northern Italy. However, the material culture suggests that the degree of interaction between each of these regions was not equal; there appears to have been a stronger connection between the northern Alpine lake-settlements and communities of central western Germany around Mainz and Frankfurt than there was between the northern Alpine forelands and the southern Alps or northern

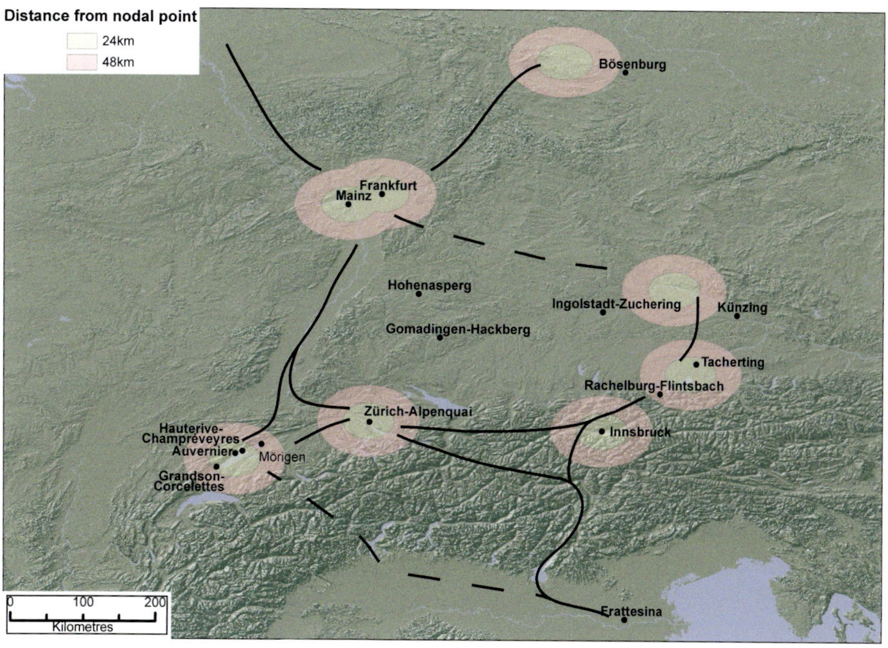

Figure 4.1: Potential nodal regions on the exchange routes running through the northern Alpine lake-dwelling region. Frattesina is shown without halo, but it is considered a trade node. The halo covering Auvernier, Grandson-Corcelettes, Hauterive-Champréveyres and Mörigen is, for convenience, centred on Lake Neuchâtel.

Italy (Figure 4.1). The distribution of materials of northern Alpine style to western France, northern Germany, Scandinavia, eastern Germany and Austria, and the Carpathian basin indicates that objects could travel significant distances from their region of origin, but whether they moved by means of a direct connection or in 'down-the-line' exchange remains uncertain. It is however possible that some objects were imported to the northern Alpine region by migrants from distant lands, such as a collection of three Nordic style items from Grandson-Corcelettes (Lake Neuchâtel) or a *Herrnbaumgarten* style razor from Chelin in the Alpine Rhône valley (Jennings 2014b: 90, 157; Nicolas 2003; Sprockhoff 1966).

The quantity of bronze objects of likely northern Alpine lake-dwelling origin found throughout central Europe in fact suggests that some of these settlements were significant centres for the production and exchange of objects. While it cannot be stated that *all* lake-dwellings were such centres of production, for example the relatively small Greifensee-Böschen or the relatively isolated Ürschhausen-Horn (see section 5.2), some of the larger sites, such as Hauterive-Champréveyres and Grandson-Corcelettes (Lake Neuchâtel) or Mörigen (Lake Biel), which have produced indications of imported objects, relatively high population, and metalwork production, may be interpreted as such 'central' sites. However, the products made at these sites did not necessarily travel together or in the same direction. For instance the casting and circulation of *socketed* and *solid handle* knives (*Tüllenmesser* and *Phantasiemesser*) are indicated through moulds and knives at sites around Lake Bourget (France) and Lake Neuchâtel in western Switzerland, but moving away from this region the *socketed* form is dominantly more westerly

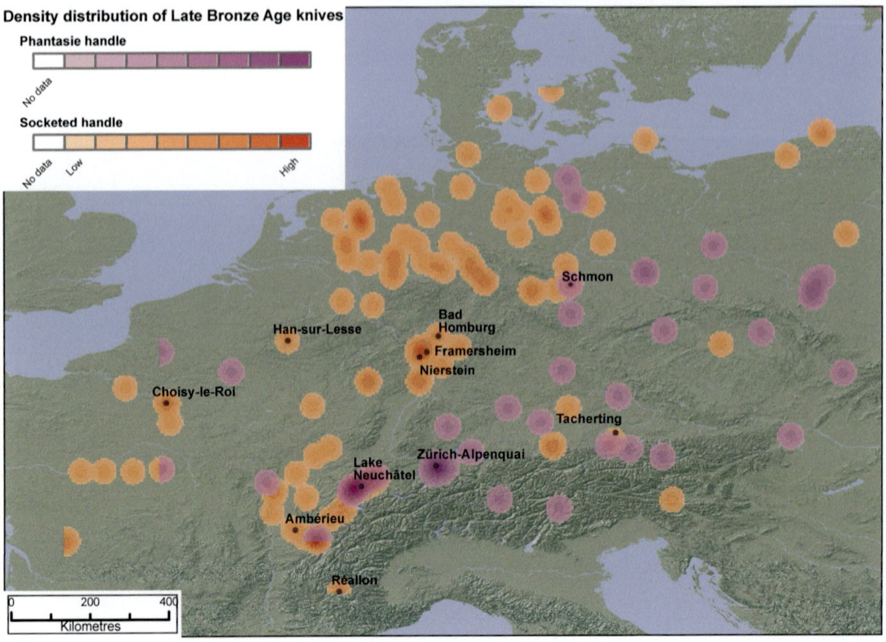

Figure 4.2: Comparative distribution of socketed and solid handled knives. It is clearly evident that the two forms followed different trajectories through Europe.

orientated, while the *solid handle* type are more easterly orientated (Figure 4.2). Such difference does not only occur on an inter-regional scale, but also within the northern Alpine forelands; many of the items and styles well represented in the region of Lake Neuchâtel are rare occurrences in the eastern zone (Jennings 2014b: e.g. Razors, Arm-and Leg-rings; Rychner 1979).

Summarizing a range of forms of Late Bronze Age material culture (see Jennings 2014b), several potential routes of interaction can be suggested flowing through the lake-dwelling region (Figure 4.1). The primary axes of interaction link both western and eastern Switzerland to the Rhine and Main valleys as far as Mainz and Frankfurt, even though there appears to be a relatively weak direct link between eastern and western Switzerland (see Rychner 1979). A secondary axis links the northern Alpine forelands to the southern Alpine region and Po Plain, most likely following valleys and passes across the Alps in eastern Switzerland and Austria, for example across the Brenner Pass and along the Inn valley (Della Casa 2002, 2007). Eastern and western Switzerland show low intensity exchange systems with, respectively, Austria and central and western France. Finally, the distribution of certain Late Bronze Age swords, for instance the *Mörigen* type, and razors also suggest a route of exchange and participation in similar systems of style and symbolism extending from Lake Neuchâtel to southern France along the Rhône and Saône valleys.

Identifying the routes of exchange and interaction flowing through the northern Alpine forelands during the early Iron Age is more difficult than for the Late Bronze Age predecessors. Two factors contribute to this difficulty: firstly, the generally poorer state of preservation of ironwork objects makes typological classification an issue, and secondly, the reduced representation of, especially early, Iron Age sites within the region means that the primary source of material is that recovered from burial contexts (Ebersbach *et al.* 2010). Material culture from known sites suggests that there was more of a continuation than revolution between the Late Bronze Age and Iron Age material culture styles (Dunning and Rychner 1994; Ruoff 1974). There does, however, appear to be a significant change in the involvement of the area in wider exchange patterns. Instead of holding a central place in the circulation of numerous forms of material culture, the former lake-dwelling area in fact appears to be relatively marginalized. Those early Iron Age materials, for instance types of ring jewellery, which are known suggest that even within the Alpine forelands styles and distribution became far more regionalized (Jennings 2014b: 129-30). The distribution of the *Gündlingen* type early Iron Age (Hallstatt C period) sword also suggests that the northern Alpine forelands were somewhat marginal in the distribution of these prestige weapons. The European distribution of *Gündlingen* form is reminiscent of the *Mörigen* type, with extension into southern France along the Rhône and Saône valleys and arcing across into southern Germany and along the Danube, but this time Switzerland is generally absent from the distribution (Cowen 1968). During the Hallstatt D period, however, the occurrence of short swords and daggers similar to those of southern Germany indicate that the northern Alpine forelands were once again incorporated – to some extent – in wider systems of exchange (Jennings 2014b: 59-61).

From the later stages of the Hallstatt era, and continuing into the La Tène period, Attic ware ceramics reached sites north of the Alps, particularly the well-known '*Fürstensitze*', such as the Heuneburg (D) and Mont Lassois (FR), but also in burials and smaller settlements (Guggisberg 2011; Krause *et al.* 2008; Pape 2000). There are several sites with Attic ceramics in the northern Alpine region, including *Fürstensitzen* at Châtillon-sur-Glâne and Üetliberg (Bauer, I *et al.* 1991; Béarat and Bauer 1994; Lüscher 1991; Pare 1991). It was not only Mediterranean ceramics travelling to regions north of the Alps, but also various forms of bronzework, such as the Etruscan *Schnabelkannen* (Vorlauf 1997). Although many of these bronze pouring jugs are recorded from sites and burials in central and southern Germany and parts of southern Switzerland, they are conspicuously absent from the northern Alpine forelands (Jennings 2014b: 155; Vorlauf 1997). The distribution of *Attic* and *Etruscan* ceramics and bronzes suggest that both the Rhône-Saône and trans-Alpine routes were employed to move goods from the Mediterranean to central Europe. Thus, while communities inhabiting the northern Alpine forelands may have assisted objects along routes of exchange between central and northern Italy and central Germany, they were not particularly able to extract materials from the exchange system or participate in the use of such objects.

4.1 Biographies of objects

Through the study of a wide range of material culture objects, and the reconstruction of hypothesized "ideal biographies" it has been suggested that it might be possible to identify instances of specific migration to – or from – the northern Alpine region, and also that there was a relatively little transfer of culturally associated values of objects as they were exchanged between different regions of Europe (Jennings 2014b). Such a study draws upon the ability of the biographic approach to address the various attitudes towards, and valuation of, objects in contemporaneous but spatially separated locations. The biographic approach also enables the theorization of object values within a single spatial setting over an extended duration. In this situation the aim is not to examine how the valuation of objects was influenced by external factors, but to observe endogenous cultural development.

4.1.1 Glass and amber jewellery beads

One of the best indicators for the incorporation of the Late Bronze Age lake-dwelling communities in exchange networks linking to northern Italy are the so called *Pfahlbauperlen* (Figure 4.3) – lake-dwelling beads – comprising blue glass barrel shaped beads with white inlay or blue based pointed beads with inlaid white 'eyes' (Bellintani and Stefan 2009; Haevernick 1978). Despite their abundance in the northern Alpine region the presently known production sites for these beads are in the Po Plain (Angelini *et al.* 2005; Angelini *et al.* 2009). Widely circulated during the Late Bronze Age, the *Pfahlbauperlen* are recorded in many lake-settlements of Switzerland and the northern Alpine region, but relatively few burials (Jennings 2014b: 32). When found in burials, such beads may be associated with both female and male identities (Beeching 1977; Kaenel and Klausener 1990;

Moinat and David-Elbiali 2003). With the decline of Frattesina in the early Iron Age, and changing glass production practices in northern Italy, the production and circulation of these beads ceased (Angelini *et al.* 2005; Polla *et al.* 2011).

Initial replacement of the *Pfahlbauperlen* may have incorporated beads produced locally north of the Alps – such as the black glass *Hagenauer* form (Haevernick 1975) – and later by the well-known *stratified eye* beads during the Hallstatt D and La Tène periods (Frey and Roth 1983; Frey *et al.* 1987; Kunter and Haevernick 1995; Venclová 1983). These Iron Age beads are predominantly found in burial contexts, typically female, and in larger numbers than their Late Bronze Age predecessors (Jennings 2014b: 33).

One of the materials identifiable as flowing in the opposite direction to the *Pfahlbauperlen* is amber. Early Bronze Age finds – such as an amber bead covered in gold foil from Zurich-Mozartstrasse (Barfield 1991; Gross *et al.* 1987; Schmidheiny 2006) indicate that amber was reaching the northern Alpine region significantly before the Late Bronze Age (see also Stahl 2006). The Late Bronze Age amber find locations are again predominantly from lake-dwelling sites, with relatively few finds from burials or other contexts, and are of amber used to create individual beads of northern Alpine style, while those of southern Alpine form were largely rejected (Jennings 2014b: 28). In contrast, Iron Age amber beads are generally found in burial contexts, with few from settlement locations, and while still used to create individual beads, can also be combined with other materials to adorn larger objects, such as fibula (e.g. at Aarwange, Cama, and Langentahal, Stahl

Figure 4.3: Jewellery beads from lake-dwellings. Faience and amber beads are known from the Early Bronze Age site at Arbon-Bleiche 2. Amber, glass – including the so-called Pfahlbauperlen – and jet beads have been recovered from Ürschhausen-Horn. (Photograph © and courtesy of Amt für Archäologie des Kantons Thurgau, Daniel Steiner, www.archaeologie.tg.ch).

2006) or composite necklaces (e.g. Waltershausen and Niedererlbach, Stahl 2006), or – in the wider northern Circum-Alpine region – sword hilts (e.g. *Mindelheim* type sword in a burial at Marainville-sur-Madon, France, Stahl 2006).

4.1.2 Ring jewellery

Bronze and Iron Age arm- and leg-ring jewellery from Switzerland and adjoining regions has been catalogued under the *Prähistorische Bronzefunde* series, providing a relatively up-to-date reference for the material (Pászthory 1985; Schmid-Sikimić 1996). The quantity of Late Bronze Age rings is much higher than their Iron Age counterparts, and in fact, they are one of the most numerous forms of bronzework excavated from Late Bronze Age lake-dwellings and terrestrial sites (Figure 4.4). Ring jewellery types also provide one of the main indicators for the involvement of the lake-dwelling communities in Late Bronze Age exchange systems in central Europe, and their dominance of those systems for the production and export of quantities of cast bronzework (Jennings 2014b: 139-40). Within the northern Circum-Alpine region ring jewellery is primarily known from lake-dwelling contexts during the Late Bronze Age, but are also recorded from both male and female burial assemblages (e.g. Beeching 1977; David-Elbiali and Moinat 2005; Moinat and David-Elbiali 2003), and structured – hoard – deposits within the boundaries of lake-dwellings (Fischer, V 2012; Kimmig, W 1992; Rychner 1987). Within their broader distribution ring jewellery of likely lake-dwelling origin are mainly found in hoard deposits (Jennings 2014b: 124-44). While some types of ring are relatively simple and formed from twisted bronze wire (e.g. *Morges* type), the cast pieces can incorporate varying levels of decoration from simple ribbing (e.g. *Mörigen* and *Sion* types) to complex inscribed or stamped patterns (e.g. *Corcelettes* and *Auvernier* types), though some undecorated examples are also known (Pászthory 1985).

In contrast to the widespread distribution of the Late Bronze Age forms of ring jewellery, the early Iron Age varieties are significantly more regional and found in fewer quantities. In terms of context, the Iron Age forms are primarily recorded from – typically female – burials. Other jewellery items found in association with the rings have been used to reconstruct jewellery sets, which the eligibility to wear may have been dictated by age and social status (Schmid-Sikimić 1996: 5). Some forms of the Iron Age ring jewellery continue the twisted wire style of the Late Bronze Age (e.g. the *Valangin* type) and other forms (e.g. the *Lyssach* type) provide a continuation of decorative style and motifs from the Late Bronze Age, with relatively minor changes and re-arrangements (Schmid-Sikimić 1996). The large barrel armbands recorded from HaD sites in Switzerland are some of the most elaborately decorated pieces, with complex banding and zonation of repetitive designs (Schmid-Sikimić 1996) reminiscent of Late Bronze Age styles (Figure 4.5).

4.1.3 Swords and spears

Weapons are another of the object categories for which a large corpus of material is available from the Late Bronze Age lake-dwellings in the northern Alpine region. In fact, several forms of sword, such as the *Mörigen* and *Auvernier* types, are named

Figure 4.4: Late Bronze Age bronzework typical of the lake-settlements. A wide range of bronze objects have been recovered from the lake-dwellings, and also inland locations, including various styles of ring-jewellery, sickle, spearhead, razor, axe, and knife. The assemblage illustrated here is from hoard deposit at Elisabethenschanze, Basel, but the objects, particularly the 'Corcelettes' type arm-rings (circle, half-circle and zig-zag decoration), are well known from lake-settlements, and particularly around Lake Neuchâtel, over 75km to the south-west of Basel. (Photograph © and courtesy of Peter Portner, Historisches Museum Basel).

after lake-dwellings where they were found, but there is no direct evidence for the manufacture of such swords at the sites. Evidence for the production of Bronze Age swords across Europe as a whole is very scarce, but a mould for an early Late Bronze Age sword from the lake-dwelling Font-La Pianta, Lake Neuchâtel

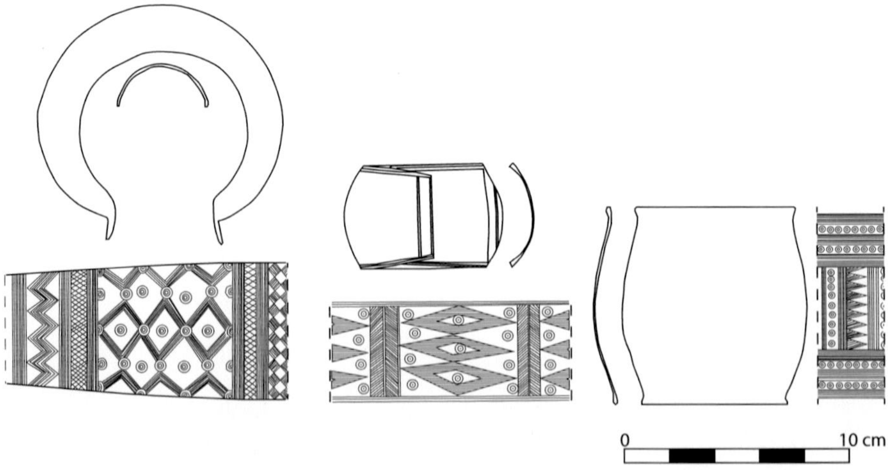

Figure 4.5: Continuation and elaboration of decorative elements can be seen through the Late Bronze Age and Iron Age. Ring jewellery particularly demonstrates the continuation. Left: Late Bronze Age (HaB2-B3) 'Corcelettes' type arm-ring from Grandson-Corcelettes (Swiss National Museum Inv. No. 9208); Centre: early Iron Age (HaD) arm-band type 'Wetzikon' from Wetzikon "Stegen/Schöngau" (Swiss National Museum Inv. No. 3257e); Right: early Iron Age (HaD) 'short tunnel arm-band, type 1' from "La Béroche" (Cantonal Museum of Archaeology, Neuchâtel without Inv. No.) (images redrawn from Pászthory 1985: no. 1349; and Schmid-Sikimić 1996: nos. 126 & 48).

(Mödlinger 2011; Schauer 1971), indicates that such items were being produced in the northern Alpine region. Predominant find contexts of Late Bronze Age swords in Switzerland are in lake-dwellings, with few from other forms of site. In neighbouring southern Germany and Austria, it is evident that a fluctuation of deposition patterns occurred during the Bronze Age, with variable deposition in burials, hoards, or wetland locations, tending towards primary deposition in wetland locations – and seldom burials – during the latter stages, i.e. HaB2/B3, of the Late Bronze Age (Krämer 1985; Roymans 1991; Schauer 1971; Torbrügge 1972).

In contrast to the relative lack of evidence for sword production, there are several sites, for instance Auvernier, Cortaillod-Est, Grandson-Corcelettes, Hauterive-Champréveyres, Mörigen, and Zug-Sumpf, which have produced casting moulds for spearheads in the northern Alpine forelands (Arnold 1986; Bauer, I and Northover 1998; Bernatzky-Goetze 1987; Colomb and Muyden 1896; Rychner-Faraggi 1993; Rychner 1979; Weidmann 1982). The distribution of spearheads with a specific shape and form of decoration – ribbing around the base of the socket – has been used in support of the so-called "*Pfahlbau*" route linking the Alpine region and northern Europe (Jacob-Friesen 1967: 262; Kristiansen 1998b). Spearheads are again primarily recorded from lake-dwelling contexts in the northern Alpine region, though some are recorded from hoard assemblages within these settlements, for instance at Auvernier-Nord (Fischer, V 2012; Rychner 1987).

Moving to the beginning of Iron Age, there are relatively few swords recorded from Switzerland, but during the HaD period a number of short swords and daggers are known (Sievers 1982). As previously detailed (see above), the HaC period swords, such as the *Gündlingen* type – suggest that the northern Alpine forelands were largely excluded from the circulation of wider European styles. Daggers relating to the HaD period indicate that the region was once again re-integrated – to a degree – in wider European styles, with similar forms found across Switzerland, southern Germany and Austria (Sievers 1982). Iron Age swords and daggers are primarily found in burial contexts, and occasionally – outside of Switzerland – show the adornment of the hilt with other materials, such as amber and ivory (e.g. Marainville-sur-Madon, France (Stahl 2006), Hallstatt, Austria (Gerdsen 1986), and Trommetsheim, Germany (Schauer 1971)). Such applied decoration is an unusual occurrence on Late Bronze Age forms, and when applied consisted of inlaid iron or other metal (for instance from Mörigen and Grandson-Corcelettes (Bernatzky-Goetze 1987; Krämer 1985; Quillfeldt 1995)). The use of small quantities of iron – and other metals – to decorate various objects during the Bronze Age may represent attempts to individualise specific objects and increase their status or prestige through achieving specific colour combinations or the incorporation of novel or rare materials (Berger, D 2011; Jennings 2014b: 161-65).

Spearheads have rarely been recorded in the northern Alpine forelands from early Iron Age (HaC-HaD) contexts, and where they have been the preserved remains make an identification of form or style more difficult than for their bronze predecessors (e.g. Drack 1973). Although some works have considered the spearheads found in votive deposits of the Alpine range (Pernet and Schmid-Sikimić 2008; Wyss 1981), those known from the Alpine forelands primarily provenance from burials. However, in burials of northern Switzerland, southern Germany and eastern France there appears to be a reduction in the combination of spearheads with other weapons, particularly *Gündlingen* swords, in HaC period burials (Jennings 2014b: 76), with the return of such associations in burials containing daggers in southern Germany and Austria during HaD (Sievers 1982).

4.1.4 Knives and razors

Many knives have been recovered from Late Bronze Age lake-dwellings in the northern Circum-Alpine region, but they have generally been classified under a scheme unique to Switzerland and not directly comparable to other catalogues available for central Europe (Bauer, I *et al.* 2004; Bianco Peroni 1976; Hohlbein 2008; Jiráň 2002; Prüssing 1982; Říhovský 1972; Rychner 1979). Similarities do exist between the forms known in Switzerland and from other parts of central Europe, with several types, such as *Baumgarten* reported as belonging to the "lake-dwelling" group of knives (*Pfahlbaumesser*) (e.g. Jiráň 2002: 57). Various styles of decoration were applied to the knives, with assorted motifs including triangles, crosses, lines, circles, half circles, and hatchings appearing on both the blade face and ridge, while grooves cast into spacing areas between the blade butt and handle became common during the HaB2/B3 period (Jennings 2014b: 95-101). It has been suggested that a distinction can be drawn between knives incorporated in burials and items found in settlements based on decoration (Říhovský 1972: 71), but in Switzerland the majority of both decorated and un-decorated knives are recorded from lake-settlements.

A large number of single sided razors are also recorded from Late Bronze Age lake-dwellings of eastern and western Switzerland, but proportionately more are found in the western area (Jennings 2014b: 80-85; Jockenhövel 1971). In contrast to the forms of objects discussed above, Late Bronze Age razors are primarily regional in their distribution, with few examples travelling outside of main cores of distribution – although there are some notable exceptions, such as a *Villanovan* type at Mörigen and a *Herrnbaumgarten* type at Chelin (Jockenhövel 1971) – and regions of stylistic dominance (Hennig, Hilke 1986: Fig. 12). Although the vast majority of razors in Switzerland are recorded from lake-dwellings, and a high proportion are recorded from lake-settlements in adjoining southern Germany and eastern France, inclusion in burial or hoard assemblages was the primary mode of deposition for razors in central Europe (Jennings 2014b: Fig. 42). Very few of the HaB period razors were decorated, and some of which is inherited decoration from converted objects (Jennings 2014a, b: 86-88), unlike their counterparts from the Italian peninsula (Bianco Peroni 1979), which may suggest a reduced social function of these as objects of status or identity creation when compared to, for example, the richly decorated knives incorporated in burial assemblages.

The situation with Iron Age knives and razors is less clear, with significantly fewer recorded in the published material – at least partly due to preservation factors resulting from the predominant replacement of bronze with iron as the primary material used for these objects. When these items are recorded, they are mainly known from burial contexts (e.g. Drack 1973), reflecting the common practice of depositing items of personal equipment in burials. Evidence from the Italian peninsula suggests that razors were not an object with exclusively male association (Bianco Peroni 1979), but remain an unusual occurrence in female burials north of the Alps, while iron knives are recorded from both male and female burials (Lüscher 1989; Lüscher and Müller 1999).

4.1.5 Late Bronze Age to Iron Age biographical changes

From the brief discussion of various forms of material culture it is clear that some changes in the biographical and cultural value associations of objects occurred between the Late Bronze Age and early Iron Age. The primary difference is observed in the find contexts of objects: with dominance of lake-dwellings in the Late Bronze Age and burials in the Iron Age (Figure 1.6). Some of this apparent difference must be attributed to the changes in social deposition practices – with greater quantities of objects included in Iron Age burials than the cremation burials of the Urnfield period – and the general 'invisibility' of the lake-dwelling communities burial practices (see section 6.1), as well as the over-representation of lake-dwelling settlements compared to inland settlements of both the Late Bronze Age and early Iron Age.

It is however possible to suggest some value changes which occurred for various object classes between the two periods. Glass beads of the Late Bronze Age, and particularly the *Pfahlbauperlen*, were objects imported to the northern Alpine region. In their region of production these beads were primarily found in multiple numbers and associated with female identities (Bellintani and Residori 2003: 490), but in the northern Alpine region they can be found in typically low numbers and with both female and male associations (Beeching 1977; Kaenel and Klausener 1990; Moinat and David-Elbiali 2003). Multiple correspondence analysis of the assemblages containing *Pfahlbauperlen* from different regions of Europe suggests that those from Italy form a relatively coherent group, with those from north of the Alps displaying more variability in object associations but remaining different from the Italian assemblages (Jennings 2014b: Chart 1). Although the social valuation of these beads changed as they travelled across the Alps, their movement gave them a new value in the northern Alpine regions based around their status as imported objects of foreign origin; they were now used as indicators of status and identity and the ability to access exchange networks.

With the cessation of the production of *Pfahlbauperlen* in northern Italy during the early Iron Age local replacements were sought in the northern Alpine region. The production of these beads in native regions resulted in a change of association, and instead of being used as indicators of status and the ability to co-ordinate exchange systems they indicated locally specific identities. The majority of such early Iron Age beads are recovered in high numbers from female burials, such as at Subingen and Bonstetten (Drack 1985; Haevernick 1975). It is possible that some of the HaD and La Tène period glass beads were imported to the northern Alpine region from wider central Europe (Frey and Roth 1983; Frey *et al.* 1987; Venclová 1983), but the beads continue to be associated primarily with female identities, thus representing a continuation of gender association throughout the Iron Age.

Amber from Hauterive-Champréveyres has been identified as originating in the Baltic region (Beck *et al.* 1993), directly illustrating that amber was reaching the northern Alpine region during the Late Bronze Age, and undoubtedly for considerably longer (e.g. the gold covered amber bead from Zurich-Mozartstrasse). The production and circulation of amber should be seen as a combined event progressing away from the Baltic region, with pieces of raw amber being extracted from circulation and produced into beads at various points, while a portion of the supply or raw material was passed further along the route to communities and regions further south. In this manner amber could represent both a local object – with regionally specific forms of bead being produced at numerous locations – but also a foreign and novel item due to its lack of availability in the region and necessity of import. This may present one explanation as to why Mediterranean styles of bead, such as the *Allumiere* type, found relatively little acceptance north of the Alps, despite the fact that the *Pfahlbauperlen* – which were produced in the same region and likely site at Frattesina – became very popular in the north.

As the majority of amber recorded from the Late Bronze Age contexts in Switzerland is from lake-settlements, it is unclear as to whether they were combined with beads of other materials or adorned larger jewellery objects. Such associations are more visible in the Iron Age, when they are found in burials in both small and large, with other jewellery objects, and also – particularly during the La Tène period – adorning other items such as fibulae and needles (e.g. Aarwangen, Langenthal, Murzelen, and Trüllikon, see Stahl 2006). This again represents a change in the biography and social value of the object, no longer was a small number of beads sufficient to display status or identity, but necklaces produced from many multiple beads were used, in addition to the decoration of regular objects to emphasise their form and provide status differentiation within secondary artefact groups. Such a deflationary effect on the value of amber could be a result of more intensive circulation of the material from the Baltic region, but may also represent the dominance of access and restriction of consumption by a few individuals. It is unclear whether amber held any specific gender associations during the Late Bronze Age, but the burial associations from the Iron Age suggest that it formed a part of female costume (Stahl 2006). This female association was however not exclusive, as the adornment of weapon hilts known from burials in Austria, France, and southern Germany demonstrates.

For the various forms of metalwork weapons, jewellery, and equipment, the primary changes appear to be in their association to individuals and employment as indicators of identity. During the Bronze Age such objects are irregular and sporadic occurrences in the known burials, with primary deposition in hoards or as isolated depositions. In contrast, in the Iron Age they were primarily placed in burials with individuals, and form parts of more regularised assemblages. In this manner the deceased were equipped with objects which they would require for the afterlife, and also with objects defining their status and identity. The use of primarily local styles and objects in the burials may also indicate that 'foreign' associations were not widely exploited as a method of generating status or symbolising identity in the mortuary sphere, even if it may have been during life. It is the change in deposition trends, and biographical culmination of objects, between the Late Bronze Age and Iron Age which demonstrate the wider development of an increased emphasis on the association of objects with specific individuals for identity construction than were previously evident through the somewhat 'communal' deposition of items in hoards during the Late Bronze Age (see Chapter 6).

4.2 Material indications of cultural change?

It is relatively rare that an entirely new form of material culture, and one which may provide a good indication of social change, appears in the archaeological record, but such an event can be seen in the finding of a number of 'keys' at lake-dwellings of the northern Circum-Alpine region (Speck 1981c; Vogt 1931).

4.2.1 Keys north of the Alps

Likely made using the lost wax method, some with plastic decoration incorporating the typical Late Bronze Age waterbird motif (e.g. Zurich-Alpenquai, -Grosser Hafner; Figure 4.6) and the ribbing typical of Late Bronze Age lake-dwelling metalwork (e.g. Mörigen), these pieces vary in both length and curvature. Although

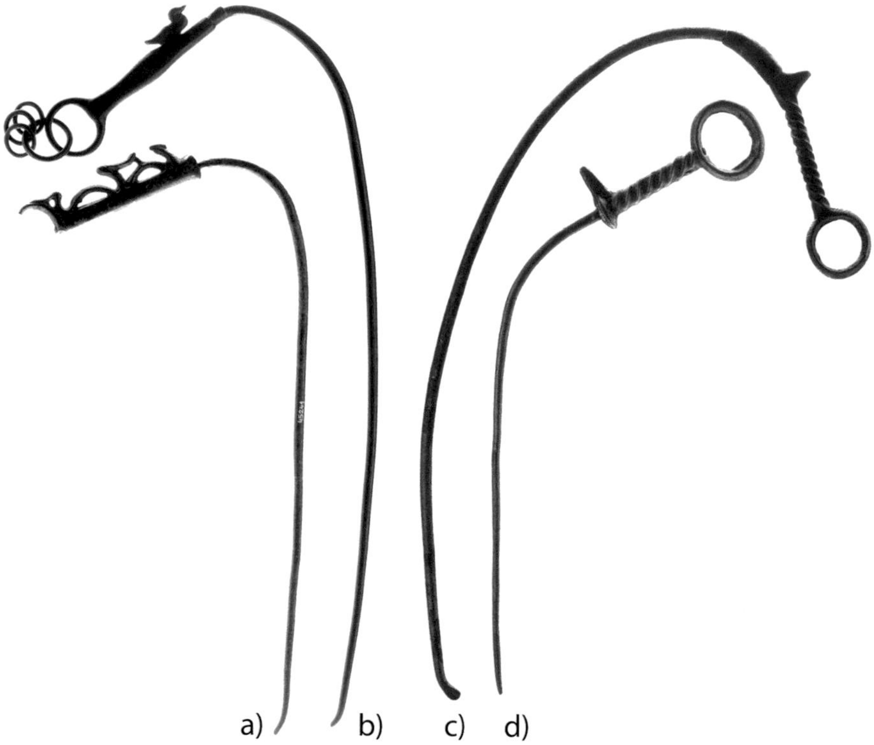

Figure 4.6: Keys from Late Bronze Age lake-dwellings. A number of keys of various styles have been recovered from lake-dwellings including a & d) Zurich-Grosser-Hafner, b) Zurich-Alpenquai, and c) Zurich-Wollishofen-Haumesser. (Images © and courtesy of the Swiss National Museum, Zurich. Object inventory numbers A-1034.1, A-86029, A-25748 and A-45241).

it has been suggested that these items are skewers or roasting spits (Mohen 1977; Needham and Bowman 2005), it is now generally accepted that they are more likely to have been used as keys (e.g. Speck 1981c; Van Willigen 2011). Keys are an exceptionally rare occurrence in European Late Bronze Age contexts, and are almost exclusively found in lake-dwelling settlements, but examples have also been discovered at the hilltop settlement Montlingerberg (Switzerland), and possibly from a hoard at Hohenhewen (D). Early Iron Age keys are known from several sites north and south of the Alps, from settlements, burial contexts and hoards, but these are again rare occurrences.

A number of wooden doors have been recovered from the northern Alpine Neolithic lake-settlements of Robenhausen and Pfäffikon-Burg (Lake Pfäffikon, (Eberli 2010; Eberschweiler 1990b)) and Zurich-Opéra (Bleicher *et al.* 2011) (Figure 4.7), but these show no direct evidence of locking mechanisms. Simple wooden cylinders were recovered during the excavation of Wasserburg-Buchau (D), which it has been suggested could potentially have been used as bar locks, operated using a key through a small hole in the door face (Speck 1981c) (Figure 4.8).

Figure 4.7: Wooden door recovered from the Neolithic Horgen cultural layer at the site Zurich-Opéra. Although there are no indications on the door of a locking mechanism such as that proposed for the Late Bronze Age, it is possible to observe the cleats on the individual door panels which secured cross beams to hold the door together. Following deposition of the door further settlement phases resulted in piles being vertically driven through the assemblage. (Photograph © and courtesy of City administration Zurich Office for urbanism, Competence centre for underwater archaeology and dendrochronology).

The keys found in early Iron Age burial contexts illustrate that there are no particular social associations which may be identified through their inclusion in burial assemblages. Keys are known from Burial 271 at Este (Italy) with the remains of an adult man, woman, and a child, from a burial at Dürrnberg (Austria) with a child, with a couple (man and woman) at Most-Soci (Slovenia), and with separate male/female burials at Tolmin (Slovenia) (Mäder 2001; Teržan 2004). A common feature across all of these burials is their apparent status as rich burials (Teržan 2004: 224), and also the fact that the keys occur as single items: one person or unit possessed one key. In contrast to the deposition of single keys in the early Iron Age, multiple instances of keys relating to the Late Bronze Age are known from several lake-dwellings north of the Alps; for example at Zurich-Wollishofen-Haumesser 13 were recovered. The occurrence of keys in lake-dwellings has been interpreted as part of a practice of votive offerings (Müller 1993; Teržan 2004: 223). However, the deposition context only depicts the culmination of the social practices, and not the causes for the prevalence of keys in these communities.

As keys are exceptionally rare from Late Bronze Age contexts north of the Alps, and none are so far known from south of the Alps, it is unclear whether they represent a local development in communities of the northern Alpine region or

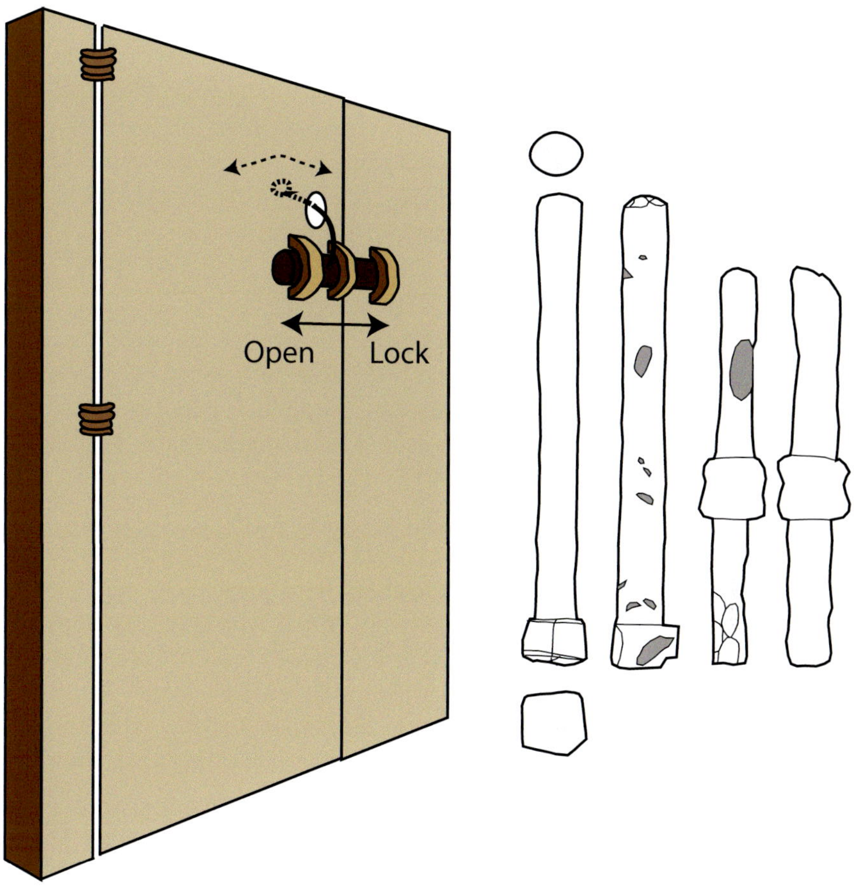

Figure 4.8: Possible wooden bar locks and method of operation. Wooden cylinders from Wasserburg-Buchau may have been bar locks (right, length 25.4 cm and 32 cm; (re-drawn from Kimmig, W 1992)) and the possible method for operation of lock with the known keys (modified after Speck 1981c: 10).

were imported from elsewhere. It is also possible that keys manufactured from other materials, such as wood, were used prior to the bronze keys discussed here, but there is currently no evidence for this. The above mentioned key from Mörigen, with typical LBA lake-dwelling groove decoration on the handle, suggests a local manufacture of the key. While the waterbird motif was widespread across Europe through the Late Bronze and early Iron Ages but relatively uncommon in the northern Alpine region (see section 6.3), and the torsion decoration on examples from Wollishofen-Haumesser (Figure 4.6), Zurich-Grosser Hafner and -Pressehaus (Speck 1981c: Fig. 7) is reminiscent of torsion, and false torsion, fibula from both north and south of the Alps (Betzler 1974; Eles Masi 1986). The hilltop settlement Montlingerberg, situated on a river valley trade route, shows extensive evidence of inter-regional contacts, and links to the Laugen - Melaun cultures of the central Alpine region (Frei, B 1955b; Steinhauser-Zimmermann 1989). It has been suggested that the concept and use of keys may have been transferred between the southern and northern Alps through this valley trade route and via Montlingerberg (Speck 1981c: 238-39). Whether or not the keys from north of the Alps, and lake-dwellings in particular, represent indigenous development or importation of ideas may be of secondary importance, as the material culture from lake-settlements displays many indications of foreign contacts. However, the keys may also be indicative of changing social structures in the lake-dwelling communities during the Late Bronze Age.

Keys as indicators of social structures

The adoption of keys in Late Bronze Age society may be connected to several factors, which can be grouped into two categories: 1) demographic influences, which relate to the increasing settlement size, density and population evident in some lake-dwellings, and 2) social influences, concerning the control of access and the display of power and status.

Demographic influences

The process of increasing settlement density, settlement size, and (in some researchers opinions) 'proto-urbanism' (Arnold 1990a) evident in Late Bronze Age lake-settlements may provide an indication for the adoption of keys and locking systems by the inhabitants of those settlements. It could be argued that with an increasing population density and settlement size, individuals were spending more time further away from the settlement core (and their dwellings), for instance for agricultural practices, and felt the necessity to secure houses and possessions. An examination of excavated and estimated settlement sizes from Early and Late Bronze Age contexts indicates a complex situation (Table 4.1). It is evident that some of the LBA settlements from which keys have been recovered are comparatively small, such as Greifensee-Böschen, while others were quite large, e.g. Zurich-Alpenquai and -Wollishofen-Haumesser.

However, settlement size itself is only one factor which may have influenced the desire to secure structures. Increasing 'foreign' relations, evidenced through material culture, may have introduced new members to societies, from either distant regions or local communities. This may have induced members of the lake-dwelling communities (and sites such as Montlingerberg) to secure their dwellings if they were distrustful of the 'immigrant' members of the community. Such a supposition is purely speculation, and a xenophobic attitude or outlook is not evident through the material culture, which illustrates a ready adoption and incorporation of selected 'foreign' elements of material culture.

In support of a widespread individual desire to secure households, and to the detriment of the concept of keys as prestigious objects (see below), are the 13 keys recovered from Zurich-Wollishofen-Haumesser, and the multiple instances from Montlingerberg and Morges, which suggest they may have been relatively common in these communities. While the exact size of Wollishofen-Haumesser and number of structures at the site are unknown, it is clear there were 13 keys present in the village. The design of the keys/locks would mean that the effectiveness of locking buildings/structures would have reduced with increasing numbers of keys

Period	Site	Size (m²)	No. Buildings	Settlement arrangement	Key/ Lock	No. keys
Early Bronze Age	Concise	> 2 500	18/23	Compact		
	Siedlung Forschner	≈ 12 000	≈ 25	Loose		
Late Bronze Age	Bevaix-Sud	≈ 4 500	≈ 20	Compact		
	Cortaillod Est	≈ 5 200	≈ 27	Compact		
	Estavayer-le-Lac	≈ 30 000	?	?	K	1
	Frattesina	≈ 100 000	?	Loose		
	Grandson-Corcelettes	> 40 000	?	Compact		
	Greifensee-Böschen	≈ 2 500	24	Loose	K	1
	Hauterive-Champréveyres	≈ 8 700/ ≈ 9 300		Compact		
	Morges-Grande-Cité	≈ 10 000	?	?	K	5
	Mörigen	≈ 16 000?	?	?	K	1
	Montlingerberg	≈ 26 000?	?	?	K	3
	Unteruhldingen	≈ 12 000	≈ 80?	Compact		
	Wasserburg-Buchau	≈ 14 000	?	Loose	L	
	Zurich-Alpenquai	≈ 28 000	?	Compact	K	3
	Zurich-Grosser-Hafner	≈ 8 400	?	?	K	1
	Zurich-Pressehaus	?	?	?	K	1
	Zurich-Wollishofen-Haumesser	≈ 24 000	?	?	K	13

Table 4.1: Examples of settlement sizes from Early and Late Bronze Age settlements and Swiss sites with keys. (Data from Bernatzky-Goetze 1987: 13-17; Palafittes 2010; Primas 2008: 39; Rychner-Faraggi 1993: 11; Schöbel 1996; Speck 1981c; Steinhauser-Zimmermann 1989).

available; the locking system proposed for the keys (Figure 4.8) is so simple, and keys of such similar design (Figure 4.6) that any of the keys would potentially have been sufficient to open any of the locks. In this light the function of such keys becomes more symbolic in their ability to represent control and access to areas and to permit or deny entrance into buildings, rather than a functional ability to do so.

Social influences

The early Iron Age keys known from northern Italy and Slovenia (the south-eastern Alpine region) occur in rich burial assemblages, illustrating that while the individuals buried need not have been of a particular social group (e.g. man or woman, adult or child), they were of high status. It is also recorded from antiquity that key holders were seen as 'temple guardians' with special religious and social roles (Tomedi 2002: 1224-26). Possible Iron Age keys, without specific deposition context, are recorded from deposits likely relating to Hallstatt phase D at Heuneburg (outer and fortified settlement (Kurz 2000: 112; Sievers *et al.* 1984: 68)), and also from Oggelshausen-Bruckgraben (Köninger In Preparation: Tab. 7.84) (see section 5.2.4). Associated finds with the single key from the Late

Bronze Age to early Iron Age hoards at Dürrnberg and Grossweikersdorf (both Austria) suggest that these assemblages were no different to other Late Bronze Age hoards, consisting of sickles, axe heads, and spears; the only unusual element are the possible keys.

Unfortunately the majority of keys from Late Bronze Age contexts are predominantly from 19th and early 20th century excavations, with little specific context or associated find information. Furthermore, the apparent lack of differentiation in structures comprising Late Bronze Age lake-villages makes the identification of special buildings that may have been the domain of social elites difficult (cf. Dunning and Rychner 1994: 69). One exception to this trend is the settlement of Greifensee-Böschen, excavated in the late 20th century, with a large central platform supporting two buildings (see section 5.2.2). Although there are no indications that the key from this site was used to access either of the two central structures, it was found near the perimeter palisade and some 60 metres from the double building platform and without listed associated finds, such a situation remains a hypothetical possibility.

While it may not be possible to identify special structures to which access was controlled through the use of locks, there are some hints at features to which access may have been restricted. At Zurich-Alpenquai, Greifensee-Böschen, and Eschenz Insel-Werd , several fragments of what were apparently exceptionally large storage vessels have been recovered (Primas 2004: 119). The internal distribution of these vessels (Zurich-Alpenquai: "hut" (house) 18 (Mäder 2001: 91); Greifensee-Böschen: structures H-J; L; M; N; O; R; W (Eberschweiler *et al.* 2007: Figs. 68-76); Insel-Werd: settlement perimeter and centre (Primas *et al.* 1989: 27)) indicates that certain individuals had the ability to store large quantities of goods, or that goods were stored in multiple locations by a central authority. In the case of individual resource hoarding keys/locks would be beneficial to secure the stockpile, while in the case of centralized stockpiling they would control access to the resources to specific members of the community.

The symbolic function of keys and locks is possibly the most significant factor to be considered, with the low quantity of keys recovered and their fine decoration, being seen as an indication that they were not mundane objects, but rather utilized in special situations and circumstances (Van Willigen 2011). However, the nature of these circumstances is open to question, and it must be remembered that 'ritual' and mundane activities and practices in prehistory often overlapped (e.g. Bradley 2005). In communities where social differentiation was apparently very limited, i.e. lake-dwellings - at least in terms of physical architecture, the possibility to control access to structures and resources could have provided a significant indication of social status. Whether this was simply the control of a domestic dwelling or a communal structure for use at certain times by the whole (or sub-sections of) community, the individuals in a position to control that access may have taken on a special significance in the community, and this would have acted as a method of social identification and segregation. The fact that so many of the keys terminate in loops – over 50% of the Late Bronze Age examples – raises the possibility that they were designed to be worn. Hanging from a belt the long metal rods would have provided an ostentatious display of the fact that the wearer had the ability to secure areas and control whom had access to locations and the materials and resources contained within. Thus, the occurrence of keys in settlements may indicate increasing hierarchization and segregation of the community, with the desire of individuals and elites to exert more ostentatious authority over other members of the community.

4.2.2 Weights

Further direct evidence of cultural change in the material record may be seen in the occurrence of a number of weights recorded from northern Alpine region Late Bronze Age lake-dwellings (Jennings 2014b). While these objects are not a new development in the lake-dwellings, and earlier examples are recorded from other parts of the Circum-Alpine arc and the Po Plain (Pare 1999, 2013), as a broad group of objects they do represent a gradual development in function. In broad terms the earlier examples north of the Alps tend to be of quite low mass, and thus hinting at relatively small or low mass items to be weighed, the later examples have a higher mass, respectively indicating the weighing of larger objects or greater quantities (see catalogue in Pare 1999). Furthermore, the occurrence of weights of apparently the same system of classification and measurement – the *Terramare* weights – both north and south of the Alps suggests that at least part of the concept of weighing may have travelled as a co-incident element along existing trade and exchange routes (Jennings 2014b; Pare 1999).

Yet the true significance of the weights lies not in the cultural connections which their distribution may indicate, but their use as instruments of commodification reflecting developments to the social systems of exchange (cf. Renfrew 2005). Although other forms of quasi-commoditized exchange are known from the Bronze Age, for example the circulation of various forms of bronze and copper ingot (e.g. Jones, M R 2007b; Rychner 1984) and fragmented objects (e.g. Primas 1986; Sommerfeld 1994), such systems are based upon the 'inherent' value of the metal as a recyclable or convertible material. It is only with the adoption of weights and scales that it becomes possible to equate the price or value of one object to another systematically and repeatedly. It has been argued that the Bronze Age economy, particularly for so-called 'prestigious' items and elite members of society was based around the principle of gift-giving (Sharples 2010: 98). In this context the adoption of instruments for enabling the direct commodification of materials, in addition to the semi-commoditized circulation of metal fragments, could have potentially induced changes to social structures resulting from the gradual diminution of the social connections generated through gift giving. Occurrence of weights belonging to the *Terramarean* system in the northern Alpine lake-dwellings suggests that the concept of commodity based exchange was influenced by trade connections to the southern Alpine region; the involvement of the lake-dwelling communities in intra-regional exchange systems brought them into contact with cultural practices and ideas which may have significantly impacted upon the traditional social composition.

While it remains possible that weights were used by a restricted section of society, as suggested for the earlier examples by their direct inclusion in burials with high status equipment (Pare 1999), or, given their low mass, for very restricted items, there are several factors which argue against such a situation. Firstly, the increased mass of the later objects suggests that they may have been used with a greater quantities or heavier goods. Secondly, the number of weights from the Late Bronze Age lake-dwellings, not only of those relating to the *Terramare* system but also to a local *Pfahlbau* group (Pare 1999), and their finding in settlements suggests that the practice was no longer confined to a restricted section of society, but was more pervasive.

It is interesting that so far few objects identified as weights come from early Iron Age contexts in the northern Alpine region, or in fact central Europe as a whole – with the exception of two possibilities from a cremation burial at Oberndorf, Germany (cf. Pare 1999: 509; Torbrügge 1965). While such an absence could be the result of lack of object identification, it may also be possible that the absence may be related to the generally increasing circulation and use of iron, a change of emphasis in the social demonstration of status, and the re-alignment of exchange routes instigated a return to gift based exchange systems in the early Iron Age communities, at least for a short period of time.

Chapter 5

Immovable Material Culture

> *It is the pervading law of all things organic and inorganic, of all things physical and metaphysical, of all things human and all things superhuman, of all true manifestations of the head, of the heart, of the soul, that the life is recognizable in its expression, that form ever follows function. This is the law.*
> (Sullivan, L H 1896: 408)

In addition to the classification of small, portable objects as material culture, it is possible to consider larger, static structures and features, such as houses, as material expressions of cultural attitudes and concepts – essentially immovable material culture. Construction methods and village plans can be highly structured and play significant roles in the formation of social identities, and have great meaning to the inhabitants (e.g. Herbich and Dietler 2009). Thus, changes in settlement form in the Circum-Alpine region between the Late Bronze Age and early Iron Age may also highlight cultural changes within the region itself, and signify attitudes of identity, ancestry, and legitimacy. A comparable, though later, example may be seen in the early medieval crannog at Lake Llangorse (Wales). This is the only known instance of this settlement form in Wales, though they are common from contemporary periods in both Scotland and Ireland; the settlement was apparently ruled by individuals of Irish descent who may have used the crannog as a method to display both power and ancestral connections (Redknap 2006: 90).

5.1 What is a lake-dwelling?

To begin with, what is a 'lake-dwelling'? Quintessentially this would seem a simple question to answer: a dwelling, or settlement, built in (on) or adjacent to a lake. Whilst this is a suitable definition of a lake-settlement, it is not an exhaustive description. A number of prehistoric settlements in Italy were built in/on rivers, or modified water courses, such as Poggiomarino (Albore Livadie *et al.* 2005), Isolone del Mincio (Piccoli and Peroni 1992), and San Pietro Canàr (Balista and Bellintani 1998). Similarly, many lake-dwelling style settlements have been discovered in marsh- and fen-land: the *Moorsiedlungen* (e.g. Gachnang-Niederwil Egelsee (Hasenfratz and Casparie 2006), and Wasserburg-Buchau (Kimmig, W 1992; Reinerth 1928)). In northern Italy, the *terramare* settlements of the Po Valley have been called "*palafitte a secco*" (Menotti 2012: 155; Strobel 1874). Thus, it is clear that pile-dwellings exist in a range of environmental locales, and not only on/in lakes.

If the definition of a lake-dwelling cannot be solely dependent upon its location, can it be further defined by the construction method? Consideration here should be given to the *Pfahlbauproblem* (Menotti 2001b, 2012) and the debate surrounding the methods of construction employed in lake-dwellings. Ferdinand Keller's (1854) original proposal of settlement structures built directly above water on wooden piles has become the traditional and romanticized view that springs to people's mind when thinking of a pile-dwelling (as well represented in much artwork from Switzerland of the period, such as the 'Neolithic lake village at a Swiss lake' by Rodolphe Auguste Bachelin (1867), now in the Swiss National Museum, and product marketing (Menotti 2012: 5, In Press)), and was primarily influenced by pacific island pile-dwellings following the European colonization of Australia and exploration of the South Pacific ocean. This interpretation was challenged by Reinerth in the 1920s. Following his excavation at Sipplingen (Reinerth 1932), he suggested that instead of being built above water, the settlements were actually built on stilts on the lake margins, with the intention of protecting the settlement from flooding during seasonal lake transgressions.

During the 1940s, further challenges came from Paret (1942) who asserted that lake-dwellings were built directly onto the ground, and, with further supporting evidence coming from excavations at Egolzwil 3 (Vogt 1951) and Zug-Sumpf (Speck 1955), the concept of lake-dwellings was changed to lake*side*-dwellings. Increasing numbers of excavations during the latter half of the 20th century have led to a reconciliation between these three views of 'lake-dwelling' construction, with evidence that, at varying times and places throughout prehistory in the Circum-Alpine region, each of the construction methods was used depending upon local environmental conditions (see Menotti 2001b: 324-26, 2012: 132-39).

Thus, a lake- or pile-dwelling, is essentially a form of settlement adapted to construction in specifically humid and damp, though not necessarily above standing water, environments. It is these adaptions which are visible in the archaeological record, but they are not the only features which set pile-dwellings apart from their terrestrial counterparts. It is notable that many of the lake-settlements are particularly high in population density (Arnold 1990a; Primas 2004). It is unclear whether this condensation of population into a small location was the result of environmental restrictions, such as preserving the maximum amount of space possible for agricultural activities, for social reasons, such as security, or as a result of successful settlements attracting more and more inhabitants.

5.1.1 Why were lake-dwellings occupied?

The decision to inhabit wetland locations was a conscious choice by communities, but the reasons behind this choice remain unclear. Various suggestions, including the potential ease of construction and life, have been proposed for influencing the decision to occupy the lakeshore (Barfield 1994: 132; Coles and Coles 1992; Menotti and Pranckėnaitė 2008; Pétrequin 1984: 321; Pétrequin and Bailly 2004; Pydyn and Gackowski 2011: 134). However, concepts of 'ease' are entirely subjective, and how much influence they had on the choice to occupy wetland environments is uncertain; particularly as inhabiting wet/humid environments may have introduced specific problems not encountered by inland communities, for example storing agricultural produce and health issues (Horden and Purcell 2000: ch. VI.5; Walsh 2014: 80-81).

It has also been suggested that defensive aspects were one of the reasons for occupation. This may have been true in some, but not all, situations. For example, while Wasserburg-Buchau (D, Billamboz 2009; Kimmig, W 1992; Reinerth 1928), Siedlung-Forschner (D, Siedlungsarchäologie im Alpenvorland XI 2009), and Greifensee-Böschen (CH, Eberschweiler *et al.* 2007), show indications of a defensive function, other settlements, such as Hauterive-Champréveyres (CH, Benkert and Egger 1986; Rychner-Faraggi 1993), Ürschhausen-Horn (CH, Gollnisch-Moos 1999), Zurich-Alpenquai (CH, Mäder 2001; Viollier *et al.* 1924), and Cortaillod-Est (CH, Arnold 1990a) do not appear particularly defensive in nature. The interaction of communities and the environment, and the availability of agriculturally productive land and natural resources may also have been a significant factor influencing where to locate settlements, and the lakeshore would have provided access to both relatively fertile land and aquatic resources (Menotti 2012: 104-06; Pydyn 2010; Vogt and Guyan 1977). It is also possible that lake-settlements were occupied to access and control marine borne trade routes (see section 3.2). Once lake-settlements were established as population centres, they may have grown through attracting artisans, e.g. metalworkers (Fischer, V 2011: 1308), which in turn may have encouraged more people to settle at the site.

With respect to the quotation of Sullivan which began this chapter, some of the developments in lake-dwellings and lake-dwelling construction can be seen as directly related to their function: different construction techniques facilitated construction above the water, hence the use of piles, or in soft marsh ground using stabilising and weight spreading foundations; defensive palisades enhanced the defensive nature of constructing in the wetland environments. However, such manifestations of technology and form only developed once the choice to settle in wetland locations was made.

Social aspects are more problematic to propose as reasons influencing the decision to settle wetland environments. It is well known that the environment, and special places/features within the landscape, played a significant aspect in the ideology of prehistoric communities (Earle and Kristiansen 2010: 252; Tilley 2010: 29). Such places are not always apparent today, as they were a specific feature of the cultural milieu during the period of settlement occupation. It is possible that some dwellings were located in relation to specific features of the landscape, or that they were inhabited because similar sites in the region had been previously occupied (see section 2.3). However, such aspects are difficult to identify through the archaeological record, and the factors behind social influences to reside in wetland environments and lake-dwellings largely remains unknown.

5.2 Northern Circum-Alpine region lake-dwellings

Extensive excavations and a long history of research in the northern Circum-Alpine region have provided a good understanding of a variety of construction techniques utilized in moor- and lake-dwellings, which varied with both time and location (Benkert *et al.* 1998; Menotti 2012: 132-39; Seifert 1996: 168-83). In general, it is possible to create a division between the construction methods employed in western and eastern parts of the region (Figure 5.1).

Settlements on the western lakes (Neuchâtel, Geneva, Biel, Murten, Bourget) were constructed using piles driven into the ground and sediment, which supported superstructures above ground (Arnold 1990a: 66-79). For Cortaillod-Est, and other lake-settlements of western Switzerland, Arnold (1990b) argued for a three aisle construction, in which four rows of posts (two wall posts and two internal posts) supported the roof of the building, which measured up to 15.5 x 6 metres in width. This three aisle plan cannot be observed in eastern Switzerland (Seifert 1996: 168).

In the eastern part of the northern Alpine region, a variety of construction techniques have been identified, including piles driven into the ground through a stabilizing plate (*Pfahlschuh*), and piles also without such a stabilizing method. Between Lake Constance and Lake Sempach a construction method termed *Schwellenbau* (sleeper beam construction) is observed, in which piles were driven into the ground through boards or planks (Benkert *et al.* 1998: 199; Gross *et al.* 1987: 67; Seifert 1996: 168-71). These boards not only provided stabilization and

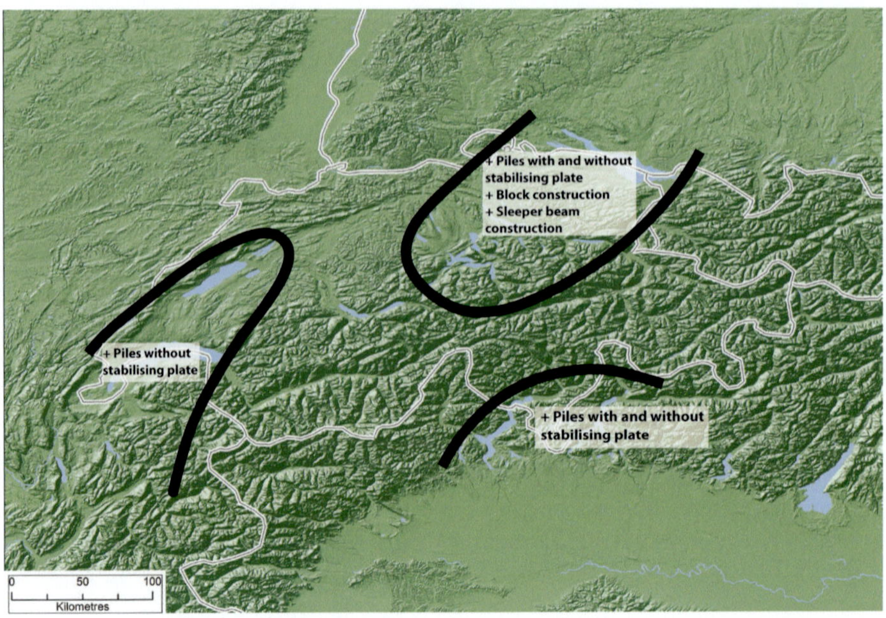

Figure 5.1: Distribution of different lake-dwelling construction methods in Switzerland during the Neolithic and Bronze Age. There is significant segregation of architectural techniques between different regions (re-drawn from Seifert 1996: Fig. 194).

support for the building posts, but also formed the base and foundations of walls. At Zug-Sumpf (CH) there is a mixture of construction techniques represented in the excavated remains. Buildings relating to an older occupation phase (dated 1056 to 940 BC through dendrochronology and 1210 to 940 cal. BC through radiocarbon dating (Seifert 1996: 46-53)) were constructed in the *Schwellenbau* and *Pfahlschuh* techniques (Seifert 1996: 54-80), while buildings from a younger phase (radiocarbon dated to between 901 and 815 cal. BC (Seifert 1996: 47)) were constructed in the block technique (Seifert 1996: 128-38).

The block construction (*blockbau*) method was common to the lake- and moor-settlements east and west of Lake Constance during the Late Bronze Age, evident at sites such as Greifensee-Böschen and Ürschhausen-Horn, and consists of layering round timbers on top of each other, intersecting and overlapping at building corners with notches/recesses to allow timbers to sit flush against each other (Menotti 2012: 134). Clearly, this method of construction is timber intensive.

The Neolithic site Egolzwil (CH) provides an example of the *packwerk* technique in the Circum-Alpine region, with foundations created by packing assorted timber in a regularized cross hatch pattern (Speck 1981b: 109-10; Wyss 1983). At Zurich-Mozartstrasse an Early Bronze Age *packwerkbau* platform was found, though there is no evidence that structures were built upon this area. The size of this platform, at roughly 200 m^2 (Gross *et al.* 1987: 70), suggests that if it was intended to be built upon, it would probably have been used to accommodate more than one structure. Other suggested functions of this unusual feature were for use as a central village place, a workspace, a herding space, a cult place, or for use as a status symbol and creating social differentiation (Gross *et al.* 1987: 70-74).

Although good levels of preservation of structural remains are not standard for the Late Bronze Age (for instance Zurich-Alpenquai has very little constructional timber remains, partly due to erosion processes (Wiemann *et al.* 2012), and house locations are theorized through areas of clay and/or loam (Künzler Wagner 2005)), a brief summary of evidence from some specific settlements is possible.

5.2.1 Ürschhausen-Horn

Ürschhausen-Horn (CH), constructed on a peninsula of Lake Nussbaum provides an insight into a Late Bronze and early Iron Age lake-settlement from eastern Switzerland, with a construction phase between 870 and 850 BC and occupation of varying intensity until around 800 BC (Gollnisch-Moos 1999; Hasenfratz and Schnyder 1998; Nagy 1999). A second occupation of the site is noted during the early Iron Age, between c. 663 and 638 BC (Billamboz and Gollnisch 1998; Gollnisch-Moos 1999: 122-27).

The late Bronze Age settlement shows a mixture of building techniques utilized to construct rectangular buildings of 10 to 25 m^2. Individual buildings were constructed using either the plank-pillar technique or *blockbau* construction. A number of approaches were taken to the foundations of buildings in order to compensate for marshy ground conditions and topographic undulation, varying from loam floors being laid directly on the ground with surrounding timber lintels, to cross and grid-work timbers being placed within the surrounding lintel structure to provide extra support for the floor. The most elaborate foundation system involved the raising of buildings on platforms constructed in a simple *blockbau* technique with the insertion of the floor timbers at an intermediary level of the structure (Gollnisch-Moos 1999: 21-71). Evidence of the structures relating to the early Iron Age settlement are less clear than those of the LBA settlement, meaning little of the building techniques can be interpreted, but it is clear that new timber constructions were laid (Amt für Archäologie Thurgau 2010: 306).

The settlement sequence (Figure 5.2) of the site proposed by Gollnisch-Moos (1999: 133-39), although somewhat at odds with that suggested by Nagy (1999), provides an interesting account of the development of this Late Bronze Age village. Initial buildings appear to spread over the settlement area, while further

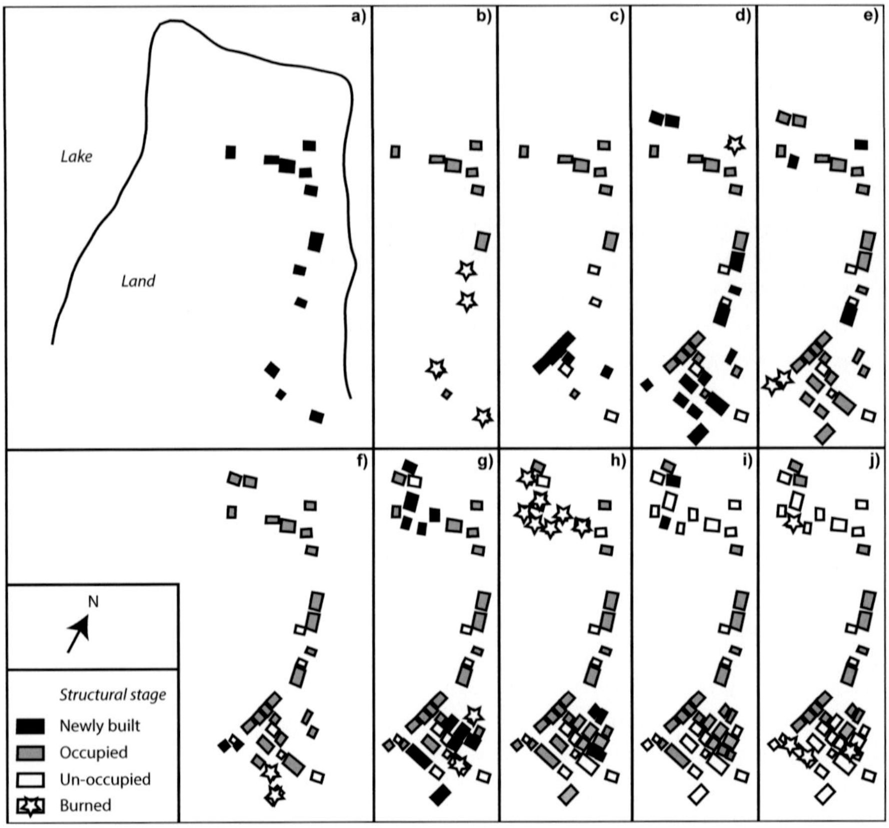

Figure 5.2: Proposed development of the Late Bronze Age Ürschhausen-Horn settlement. Gollnisch-Moos (1999: 133-39) proposed a 10 stage development of the settlement: construction initially began dispersed across the settlement (a), before some buildings were rapidly surplus to requirements (b). The southern half of the settlement was more densely built than the northern half (c-e), with some buildings destroyed or cleared by fire. The northern half of the settlement appears to have remained relatively stable until the latter stages, when most of the buildings were abandoned before being burned (f-j), though some minor rebuilding may have occurred (g, i). A similar pattern, though considerably more dynamic, is visible in the southern half of the settlement, with buildings being abandoned, renovated and reoccupied, or destroyed by fire (re-drawn from Gollnisch-Moos 1999: Figs. 222-24).

construction events fill in the gaps, though there appear to remain two fairly distinct areas of the settlement – a more dispersed area in the north, and a more compact, dense, and semi-regularized area to the south. An undeveloped space to the centre-west of the village may have been used as a communal area. No palisade was found around the village, but apparent high-water barriers were observed in areas around the settlement (Gollnisch-Moos 1999: 188), suggesting that some preparations were taken to protect against inundation (cf. Menotti *et al.* 2014).

It is interesting that relatively little metalwork was found at the site, suggesting that some of the buildings were cleared before their deliberate abandonment, and possibly, destruction (Nagy 1999). Furthermore, distribution of the pottery at the settlement indicates that ceramics were placed along the outside of buildings, and that fragments of individual vessels were dispersed amongst several structures (Gollnisch-Moos 1999; Nagy 1999). Ethnographic studies (e.g. Deal 1985; Hayden and Cannon 1983) have demonstrated that ceramics may be temporarily stored along the outside of buildings following breakage, and in the event of abandonment such vessels are left (*in situ*) while intact and useable vessels are removed. These studies also indicate that the dispersal of broken vessels and sherds across a site can be the result of children's play activities or the innovative use of ceramic fragments for specific functions. Both the lack of metalwork and distribution of ceramics at the site may suggest planned abandonment and destruction of buildings rather than accidental fire or hurried evacuation.

5.2.2 Greifensee-Böschen

The settlement Greifensee-Böschen (CH) is an interesting Late Bronze Age village, which was occupied for roughly a decade between 1051 and 1042 BC (Eberschweiler *et al.* 2007: 97-120). Construction of the settlement began with the first structures in 1051 BC, before a complete row of houses was finished around 1049/1048 BC. A surrounding palisade and "hedgehog" like structure, built of piles driven into the ground at an angle on the landwards side of the settlement, constructed around 1047 BC (Eberschweiler *et al.* 2007: 114), would have acted as both defensive measures and wind breaks. Further village expansion occurred in subsequent years, including some structures built outside of the surrounding palisade but within the hedgehog structure, suggesting that the palisade fell into disrepair or that these buildings were intentionally separated from the main area of settlement. All building work at the site appears to have been completed by 1042 BC (Figure 5.3).

Structures at Greifensee-Böschen were constructed in an elaborated *blockbau* technique (Eberschweiler 1990a; Eberschweiler *et al.* 2007: 38-96). Instead of simply layering timbers or beams on top of each other, various degrees of stabilization methods were utilized to ensure that the timber structures could not move around. Firstly, timbers or beams were secured together at their overlapping ends with treenails or binding to limit the amount of lateral movement that could occur within the structure itself. Secondly, stabilization was provided by pinning the *blockbau* structure into place with alignment piles or pegs, reducing the potential for the entire construction to move. To reduce the possibility of

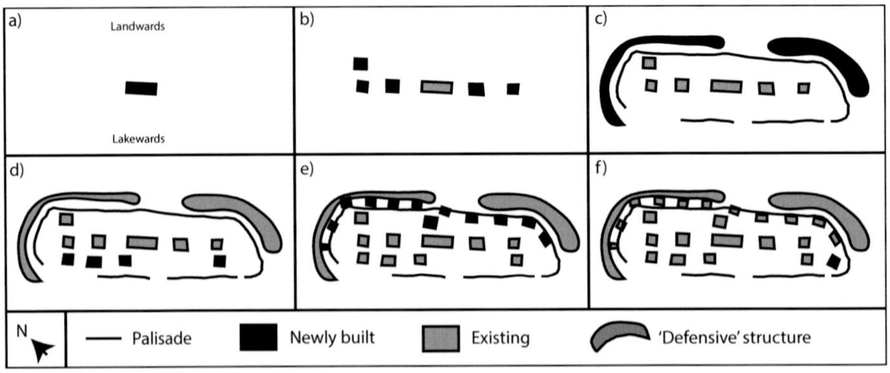

Figure 5.3: Development of Greifensee-Böschen. Beginning in 1051 BC the settlement was established with a double structure standing on a single platform (a). Expansion of the settlement occurred in 1048 BC (b), with a palisade and defensive (?) structure constructed in 1047 BC (c). A second phase of expansion spread further into the lake during 1047/46 BC (d) before expansion on the land side of the settlement in 1045 BC (e). The final building of the settlement was constructed in 1042 BC (f) (re-drawn from Eberschweiler et al. 2007: Fig. 373).

the structure sinking into the ground the guiding piles were driven into the ground through pre-cut timber boards that acted as weight spreaders for the above building structure, in some cases the bottom layer of logs were also bound to timber boards. Occasionally, wooden boards were placed under the perimeter of the whole *blockbau* structure (e.g. house R), or with cross boards running across the long edges of the structure (e.g. house H), which would also have assisted with weight distribution, and is similar to the *Schwellenbau* technique described above.

Although little material relates to the upper elements of the building structures, building platforms have been inferred from piles and pile plates positioned around the *blockbau* foundations. These piles would have provided support for a platform that extended beyond the edges of the foundations. The theorized platform area suggests that single buildings were built on them, though it is apparent that the earliest structures (buildings H and J) were built on a single large platform. Whether the settlement was permanently above water is currently unknown, but the measures taken to stabilize the *blockbau* structure and elevation of the building platform suggest that the buildings were constructed in shallow water (Eberschweiler *et al.* 2007: 259-68).

5.2.3 Wasserburg-Buchau

The Late Bronze Age settlement of Wasserburg-Buchau, constructed and occupied at successive periods between 1058 and 852 BC (Billamboz 2006b, 2009), was most likely built on a low hill/rise in the hinterland of Lake Feder, Germany, and surround by a swampy marshland (Kimmig, W 1992; Reinerth 1928). It is possible that the lake edge was in proximity to the settlement, and that on occasion high-water levels reached the edge of the settlement area. Successive palisades were constructed around the settlement, culminating with a final encircling palisade with proposed entrance gateways/towers on opposing sides of the settlement

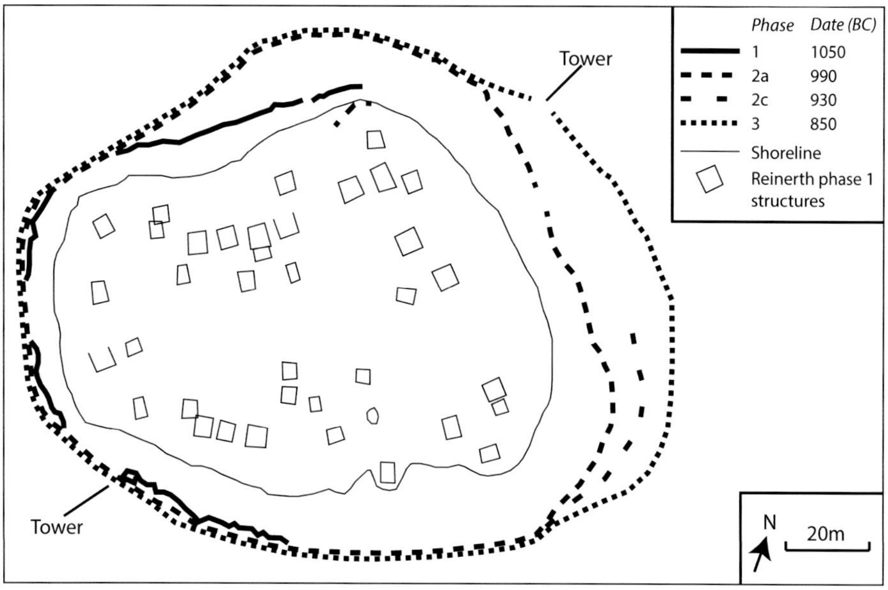

Figure 5.4: Development of the perimeter palisade at Wasserburg-Buchau. Dendrochronological dating has suggested that the 'winged' structures originally proposed by Reinerth (1932) are actually successive overlaying and displaced constructions (re-drawn from Billamboz 2006b).

(Figure 5.4). Such gateways and the presence of trackways in the Federsee area, e.g. the Wuhrstraße (Billamboz 1998; Schlichtherle 2002; Schlichtherle and Strobel 1999: 25-26), and the discovery of wagon-wheels and axles (Kimmig, W 1992) are further indicators the settlement was not permanently surrounded by water.

Several phases of construction have been proposed for the settlement. An older settlement, consisting of a number of quadrangular buildings, is dated to around 1050-990 BC, with best evidence coming from successive palisade construction events (Billamboz 2006b: 102-03, 2009). Suggestions of a younger settlement phase with larger, winged buildings have been disproved and replaced by several phases of construction and repair continuing into the mid-9th century BC (Billamboz 2006b, 2009; cf. Reinerth 1928). Structures were built in the *blockbau* technique, with adjacently laid round wood timbers to create a floor surface. Cross beams were positioned under the floor timbers to provide stability, though a full *packwerkbau* system was not evident (Reinerth 1928).

5.2.4 Oggelshausen-Bruckgraben

Oggelshausen-Bruckgraben (D) is not strictly a lake-settlement, but a fish trap complex situated in a former section of the Lake Feder, dated to between 730 and 621 BC (Köninger 1998, 1999, 2000, 2001, 2001/2002: 51). This site is important to understand changing attitudes towards lake use between the Late Bronze and early Iron Age. Construction elements at the site relate to the arms of the fish traps, which were used to funnel fish into the catchment area. These arms were formed from piles driven into the lake sediment, with smaller timbers woven between the vertical poles to create a funnel system, standing in between 1.2 and 1.5 metres of water (Köninger 2001/2002: 38). Groupings of piles in four points around the confluence of the arms have been interpreted as foundation piles at the corner of huts built above the end of the fish trap. This proposal is strengthened by the presence of collapsed hearths and artefact finds from these areas, but there are no structural remains of these buildings, which would have been elevated above the water surface on piles. Whether these huts were occupied on a long-term basis, or simply for a few weeks a year when the fish traps would have been active during the fish migration season is unknown. Studies of ceramics from the site have shown that the pottery was produced on the Swabian Alb, some 25 to 30km to the west of the site; clearly the fishing trap system at Oggelshausen was not driven by the local population of the Federsee region (Köninger In Preparation).

5.3 Settlement biographies

In contrast to the statement of Sullivan quoted at the beginning of this chapter, it is widely accepted that settlements and buildings (of all time periods) are not simply functional, but actively manipulated to promote and display social and community identity, prestige and power (e.g. Johnson 1989; Liddiard 2005; Sharples 2007), but of course these aspects could also be interpreted as a 'function' of the strucutres. Recent publications (e.g. Arnoldussen 2013; Brück 1999; Gerritsen 2003, 2008; Jennings 2012a) have attempted to study the individual or typical social biography of houses and buildings (Figure 5.5), as an 'immovable' form of material culture. Late Bronze Age lake-settlements from the Circum-Alpine region present some

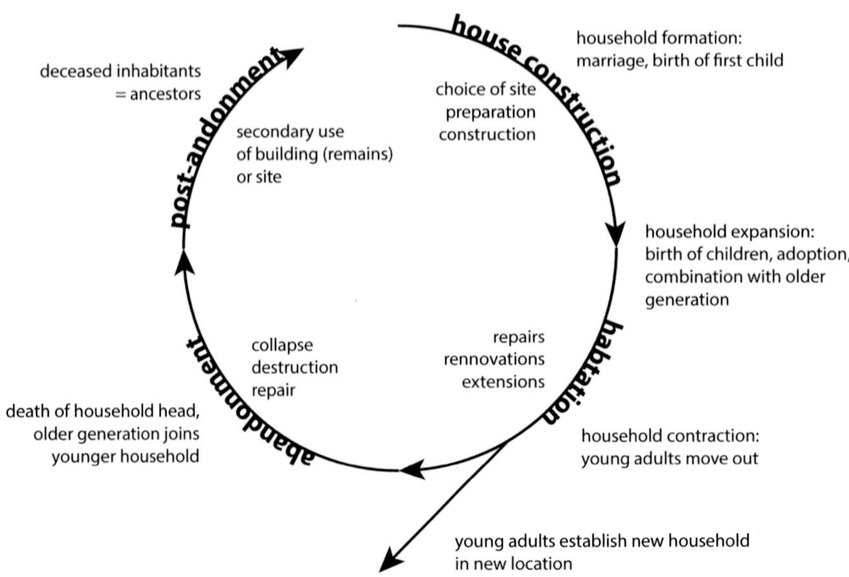

Figure 5.5: The potential biography of a single-phase farmstead (in northern Europe) in relation to the biography of an inhabiting household. (Modified after Gerritsen 2003: Fig. 3.1).

difficulties in considering the biography of individual buildings, in that many settlements do not have preserved habitation layers or building remains (e.g. Zurich-Alpenquai), or the settlement was of limited duration (e.g. Greifensee-Böschen), when compared to settlements from earlier periods (e.g. Arbon-Bleiche 3) where interesting research has been completed on the re-use of buildings and household identities (Doppler 2013; Doppler *et al.* 2010; Ismail-Meyer and Rentzel 2004: 76-78). Two settlements with greater potential for interpreting building histories and sequences of occupation are Ürschhausen-Horn (Gollnisch-Moos 1999; Nagy 1999), and Wasserburg-Buchau (Billamboz 2006b; Kimmig, W 1992).

While the LBA Circum-Alpine lake-dwellings may have limited potential for considering the biographies of individual buildings, there may be greater possibility for considering the biography of villages and settlements as a collection of buildings, through examination of the construction, development, layout, and abandonment of settlements over time and the movement of settlements in a region or "*Siedlungskammer*" (Ebersbach 2013: 295-96). The concept of "*Hausplatz*" (Billamboz 2006a; Ebersbach 2013: 291) was developed to explain the fact that buildings were often constructed in the same location as (i.e. on top of) former buildings, sometimes after significant interludes, and with spaces left deliberately empty and open for future constructions. Such a concept implies that not only were settlements actively planned, but also that locations had socially acceptable biographies and uses, and settlement location was guided by previous structures/sites (Jennings 2012a).

5.3.1 Lake-settlement areas of the northern Circum-Alpine region

To develop an assessment of the biography of lake-settlements of the Circum-Alpine region a number of areas are selected for further investigation depending upon the presence of Late Bronze Age/early Iron Age settlements, the presence of earlier settlements, and the level of excavation that has been conducted on those settlements.

5.3.1.1 Lake Feder

Evidence of lake-dwellings ranging from the 5th millennium (Aichbühl) to the early 1st millennium BC (Wasserburg-Buchau), and a fishing complex from the mid-1st millennium BC (Oggelshausen-Bruckgraben) are known from Lake Feder (Schlichtherle 2002, 2004). The available dating evidence suggests that many of the Neolithic settlements underwent multiple phases of occupation and construction (e.g. Alleshausen-Grundwiesen (Table 5.1)), with gradual movement of settlements around the lake and subsequent re-occupation (Schlichtherle 2009). The only recorded settlement of the Late Bronze Age is Wasserburg-Buchau, with evidence for several phases of rebuilding and development, covering both the buildings themselves and also the surrounding palisade (see section 5.2.3). Unfortunately, the limited dating evidence for structures of the settlement interior makes further interpretation of building construction phases difficult. However, inferences may be made from the palisade modifications, suggesting three main phases of construction and occupation (Billamboz 2006b). Perpetuation of the palisade location along the south-east to western sides of the settlement over all phases suggests a constraint in this area, while expansion of the perimeter along the western to north-eastern edge of the settlement between both phases 1 to 2 and 2 to 3, illustrates an expansion of the enclosed area, but without an increase in the settlement which was constrained by the 'island' area (Figure 5.4). Phases of building construction were, in some instances, in roughly the same location, with buildings overlapping and leading to suggestions of 'winged buildings' during the first excavation of the site (Reinerth 1928); but these are now recognized as multiple sequential building phases at rotated and displaced locations (Billamboz 2006b, 2009).

While the evidence concerning the constructional biography of Wasserburg-Buchau is currently insufficient to progress any further than brief statements, a history of settlement form may be more possible for the Federsee area. It is evident from the published settlement plans that Neolithic settlements around Lake Feder generally follow a regularized plan or semi-regular arrangement (Figure 5.6 and Table 5.1). The Bronze Age sites of Siedlung Forschner and Wasserburg-Buchau display a break with these regularized settlement plans, and become conglomerates of buildings with small clusters separated from each other, and all constrained by a surrounding palisade. Such a development may indicate increasing levels of social differentiation within the resident community.

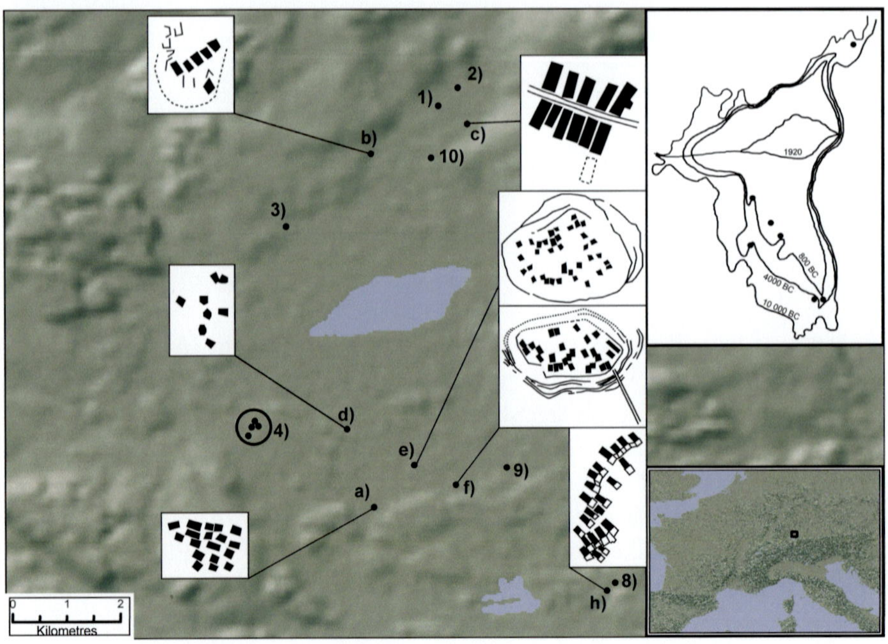

Figure 5.6: Lake-settlements in the region of Lake Feder. A change from general settlement organization can be seen between the Neolithic and the Late Bronze Age settlements (settlement plans modified after Schlichtherle 2002). Inset image shows hypothesized extent of the lake during prehistory (after Bertsch 1931). See Table 5.1 for site descriptions.

Site	Dating	Dating method	Label
Alleshausen-Grundwiesen	3020-2700 cal. BC	C14	b)
Alleshausen-Hartöschle	3920-3916 BC		1)
Alleshausen-Ödenahlen	3700-3688 BC		2)
Alleshausen-Täschenwiesen	3029-2624 cal. BC	C14	3)
	2850-2600 cal. BC	C14	
Bad Buchau-Bachwiesen I	2975 BC		4)
Bad Buchau-Bachwiesen III	3300 BC		4)
Bad Buchau-Dullenried	3332-3035 cal. BC	C14	d)
Bad Buchau-Taubried	1680-1520 cal. BC	C14	a)
Bad Buchau-Torwiesen I	3336-3102 cal. BC	C14	4)
Bad Buchau-Torwiesen II	3283-3278 BC		4)
Bad Schussenried-Aichbühl	4260-4100 BC		h)
	4390-4280 cal. BC	C14	
Bad Schussenried-Riedschachen	3871 BC		8)
Oggelshausen-Bruckgraben	730-621 BC		9)
Seekirch-Achwiesen	2860-2490 BC		10)
Seekirch-Stockwiesen	3932-3930 BC		c)
	3745-3723 BC		
Siedlung-Forschner	1767-1730 BC		f)
	1600 BC		
	1519-1480 BC		
Wasserburg-Buchau	W-B phase 1: 1058-1054 BC		e)
	W-B phase 2a: 1006-988 BC		
	W-B phase 2b: 964-945 BC		
	W-B phase 2c: 932-925 BC		
	W-B phase 3: 867-852 BC		

Table 5.1: Sites from the Lake Feder region. See Figure 5.6 for locations and plans of lettered sites. Dating method is dendrochronology unless specified (data from Palafittes 2010).

The early Iron Age fishing complex of Oggelshausen-Bruckgraben (see section 5.2.4) represents a final break with the lake-dwelling tradition on Lake Feder. Instead of viewing the lake and lakeshore as a viable location for settlement, it was seen as an area for resource extraction. Finds detailed by Paret (1926-28) relating to the LBA-EIA suggest further human interaction in the Federsee area in association with a former waterway running into the lake.

5.3.1.2 Zurich Bay

Zurich bay shows considerable continuation and concentration of settlement, with numerous sites currently known in the area (Figure 5.7 and Table 5.2), and dating evidence suggesting repeated re-occupation of sites over many centuries. While published settlement plans for Neolithic and Early Bronze Age settlements,

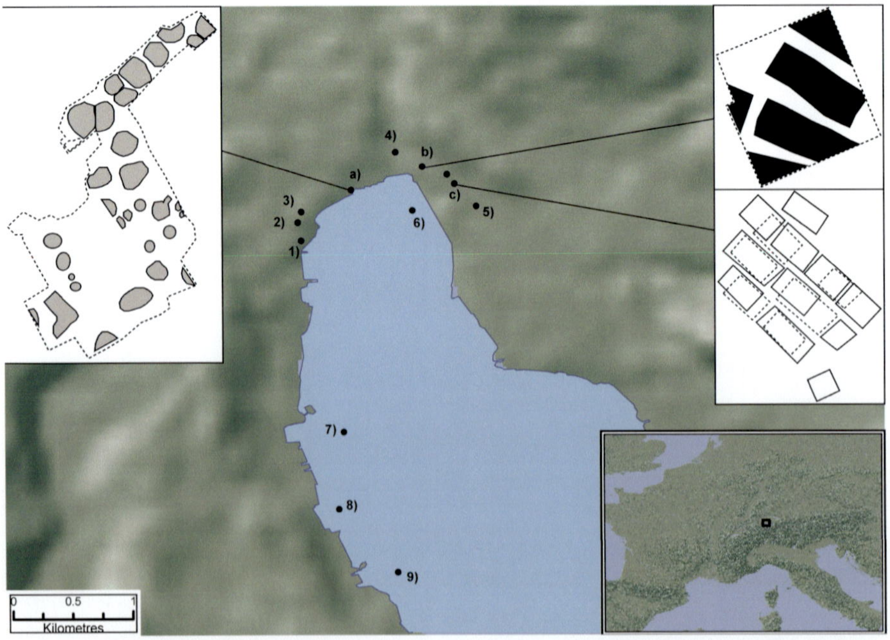

Figure 5.7: Lake-settlements from the region of Lake Zurich. Preservation issues have reduced the potential to reconstruct plans of Late Bronze Age settlements, but some researchers have suggested indications can be observed in the positioning of loam deposits and artefact distribution (Mozartstrasse modified after Gross et al. 1987; Alpenquai modified after Mäder 2001; Kleiner-Hafner modified after Suter et al. 1987). See Table 5.2 for site descriptions.

e.g. –Mozartstrasse and –Kleiner-Hafner, follow a regular/semi-regular plan as seen elsewhere, the archaeological remains make a comparison study of the Late Bronze Age settlement forms difficult. At the site Zurich-Alpenquai, for example, erosion and early 20th century dredging have made it difficult to suggest building arrangements, but possible – and tentative – structure locations and activity areas have been identified through loam deposits and artefact distributions (Künzler Wagner 2005; Mäder 2001).

Dating evidence and material remains suggests that several of the Late Bronze Age settlements may have been occupied concurrently, such as -Wollishofen-Haumesser, -Grosser Hafner, and -Alpenquai (Gross *et al.* 1987: 154-55; Mäder 2001: 76-78). Contemporary occupation of these settlements in close proximity raises questions as to how the inhabitants related to, and with, each other in terms of both physical/genealogical and social connections. What may be stated, concerning settlement development, from the number and typology of metal objects found at Zurich-Alpenquai and Zurich-Wollishofen-Haumesser, is that Wollishofen-Haumesser was the larger or more significant site during the 12th to 9th centuries (HaA-HaB2), with Alpenquai represented by significantly fewer metalwork finds, possibly suggesting a smaller settlement. During the later 9th and 8th centuries (HaB3) the situation is reversed, with Alpenquai yielding significantly more metal objects than Wollishofen-Haumesser. The co-occurrence of ceramics and metalwork of similar

Site (all Zurich-)	Cultural period							Dating	Method	Label
	Egolzwil	Cortaillod	Pfyn	Horgen	Corded Ware	EBA	LBA			
Bauschanze		X	X	X	X	X	X		Dendro, Typology, C14	4)
Enge-Alpenquai							X	1041-976 BC -844 BC	Dendro	a)
Enge-Breitingerstrasse			X	X	X				Typology	2)
Enge-Breitingerstrasse Rentenanstalt			X	X		X			Typology	3)
Enge-Mythenschloss									Dendro, Typology	1)
Grosser-Hafner		X	X			X	X		Dendro, Typology, C14	6)
Kleiner-Hafner	X	X	X	X	X	X	X		Dendro, Typology, C14	b)
Mozartstrasse		X	X	X	X	X	X		Dendro, Typology, C14	c)
Opera				X					Dendro	
Seefeld	X		X	X	X	X			Typology	5)
Wollishofen-Haumesser		X	X			X	X		Dendro, Typology, C14	7)
Wollishofen-Bad					X				Dendro, Typology	8)
Wollishofen-Horn				X					Typology	9)

Table 5.2: Chronological classification and dating of lake-dwellings from the Zurich Bay area. See Figure 5.7 for locations and plans of sites (data from Bleicher et al. 2011; Palafittes 2010).

typology at both sites suggests contemporaneous occupation or site use (Mäder 2001: 76, Fig. 68). However, the difference in resolution between typological and dendrochronological dating must be considered (see section 1.3), and it is possible that the two sites did not directly overlap in occupation, but were sequentially occupied for short durations (recall the occupation of Greifensee-Böschen for 10 years) within a period of circulation of typologically similar artefacts.

5.3.1.3 Lake Greifen and Lake Pfäffikon

The ten lake-dwellings currently recorded for Lake Greifen cover the Neolithic to Bronze Age (Table 5.3), though the most thoroughly investigated, and relevant for this study, is Greifensee-Böschen (see section 5.2.2). The site of Fällanden Rietspitz (Bauer, I 1985) suggests two construction/settlement phases during the Late Bronze Age, though no settlement plans have been published for this site, and only limited excavation took place. From Lake Pfäffikon the most relevant sites are Wetzikon-Robenhausen (Altorfer 2010: 125) and Pfäffikon-Baselrüti (Altorfer 2010: 250) (Table 5.3). While there are not as many dendrochronology dates available for settlements from Lake Greifen and Lake Pfäffikon as for other regions, typological dating of material suggests that sites were re-occupied over several periods and that settlements may have relocated around the lake (Figure 5.8, Table 5.3).

Although the low number of published settlement plans from Lakes Greifen and Pfäffikon make an overview similar to that completed for Lake Feder difficult, the settlement Greifensee-Böschen presents an excellent example to study the biography and development of a single site. As has been previously detailed (see section 5.2.2), the settlement began with the construction of two buildings on a single platform in 1051 BC. These may be interpreted as 'pioneer houses' (Ebersbach 2013: 291; Eberschweiler *et al.* 2007) constructed as foundation buildings for a new settlement, as also seen at the Neolithic sites of Arbon-Bleiche 3 (De Capitani *et al.* 2002; Leuzinger 2000) and Sutz-Lattrigen (Hafner and Suter 2004). It is unknown who these pioneering individuals were, where they came from, and how new settlement sites were selected. The multi-phase nature of many lake-settlements (but not Greifensee-Böschen) may suggest that sites were chosen because they were known to have been previously settled, either through cultural memory or direct evidence in the form of visible timbers, indicating that settlement in that location had been successful in the past (Arnoldussen 2013: 739-40).

Expansion occurred three years after the foundation of Greifensee-Böschen, with the construction of five additional, stand-alone, houses, in a regularized orientation running parallel to the lakeshore. The rapid expansion of settlements after pioneer site selection has been taken as an indicator that settlements grew through colonization rather than purely demographic expansion (Ebersbach 2013: 291). The time lag between pioneer settlement and expansion may suggest that the

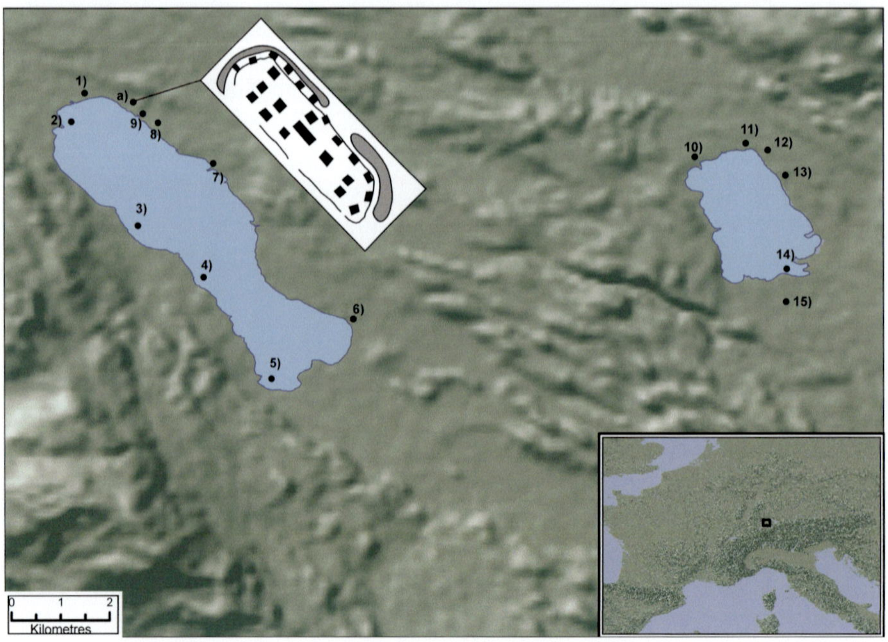

Figure 5.8: Lake-settlements from the Lake Greifen and Lake Pfäffikon. Excellent preservation and dendrochronological investigation at Greifensee-Böschen make the reconstruction of settlement plan highly accurate (Greifensee-Böschen plan re-drawn after Eberschweiler et al. 2007). For site descriptions see Table 5.3.

pioneer founders were responsible for some preparation work in the area before further colonization (e.g. clearing, timber selection, construction, etc.).

In the year following primary expansion of the settlement a surrounding palisade and elaborate 'hedgehog' structure was constructed, which may have fulfilled the defensive or windbreak function previously mentioned. In addition to purely mechanical aspects of palisade construction, social aspects should also be considered; the creation of boundaries can be used to signify community identity, cohesion and exclusion, and to define areas of the environment (see Aslan 2006; Ralston 1995; Wells 2007). Certainly, the impressive 'hedgehog' structure would appear as a defensive feature (against either humans or animals), particularly as it occurs only on the landward side of the settlement. To members outside of the Greifensee-Böschen community this structure would symbolize their exclusion from the settlement, with a single entry/crossing point representing controlled access to the interior. Furthermore, the palisade and 'hedgehog' structure effectively demarcate the potential size of the settlement; they could have been erected as a planning feature to limit both the size and spread of the village as

Site	**Cultural period**						**Dating**	**Method**	**Label**
	Cortaillod	Pfyn	Horgen	Corded Ware	EBA	LBA			
Fällanden-Rietspitz	X	X	X	X	X	X		Typological	2)
Greifensee-Böschen					X	X	1051-1042 BC	Dendro	a)
Greifensee-Furen			X	X				Typological	8)
Greifensee-Starkstromkabel			X		X	X		Typological	9)
Greifensee-Storen/Wildsberg		X	X	X				Typological	7)
Maur-Weierwiesen		X	X	X		X		Typological	3)
Maur-Schifflände		X	X	X	X		2680 BC	Dendro	4)
Maur-Uessikon		X	X					Typological	5)
Pfäffikon-Baselrüti						X		Typological	10)
Pfäffikon-Burg		X			X			Typological	11)
Pfäffikon-Riet		X						Typological	12)
Pfäffikon-Irgenhausen				X	X			Typological	13)
Schwerzenbach-Suelen						X		Archaeobotanical	1)
Uster-Riedikon		X	X			X		Typological	6)
Wetzikon-Himmerich	X	X		X				Typological	14)
Wetzikon-Robenhausen		X		X	X	X		Typological	15)

Table 5.3: Typological classification and dating for lake-dwellings from Lake Greifen and Lake Pfäffikon. For location and plans of sites see Figure 5.8 (data from database of Palafittes 2010).

a way of preventing uncontrolled expansion through immigration or population growth (Seifert 1996: 164-65). Indeed, in the three years following the erection of the barrier features more buildings were constructed in the village, including smaller buildings which expanded to the very edge of the 'hedgehog' structure and occasionally overlay parts of the palisade – effectively rendering the internal palisade redundant. Why the palisade was not required after so short a time is unknown, but it adds weight to a non-functional (e.g. not defensive) argument. Instead of a defensive function it could be suggested that the palisade was constructed after the initial expansion of the settlement to define the settlement perimeter and used to guide immigrant individuals to construct buildings within a specific area, or alternatively to prevent further immigration, with the subsequent buildings, being constructed by 'indigenous' members instead of outsiders.

After only 10 to 12 years the settlement was apparently destroyed by a conflagration (Eberschweiler *et al.* 2007). Destruction by fire appears to be a common feature in many lake-dwelling settlements, for instance also at Ürschhausen-Horn (see section 5.2.1) and Arbon-Bleiche 3, which was destroyed (and not rebuilt) after 15 years of occupation in 3370 BC (De Capitani *et al.* 2002; Jacomet *et al.* 2004; Leuzinger 2000, 2001). One explanation for destruction by fire would be to interpret these incidences as accidental events in which fire began in one building/ area and subsequently spread to others, or was successfully contained to specific buildings allowing the settlement to continue (e.g. Ürschhausen-Horn). However, such an interpretation is rather simplistic and also suggests that lake-dwellers were somewhat clumsy with their use of fire. Instead, these "burning events" could be the symbolic destruction of buildings at the end of their use life, or the demise of households (e.g. Bradley 2005: 57, 207-09; Gerritsen 1999, 2003, 2008; Rivière 1995: 197-98; Tringham 2000). Such symbolic destruction by fire has also been proposed for the inland Late Bronze Age remains identified as "*Brandschuttgruben*" in Germany and other regions (Bönisch 2005).

Destruction of single buildings may be indicative of the demise of a single household, through death, emigration to another settlement, or by attaining a certain life stage. The destruction of an entire settlement, such as Greifensee-Böschen, may represent the symbolic death of the settlement, and its potential "re-birth" through re-construction (e.g. Sutz-Lattrigen – Rütte (Hafner and Suter 2004)). In this situation it is unlikely that the destruction represents the death of the village through the death of inhabitants, but instead the emigration of occupants to another location, through choice, requirement due to environmental change or over exploitation, or by force. The occupation of Greifensee-Böschen for a single decade falls at the lower end of the predicted survival period of a pile-dwelling structure (between 10 and 15 years (Billamboz 2006a; Billamboz and Köninger 2008), but in some circumstances less (Bleicher 2009)), indicating that houses were not subjected to extensive renovation or repair, as is also indicated by the dendrochronological evidence.

5.3.1.4 Lake Chalain

The small Lake Chalain (French Jura) includes a high number of spatially concentrated pile-dwelling sites (Figure 5.9 and Table 5.4), many of which relate to the Neolithic. Significantly, the Iron Age site Chalain ML V I, located some 100 metres from the lakeshore, illustrates the possible displacement of settlements which would have occurred during periods of high lake water during the early Iron Age (Pétrequin 2013: 256; Pétrequin *et al.* 2005). Indeed, the relocation and displacement of sites away from the lakeshore raises an important point: lakes are enclosed waterscapes and they *always* have a shoreline. During times of higher – or lower – water levels this shoreline simply shifts position. From an archaeological perspective both raising and lowering of the shoreline may restrict access to the prehistoric resource.

Permanently raising the shoreline significantly may increase the depth at which the archaeological material is submerged or buried, and reduce the likelihood of its discovery simply through logistical considerations and the requirements of excavation. Raising and lowering of the lakeshore, to varying heights, will also have an impact upon the preservation and perception of lake-dwellings during excavation. If the timber is buried in standard terrestrial conditions it is more than likely to decay, leaving only staining on the ground for archaeologists to investigate in the form of postholes. Furthermore, if a lake-dwelling site was found – in a decayed state – at a displaced position in relation to the modern lake (for instance

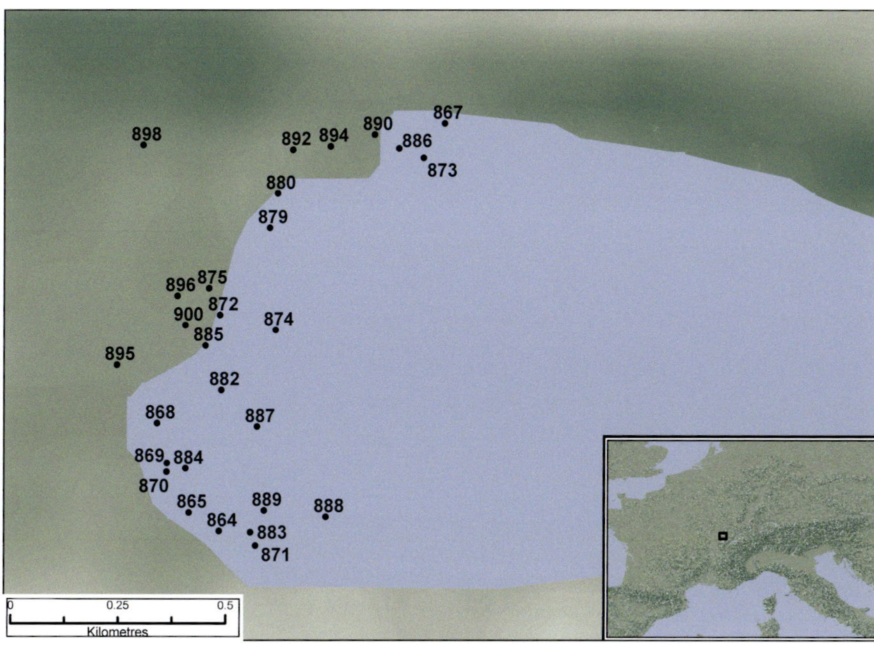

Figure 5.9: Lake-settlement locations in Lake Chalain, France. There are a remarkable number of sites in close proximity along the lakeshore, which appear to follow the rising and falling of the lakeshore during periods of fluctuating climate (data from Palafittes 2010). For site descriptions see Table 5.4.

Site	Dating period (years BC)									Label
	Dating Uncertain	4500-4000	4000-3500	3500-3000	3000-2500	2500-2000	2000-1500	1500-1000	1000-500	
Chalain 19				X						864
Chalain 18					X					865
Chalain 10	X									867
Chalain 14				X				X		868
Chalain 15					X					869
Chalain 16					X	X				870
Chalain 24					X					871
Chalain 26					X			X		872
Chalain 1					X		X			873
Chalain 30								X		874
Chalain 12					X					875
Chalain 6				X	X					879
Chalain 5					X					880
Chalain 29					X			X		882
Chalain 27					X					883
Chalain 17					X					884
Chalain 25				X	X					885
Chalain 2/3-5					X					886
Chalain 22					X			X		887
Chalain 21					X					888
Chalain 21					X					888
Chalain 20					X			X		889
Chalain 2 A-C				X	X					890
Chalain 4				X						892
Chalain 3				X	X					894
Chalain 28			X	X						895
Chalain 13				X						896
Chalain ML V I		X	X	X	X				X	898

Table 5.4: Lake-settlements of Lake Chalain, France. For location of sites see Figure 5.9. Dating categories in years BC (data from Palafittes 2010).

possibly c. 400 metres in areas of Zurich Bay by Menotti's modelling (2001a: 126)), it would require a leap of faith and palaeo-environmental reconstruction, as conducted at Chalain ML V I, to indicate its status as a lake-dwelling.

Returning to the question of the final abandonment of lake-dwellings during the early Iron Age, the possibility of not discovering (through location or preservation) or not recognising (location) of Late Bronze Age/early Iron Age settlements must be considered. The relatively recent discovery and dating of lake-dwellings on Lake Bourget, France, such as Conjux Le Port, Chindrieux, and Le Saut de la Pucelle (respectively dendrochronologically dated to 816-812 BC, 814 BC, and 805 BC, Billaud 2006; Billaud 2008; Billaud and Marguet 2005) should serve as reminders that there is still archaeological material to be discovered, excavated and dated, which may challenge current models of abandonment and cessation of the lake-dwelling tradition.

5.3.1.5 Lake Constance

Being significantly larger than Lake Feder and Lake Greifen, Lake Constance has a greater number of lake-dwellings along its shoreline (not all sites listed in this study, for full details see Palafittes 2010; Suter and Schlichtherle 2009), and a number of published settlement plans permit a brief discussion of settlement form (Figure 5.10 and Table 5.5). From the available dating evidence it is again clear that sites were occupied over several phases, often after significant intervals of time and in the same location (Table 5.5), in accordance with the *Siedlungskammer* and *Siedlungsplatz* proposals (see section 5.3). The published settlement plans for selected settlements from Lake Constance indicate a somewhat similar development to those seen on Lake Feder (see above); Neolithic settlements established in regular, or semi-regular, arrangement and the buildings were constructed on stilts to accommodate variations in the lake water level (Schlichtherle 2004: 28). Bronze

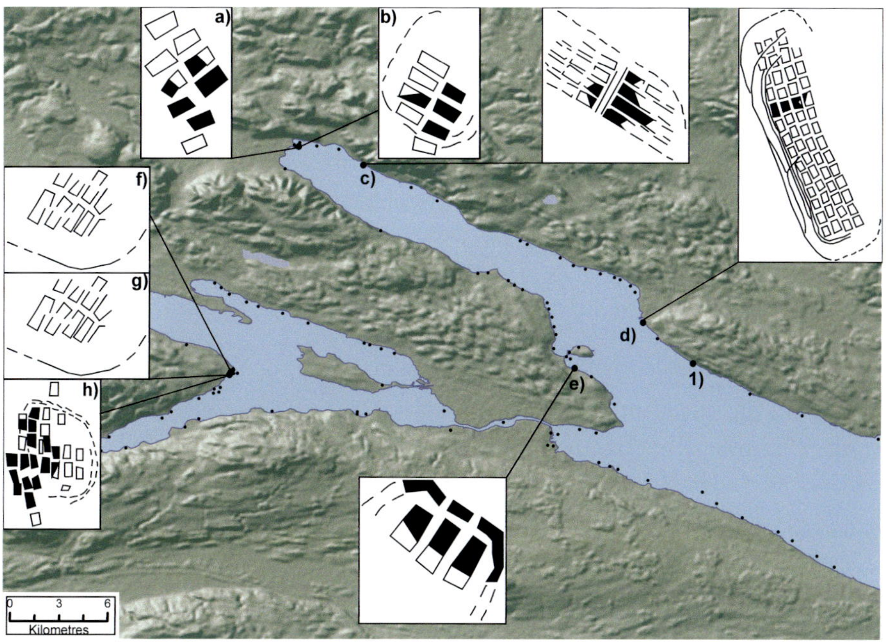

Figure 5.10: Selected lake-settlements around Lake Constance. There are many prehistoric lake-settlements along the shores of Lake Constance – see the sheer quantity of small dots – only a selection of those with reconstructed settlement plans are detailed here (data from Palafittes 2010; settlement plans re-drawn after Schlichtherle 1995). For site descriptions see Table 5.5.

Site	Cultural Period							Dating	Dating method	Label
	Michelsberg	Hornstaad	Pfyn	Horgen	Corded Ware	EBA	LBA			
Bodman-Schachen I						X		1646-1640	Dendro, C14	a)
								1618-1591		b)
								1505-1503		
Egg-Obere Güll I				X		X		3306-3023 BC	Dendro, C14	e)
								1621-1620 BC		
Hagnau-Burg	X		X	X		X	X	1050-874 BC	Dendro	1)
Hornstaad-Hörnle I		X	X					3917-3904 BC	Dendro	f)
								3586-3507 BC		h)
Hornstaad-Hörnle II			X					3870-3862 BC	Dendro	g)
Sipplingen					X			2423 BC	Dendro	c)
Unteruhldingen					X		X	Phase I: 975-954 BC	Dendro	d)
								Phase II: 930-917 BC		
								Phase III: 863-850 BC		

Table 5.5: Typological classification and dating for sites from Lake-Constance. For site locations and plans see Figure 5.10 (data from Palafittes 2010).

Age settlements on Lake Constance differ from those on Lake Feder in that they retain the regularized arrangement, surrounded by palisades, as exemplified by Unteruhldingen-Stollenwiesen (Schöbel 1996: 29-58), instead of dispersing into a looser arrangement of building clusters. The continuation of regularized settlement plans to the Late Bronze Age is evidenced by numerous other lake-dwellings, particularly from western Switzerland, such as Hauterive-Champréveyres (Pillonel 2007), Cortaillod-Est, Cortaillod-Les Esserts, Grandson-Corcelettes, and Bevaix-Sud, (Arnold 1990a). The regularization of settlement layout and increasing settlement size has been seen by some researchers as an indication of increasing levels of '(proto-)urbanization' in the Late Bronze Age lake-dwelling communities (Arnold 1990a; Pétrequin 2013: 263-64; Primas 2008: 15-46).

5.3.2 Inland settlements of the Late Bronze Age and Iron Age in the northern Circum-Alpine region

Evidence for inland settlements of the northern Circum-Alpine region relating to the Late Bronze Age and Iron Age is scarcer than that relating to the lake-dwellings, due to both preservation levels and research history (cf. Ebersbach *et al.* 2010). Excavation in advance of motorway construction revealed several Late Bronze Age sites in the hinterland of Lake Murten and Lake Neuchâtel (e.g. Morat-Löwenberg

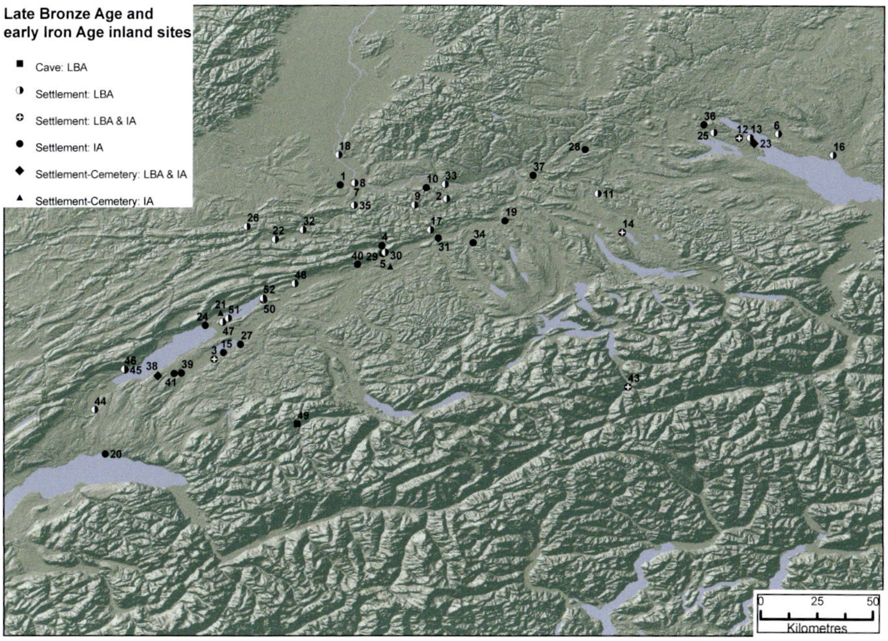

Figure 5.11: Late Bronze Age and early Iron Age settlement sites studied from Switzerland and neighbouring regions. The figure is not an exhaustive list of all sites, but gives a representative picture of the situation, particularly when comparing the relative scarcity of inland settlements compared to lake-dwellings. For site details see Appendix 1.

(Boisaubert and Bugnon 2008), Frasses-Praz au Doux (Mauvilly and Ruffieux 2008), and Onnens-Le Moti (Poncet Schmid *et al.* 2013)) and other settlements are known from further inland (e.g. Bavois-En Raillon (Vital and Voruz 1984)) (Figure 5.11). These settlements are somewhat smaller and less regularized in layout than their lakeshore contemporaries. It has been suggested that the settlement Conjux-Le Port 3 (Lake Bourget, FR) may represent an intermediary between a lake-settlement and an inland settlement (Billaud 2008). Lake-resource extraction areas may also be identified in the archaeological record, for example at Zug-Chollerpark (Lake Zug) there are possible indications of fishing stations relating to both the Late Bronze Age and early Iron Age (Eberschweiler 2004: 161-70).

Some inland settlements do, however, follow a regularized plan. For instance the Middle and Late Bronze Age highland settlement Savognin-Padnal shows indications of standardized structure size and close spatial alignment (Rageth 1976, 1986). Some inland sites and landscapes also show continuation of use between the Late Bronze Age and early Iron Age, for example in the vicinity of Morat-Löwenberg several Iron Age burials are recorded (Boisaubert and Bugnon 2008), and artefacts from sporadic excavation in Zug (CH) suggest that there was Iron Age human occupation in the vicinity of LBA lake-settlements (Bauer, I 1993).

Greater levels of information are known regarding hilltop and fortified 'highland' sites of the Late Bronze Age and early Iron Age in Switzerland (Figure 5.12), for example Montlingerberg (Steinhauser and Primas 1987), Rhinsberg (Bigler 2005),

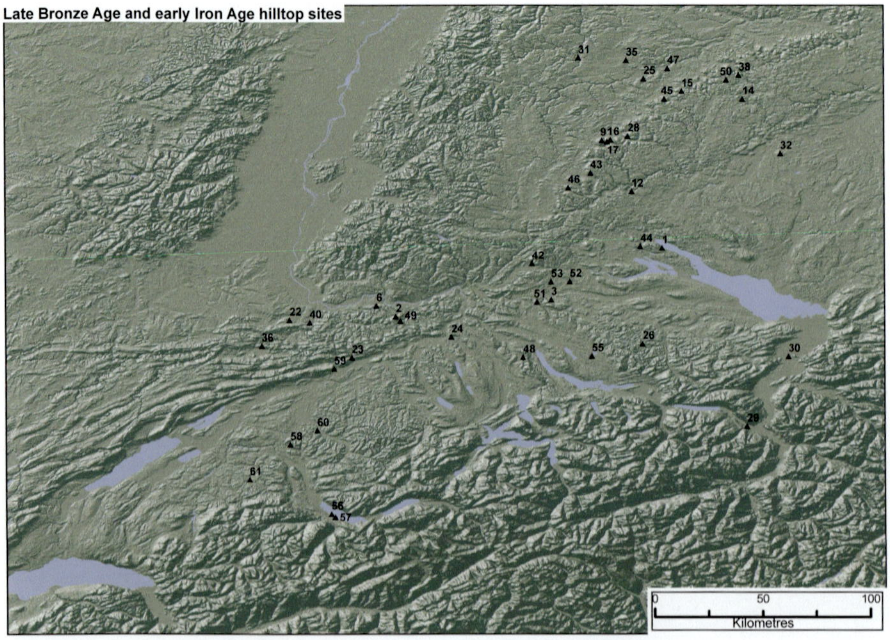

Figure 5.12: Late Bronze Age and early Iron Age highland/hilltop sites from Switzerland and neighbouring regions included in the study. For site details see Appendix 2.

Ebersberg-Berg am Irchel (Brem *et al.* 1987: 124), Wittnauer Horn (Berger, L and Brogli 1980; Bersu 1945), Scuol-Munt Baselgia (Stauffer-Isenring and Kaufmann 1983), Flueli-Amsteg (Primas *et al.* 1992), and Brig-Gils Waldmatte (Curdy *et al.* 1993). Again, some of these settlements show continuation between the Bronze and Iron Age (e.g. Montlingerberg, Wittnauer Horn, and Flueli-Amsteg). It has been suggested that many of these highland fortified sites occur on important trade routes and crossing places and became 'unavoidable' places (*zwangspunkt*) (Brem *et al.* 1987: 124; Jockenhövel 1985; Rind 1999: 3), which would have enabled a degree of control over, and participation in, exchange and communication networks (see Chapter 3). Indeed, Montlingerberg and Scuol-Munt Baselgia in particular show indications of their involvement in long-distance exchange networks. Occupation of hilltop settlements does not mark a new tradition during the Late Bronze Age or Iron Age (cf. Harding 2006; Jockenhövel 1974), and many settlements of such form are recorded from Switzerland and southern Germany relating to the Early and Middle Bronze Age, which may have been utilized as central places and formed a node in copper circulation networks (Krause 2005). However, the increased population density and elaborate fortifications of some Iron Age hilltop settlements marks a break from previous traditions and new emphasis on enclosure, separation, and display (cf. Harding 2006) and social hierarchy structures enabled larger populations (Seifert 1996: 164-65).

Some of the Late Bronze Age hilltop settlements, for example Zurich-Üetliberg (Figure 5.13) and Heidenburg, Lake Pfäffikon (Altorfer 2010: 254; Bauer, I *et al.* 1991), occur within proximity to, and show indications of contemporary

Figure 5.13: The location of the fortified settlement of Üetliberg gave it a commanding position over Lake Zurich. The settlement was situated on the distant mountain, on the highest peak from the right, from where the settlement would have a good view of the lake, and settlements along the lake-shore. Zurich-Alpenquai is towards the right hand extent of the image, and Zurich-Wollishofen-Haumesser is on the distant lake-edge in the area to the left of the church tower. (Image held by Eidgenössisches Archiv für Denkmalpflege (EAD): Sammlung VSG Verein Schweizerischer Geografielehrer, item no. EAD-VSG : Küsnacht).

occupation/use to, lake-settlements. How these sites were utilized in combination with the lake-dwellings is unclear, but material culture evidence (e.g. *Pfahlbauperlen* from Üetliberg (Bauer, I *et al.* 1991; Jennings 2014b)) suggests circulation of goods between the two settlement types. From the quantity of artefacts recovered from the hilltop settlements in the vicinity of lake-dwellings, for instance Üetliberg adjacent to Zurich bay, it may be surmised that the lakeshore sites formed the large population centres of the Late Bronze Age, with possible sporadic use of the hilltop settlements. Such a situation is further indicated by more distant 'hilltop' settlements in the Alpine valleys, such as Montlingerberg (Steinhauser-Zimmermann 1989), which show indications of higher population and extended occupation.

5.3.3 Biographies of Lake-Settlements

In discussing the biographies of settlements an important factor to consider is the possible re-use of timber over successive phases of occupation or between settlements. The construction of pile-dwellings would have required a significant quantity of timber, large amounts of which would have been used for construction of the superstructure, and so protected from possible decaying influence of ground

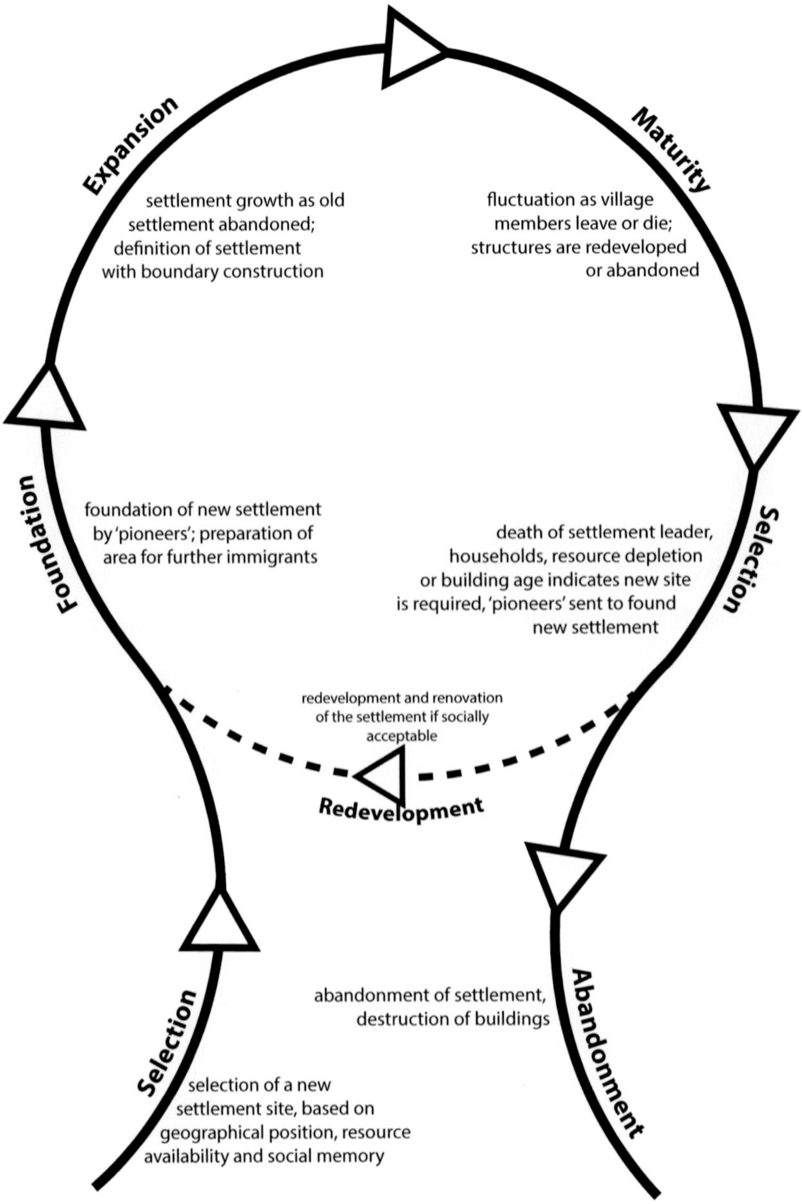

Figure 5.14: Hypothesized development sequence including a social biography for Circum-Alpine region lake-dwellings. (After Jennings 2012a).

contact. Such superstructure timber may have constituted a significant and readily available timber resource, which, in light of the current dendrochronological evidence, does not appear to have been extensively utilized. One example where timber re-use has been identified is at the settlement Conjux-Le Port 3, where initial pioneer construction may have re-used piles from an older settlement (Billaud 2011), and re-use has also been suggested for Hauterive-Champréveyres, where evidence indicates that piles were occasionally removed and possibly reworked

(Pillonel 2007: 70). The re-use of timbers, coupled with the splitting of timbers to produce multiple piles from single logs (also at Cortaillod-Est, Arnold 1986), may indicate an over exploitation of the surrounding forest resources, leading to a reduced availability of suitable size trees. Such re-use of timbers may have created a social conflict arising from the use of timbers from former settlements which, as has already been discussed (see section 5.3.1.3), were frequently destroyed by fire as a possible symbolic destruction of dwellings.

As a summary biography of lake-dwelling settlements, a development cycle has been proposed (Figure 5.14). Settlement, and building, life was likely dependant on social preconceptions of the expected, and acceptable, duration in addition to physical factors such as the survival of building materials (Gerritsen 2008: 159; Jennings 2012a).

Settlement occupation began with the choice to relocate and found a new (or old) site. This would have required the selection of a number of pioneer settlers to begin construction. The choice to found a new settlement may have been influenced by a number of factors, such as the death of elite individuals, reduced environmental resources and agricultural productivity, or the state of repair of buildings. Selection of site location may have drawn upon visible indicators of past settlement construction (see section 2.3), social memory (cf. Robinson 2013), and utilized features of the landscape to provide legitimacy for occupation (cf. Thomas, J 2013) The settlement would then expand as members gradually relocated from the previous site, were joined by immigrants, or through natural demographic expansion and achievement of life stages for individual members of the community. At this stage the decision may have been taken to actively impose a limit on the potential settlement size through the erection of perimeter palisades and fences. The layout and organization of settlements may provide some indication as to the hierarchical nature of the community; regular alignment with equal sized buildings suggests a more egalitarian society (cf. Aslan 2006), while the clustering of structures may represent the symbolism of social ties and membership of households in certain (sub)communities (Marcus 2000: 236; Marshall 2000: 96-97). However, it is important to remember that building size and position is not the only way to signify status or membership (Chesson 2003), and other methods must have been employed in the otherwise apparently un-hierarchical lake-settlements (Dunning and Rychner 1994: 69). Within the lake-dwelling tradition of the northern Circum-Alpine region, both settlements with a regularized layout and those with an open or loose organization occur somewhat contemporaneously, but the latter are more frequent in the eastern region (cf. Primas 2008: 39). It is also possible that a development occurred from the regularized to loosely arranged settlements within a specific area even in the western northern Circum-Alpine region, for example around Lake Bourget at Conjux-Le Port (Billaud 2006, 2008).

Upon reaching maturity, or a relatively stable size, a settlement may have undergone population fluctuation, as members died or left the community, buildings fell into disrepair and were abandoned/demolished or renovated, but without undergoing significant expansion. After a period of time (either short – e.g. Greifensee-Böschen – or longer – e.g. Hauterive-Champréveyres) the decision to relocate (or renovate) the settlement was made, based upon the same principles as those suggested above, which would have resulted in the loss of a few members of the community as pioneers to found the new site, followed by complete abandonment of the settlement in the following years. It has been suggested that communities of the Iberian peninsula during the Late Bronze Age and early Iron Age were based around the individual, and therefore when one person died their rights did not pass onto the next generation through principles of inheritance, meaning that the rights to building plots and involvement in exchange networks needed to be attained by each generation, resulting in shifting settlements and building locations (Blanco-González 2011; González-Ruibal 2006). Furthermore, it has been argued that a link can be seen between the increasing permanence of settlement and increasingly hereditary societies (Blanco-González 2011: 404). A non-hereditary explanation may also account for the transient nature of lake-dwelling settlements in the northern Circum-Alpine region, with inhabitants required to found new building plots once household elders died, but such practices are difficult to identify – not least because of the limited evidence for funerary practices of the lake-dwelling communities.

From the above descriptions of lake-dwelling evolution around the northern Circum-Alpine region, it is evident that a distinction can be drawn between the 'open' (in this sense used to refer to the loose and irregular arrangement of structures not in a grid like pattern, and not to the presence of perimeter palisades or defensive structures) settlements such as Ürschhausen-Horn, Greifensee-Böschen, and Wasserburg-Buchau and those of the compacted regularized type such as Hauterive-Champréveyres and Cortaillod-Est (Primas 2008: 39). Vital (1993) has tried to explain Late Bronze Age and early Iron Age changes in settlement form (rectilinear pattern of lake-settlement to compact clustered inland settlement) of the French Jura region with relation to socio-cultural changes, from individual to familial/lineage based systems of hierarchy. Late Bronze and early Iron Age terrestrial settlements from Switzerland and southern Germany with settlement plans are relatively rare. The few which have published plans, e.g. Montlingerberg (Steinhauser-Zimmermann 1989), Goldberg (D, Schauer 1995), Wittnauer Horn (Berger, L and Brogli 1980; Bersu 1945), Savognin Padnal (Rageth 1976, 1986), and the well-known Iron Age fortified settlement Heuneburg (D, Gersbach 1995; Kimmig, P 1975; Kimmig, W 2000b) indicate that condensed settlements with regularized internal arrangement were common throughout the region, but that (some of) the Late Bronze Age lake-dwellings were somewhat larger than their terrestrial contemporaries (cf. Boisaubert *et al.* 2008; Primas 2008: 39). However, it has also been argued that regularized settlement plans are so widespread across Europe and throughout prehistory that they are of little interpretative value for consideration of cultural influences; instead they may be symbolic of general periods of demographic expansion and colonization/settlement founding (Barfield 1994; also Herbich and Dietler 2009).

Instead of considering the internal settlement arrangement, a brief consideration of the settlement enclosure in the form of palisades and the surrounding ditches/walls of Iron Age settlements may suggest a partial social influence in the decision to move away from lakeshores. As discussed above, the erection of barriers takes as much a symbolic role as functional defensive role. Barrier structures in the Iron Age were likely to have been used as a method to display the prestige and power of ruling elites in an increasingly overt (when compared to the Bronze Age (cf. Brück 1999; Harding 2006)) hierarchical society, through symbolization of economic and political strength required to undertake such constructions in competitive consumption of labour and resources (Payne *et al.* 2006; Primas 2008: 44; Sharples 2007). One of the greatest examples for the presence of symbolism in the construction of surrounding works is the Mediterranean style mudbrick wall of the Heuneburg (Gersbach 1995; Kimmig, W 2000b; Ralston 1995: 71), symbolising identity, power, and status to residents, non-residents, and 'foreigners'. The settlement of Geiselhöring (D, Nagler-Zanier 1999) provides further evidence of the role of fortifications as not only physical defensive structures, but also as a method to exclude and deprive the senses of incomers by hiding the settlement interior from the route along which persons must progress until they are intended, and permitted, to view the settlement (see Wells 2007: 391-92).

Returning to the lake-dwellings previously discussed, the settlements of Greifensee-Böschen, Siedlung-Forschner, and Wasserburg-Buchau have the most prominent boundary features, all of which may (partly) have been used as a symbolic display of community and status. However, in a period of increasing individualization and stratification, settlements in wet environments may have lacked the required stability to create and maintain stratified social systems before structures decayed (see Bleicher 2009) or local resources were exploited/exhausted, forcing the relocation of settlement. Furthermore, wetland environments are not conducive to the construction of earthworks, which form the basis of many of the perimeters of the Iron Age fortified sites, reducing the ability to demonstrate power through the consumption of labour (but see the *Terramare* of the Po Plain, Menotti 2012: 155-57). The lowland nature of the lakes would also limit the visibility of settlements, reducing the potential external audience of the conspicuous consumption. The relative proximity of the Heuneburg to Lake Feder (circa. 15km to the east), the Üetliberg to Lake Zurich, and the Baarburg to Lake Zug, may suggest that the lake was abandoned in favour of 'highland' fortified sites. Thus, it must be considered a possibility that the lake-dwelling tradition declined, partly, because these settlements, and their environmental position, were unable to support the systems of social differentiation and stratification required by a newly emerging elite class.

5.4 Settlement visibility

Developments in Geographic Information Systems (GIS) and computing power during recent decades have increased the availability of approaches to assess the visibility of sites within landscapes (Fisher *et al.* 1997; Llobera 2001; Mainberger and Mainberger 2010; Wheatley 1995; Wheatley and Gillings 2002; Woodman 2000). For the purposes of interpreting the possible prominence and visibility of lake-settlements a trial GIS analysis was conducted on a region incorporating

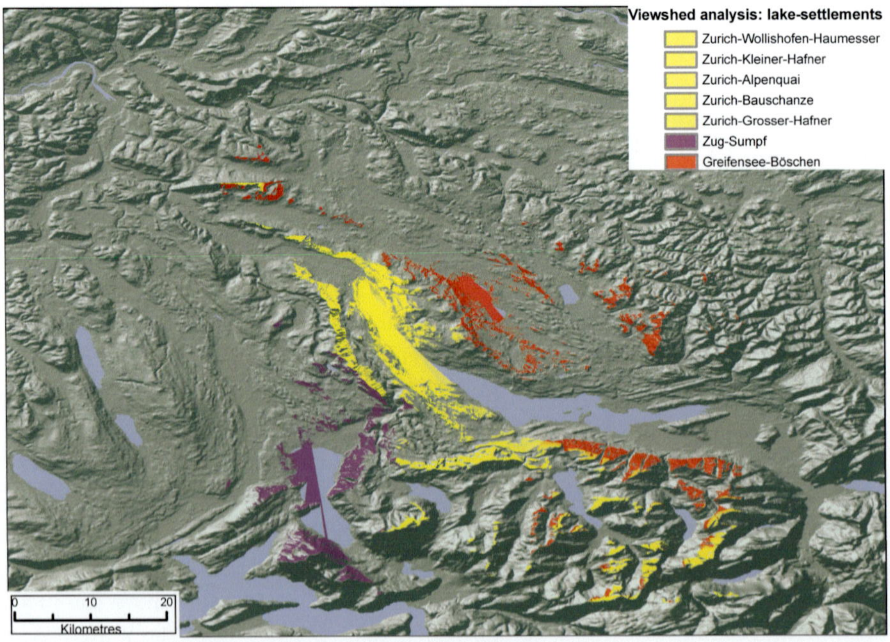

Figure 5.15: Viewshed of Late Bronze Age lake-dwellings in Zurich Bay, Zug-Sumpf, and Greifensee-Böschen. Analysis completed in ArcGIS 10 using base model and height data from SwissTopo DHM 25 (data source: Swiss Federal Office of Topography). Resultant visibility analysis data presented using SRTM background and visibility overlay. Visibility extent limited at west by extent of DHM, no maximum visibility restrictions / horizon set.

Lake Zurich, Lake Greifen and Lake Zug, with locational information for late Bronze Age lake-dwelling sites (Figure 5.15), and compared to two early Iron Age hilltop settlements: Üetliberg overlooking Lake Zurich ,(Bauer, I *et al.* 1991) and Baarburg (Stöckli 2000), overlooking Lake Zug (Figure 5.16).

Although with little direct explanatory value, such visibility modelling does make clear what may be considered as relatively self-evident observations, such as the increased prominence of the 'highland' settlements compared to the lakeshore settlements, and that the visibility of the lakeshore settlements is extensive across the lake but limited inland. However, problems with visibility analysis in archaeological applications concerning the lack of vegetation cover in GIS models, changing landscape features and the over emphasis of visual at the expense of sound or smell orientation indicators are well recognized (e.g. Conolly and Lane 2006). The impact of vegetation cover should be considered not only as an impairment to the visibility of sites, but should also be recognized as a landscape masking feature, disguising elements of the landscape which may appear significantly different were they deforested, such as ridges, slopes and even the lakeshore (Tilley 2010). Furthermore, the structures and their appearance will significantly influence their visibility in the landscape, as has been discussed in the case of the whitewashed mudbrick wall of the Heuneburg (Germany) making the site significantly more prominent within the local environment (Arnold 2010).

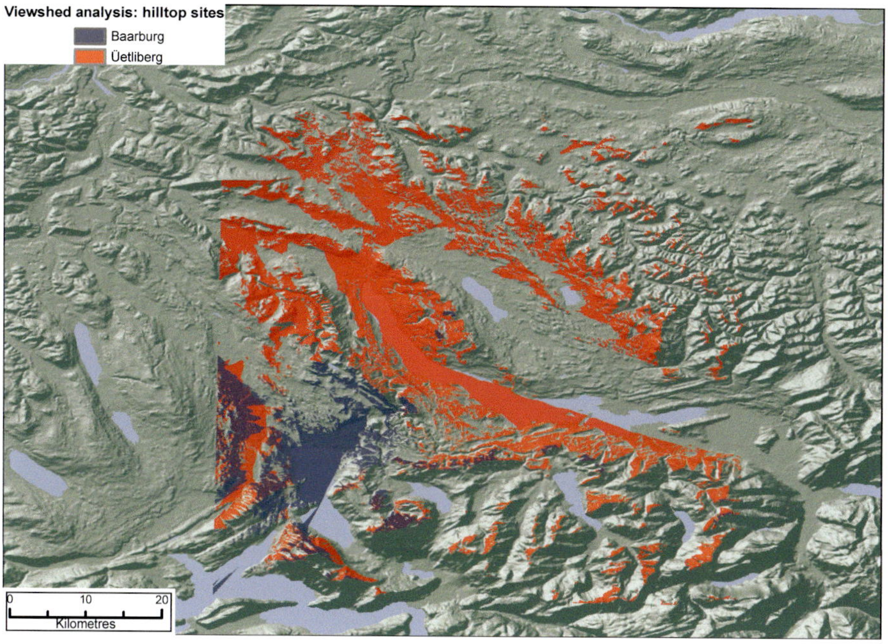

Figure 5.16: Viewshed of the early Iron Age Üetliberg and Baarburg hilltop settlements. Analysis completed in ArcGIS 10 using base model and height data from SwissTopo DHM 25 (data source: Swiss Federal Office of Topography). Resultant visibility analysis data presented using SRTM background and visibility overlay. Visibility extent limited at west by extent of DHM, no maximum visibility restrictions / horizon set.

Furthermore, preservation of the lake-dwellings has provided good indications of the sub-structural features, but little information concerning super-structures, making reconstruction of the upper levels of buildings difficult and reducing possible interpretations of their prominence within the landscape. With reference to the lake-dwellings and lake environments, weather conditions should also be noted: thick fog banks and snow cover, both of which occur regularly around the lakes of the Circum-Alpine region, would all influence the visibility and prominence of sites in the environment (Figure 5.17). While such meteorological affects would not permanently affect the visibility of such sites, they may have had significant seasonal impacts.

The conducted visibility analysis has highlighted the potential difference in visibility between specific lake-dwellings and hilltop settlements. While both settlement types may have been occupied somewhat contemporaneously during the Late Bronze Age, the lake-dwellings did not survive the transition to the early Iron Age. It is possible that the lake-settlements were located to access specific trade routes (see Chapter 3), with the hilltop sites being 'retreats' during the Late Bronze Age. During the Iron Age the hilltop sites became more elaborately fortified, and the occurrence of imported objects (e.g. Attic ceramics (Dietrich-Weibel *et al.* 1998; Guggisberg 1991; Lüscher 1991)) suggests that they were now centres of trade and political power, even though they may have continued to access and/or direct trade along the same water routes as used in previous eras. Thus, it would

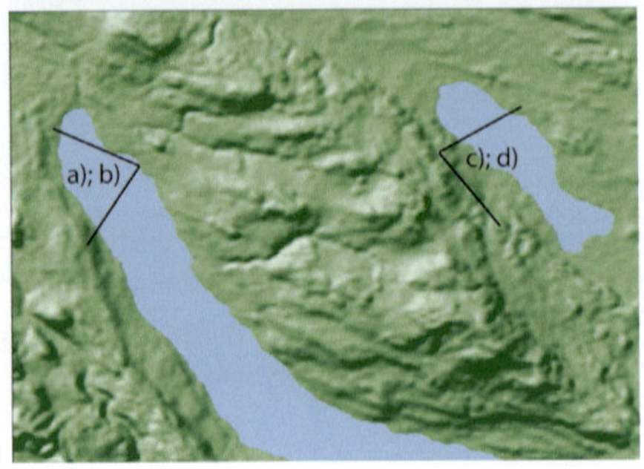

Figure 5.17: Influences of climatic conditions on the visibility of the environment. Looking west across Lake Zurich in clear weather (a) and foggy conditions (b), and east across Lake Greifen during clear (c) and foggy (d) conditions there is a marked difference on the visibility of locations and the landscape. Map (e) shows viewing directions for photographs. (Photographs courtesy of N Bleicher (Zurich)).

appear as though the visibility of such sites was more important than their direct location upon waterways to restrict access to trade traffic.

Combined with the issue of visibility, and also to the movement of trade and communication routes, is the general progress of landscape clearance and the opening of the environment throughout prehistory. On- and off- site surveys of botanical indicators suggest that the environment was gradually being opened and forests cleared throughout the Bronze Age (Brombacher and Klee 2009; Rachoud-Schneider 2009), with a pronounced reduction in the prevalence of tree pollen in some regions, corresponding to an increase in the representation of grass species and thus reflecting a possible deforestation of the landscape for agricultural purposes (e.g. Jacomet and Brombacher 2009; Jacomet *et al.* 1999: Fig. 40; Magny *et al.* 2013). Such environmental modifications were precipitated by the creation of a feedback loop between technological developments, such as the production of bronze and iron tools and the improvement of agricultural practices including the ploughing techniques (Jacomet *et al.* 1999: 109-11), and demographic and social requirements for greater production of food stuffs. A side effect of the opening of the landscape would have been a reduction in the general tree and forest cover (Bogaard 2011: 275), enabling easier navigation of the natural – but not necessarily social – environment for purposes of exchange, and also increasing the potential visibility of sites across the landscape.

Chapter 6

Religion, Rituals, and Symbolism

Ritual and religion are, as suggested in Hawkes' (1954) 'ladder of inference', some of the most problematic aspects of prehistoric society to understand from the archaeological record. Possibly the best indicators for past ritual and religious practices are the burial structures and remains, from which burial goods and treatment of the bodies provide indications of cultural attitudes and practices. The study of material culture items from the lake-dwelling regions of Switzerland has shown that objects were seldom deposited in burial contexts in these communities during the Late Bronze Age (see Chapter 4). In fact, due to the limited number of burials associated to the lake-dwelling communities their funerary practices are poorly understood (Ebersbach *et al.* 2010; Primas 2004: 113). Some cemeteries are however known, for example Le Boiron (Beeching 1977), and burials at Vidy-Chavannes (Kaenel and Klausener 1990; Moinat and David-Elbiali 2003), but the burial practice of lake-dwelling communities remains largely enigmatic.

6.1 Burial Practices

When considering burial traditions of any period, it is important to remember that the burial rites were not carried out by the individual placed in the burial, but by the members of society who survived them; "the dead do not bury themselves, but are treated and disposed of by the living" (Parker Pearson 1999: 3). Thus, the objects which were placed in burials as offerings and equipment may not only have represented the personal belongings or identity of the individual, but signify the relationships and roles that they held and fulfilled in society (Fontijn 2002: 241; Joy 2010: 76; Parker Pearson 1999: 84). However, burial goods need not be biographical in only the strictest sense, but may also be symbolically biographical, as essentially argued by Whitley (2002) for Late Bronze Age and early Iron Age warrior burials in Greece: individuals were buried with the ornaments of warriors because the position they held in society dictated that they *were* warriors, despite the fact that their age and physiology suggests they (possibly) *were not*. The objects chosen for inclusion in burials may have been specifically made for this purpose, to recreate identities that were destroyed in cremation process (Fontijn 2002: 240; Parker Pearson 1999: 85), and also as a display of wealth and power to observers of the burial – not only of the individuals entombed, but also those performing the ceremonies. Burials were also arenas for political and social deception, for example the Bronze Age trunk burial at Borum-Eshøj (DK), in which a dagger was placed inside a sword scabbard in the burial, both deceived observers of the ceremony with a false deposition, and simultaneously deprived the deceased of their appropriate burial items (Parker Pearson 1999: 85-87).

Cemeteries and burials associated with Late Bronze Age lake-settlements are very uncommon, which makes a comparative analysis of burials and their incorporated items difficult. The few examples which are known (Table 6.1) show that while a range of 'accessory' goods were included in burials (for example glass beads, arm-/leg-rings, needles, and plain ceramics), 'functional' objects such as arrows, spinning whorls, fish hooks, razors, knives, swords/weapons, and richly decorated ceramics were seldom deposited in this manner (cf. David-Elbiali and Moinat 2005: 161-62; Primas 2004). The low number of burials and relatively low frequency of deposition at these locations suggests that a small proportion of the communities living in these regions are represented. Late Bronze Age inland cemeteries within Switzerland, illustrate a similar style and frequency of burial to their lake proximity counterparts, but also demonstrate the continuity and re-use of Middle Bronze Age cemeteries (e.g. Morat-Löwenberg). Small, short duration cemeteries are evident in southern Germany, where they have been interpreted as a reflection of short duration, mobile, settlement trends (Brestrich and Wahl 1998: 307). Such a system of mobile inland settlements may be similar to the pattern evident for lake-settlements (see section 5.3), and it is possible that cemeteries and burial grounds associated with the pile-dwellings would be similarly small and of short duration.

Site	Dating period	Inhumations	Cremations	Qty	Lake-dwelling or Inland association
Le Boiron	HaB	X	X	36	L-D
Vidy-Chavannes	HaB-HaC	X	X	16	L-D
Saint Prex-La Moraine	HaA2		X	<60	L-D
Vidy-Musée romain	HaB1-HaB2	X	X	3	L-D
Cortaillod-Aux Murgiers	HaA1		X	2	L-D
Le Landeron-Les Carougets	HaB1-HaB2	X	X	1	L-D
Delémont-En La Pran	HaB1		X	40	Inland
Morat-Löwenberg	HaB	X		1	Inland
Sion-Rue De Lausanne;					Inland
-Maison Solioz;	Bronze final	X	X	?	
-Maison de Torrenté;	HaB2-HaB3	X	X	1	
-Maison Cocatrix;	Bronze final		X	?	
-l'Hôtel de la Poste;	Bronze final			?	

Table 6.1: Selected Late Bronze Age burials and cemeteries related to lake-dwellings and inland settlements within Switzerland. L-D = Lake-dwelling. (Beeching 1977; Boisaubert and Bugnon 2008; Bouyer and Boisaubert 1992; David-Elbiali and Moinat 2005; Gallay and Kaenel 1986; Hapka 1995; Hofmann 1991; Hofmann Rognon and Doswald 2005; Kaenel and Klausener 1990; Moinat and David-Elbiali 2003; Pousaz et al. 2000). (List is not exhaustive – for further sites and references see Moinat and David-Elbiali 2003 and Figure 6.1).

Excavations in advance of the A1 motorway in western Switzerland revealed a higher inland settlement density for the Bronze Age than had previously been assumed (Boisaubert *et al.* 2008: 446). Particularly intensive areas of occupation over distances of less than 10km in the hinterland of Estavayer-le-Lac and Lake Murten were identified, yet few cemeteries were found in these regions (Mauvilly 2008: Fig. 1). It is possible that these cemeteries were utilized by more than one community within the area, and do not only relate to the closest settlement. Evidence from Late Bronze Age settlement and cemetery association in other regions, such as Frattesina and Il Narde in the Po Plain, separated by c. 800 metres (Salzani and Colonna 2010), Rhenen and Remmerden (NL) separated by less than 1km (Fontijn 2010: 139), and suggestions of up to 5km separation in central Switzerland for the early Iron Age (Brun 1992: 195), indicates that not inconsiderable distances occurred between communities and their cemeteries. During the Iron Age, separation between some burials and the assumedly associated settlement becomes even greater, particularly for elite burials, such as between the Hochdorf and Hohenasperg (D) at c. 12km, (see Brun 1992: 199-201). Thus, it is quite possible that the lake-dwelling communities utilized some of the cemeteries within the immediate lake-hinterland (cf. Fischer, V 2012: 143-

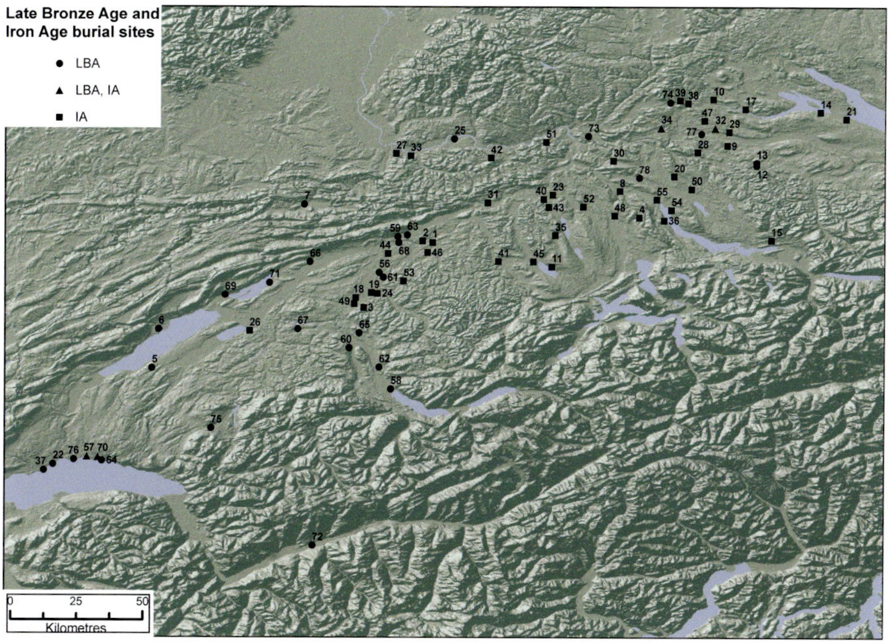

Figure 6.1: Selected Late Bronze Age and early Iron Age burials and cemeteries in Switzerland. It is evident that several burial sites have been located along the immediate lake-hinterland, but it is also apparent that some are located further inland (for site list see Appendix 3). The map is not exhaustive, especially considering Iron Age sites, but well demonstrates the relative disproportion in representation of Late Bronze Age and Iron Age burials in the region. A great number of Iron Age sites – not mapped here – are apparent in the Canton of Bern (central-western Switzerland), as well demonstrated by Ebersbach et al. (2010).

44), as may be indicated by some of the (rare) items included in burials – e.g. arm-/leg-rings and glass beads at Le Boiron (Beeching 1977) and Vidy-Chavannes (Fischer, V 2012; Kaenel and Klausener 1990; Moinat and David-Elbiali 2003). At present, however, there is little direct evidence to suggest that such joint use of inland cemeteries occurred (Figure 6.1), and given their relatively small size when compared to the potential population of lake-settlements it is questionable as to how many communities co-shared the use of cemeteries or what percentage of the population was buried in this manner.

Human remains, but not burials, are known from locations within several LBA lake-settlements of the northern Circum-Alpine region. The most well recorded remains are from Ürschhausen-Horn (CH) and Wasserburg-Buchau (D), where, respectively, remains of a seven year old girl and of seven individuals were recovered (Baumeister 2009: 11, 53). However, these instances do not appear to be burials *sensu strictu*, but possibly, ritualistic offerings in significant places within the local environmental setting. Occurring at the edge of the lakeshore, they may have been offerings or sacrificial depositions in an attempt to prevent water levels rising further (Menotti *et al.* 2014). Fragments of human bones, typically cranial, are known from a number of lake-settlements, both Neolithic (proportionately more) and Bronze Age (less), though such occurrences are by no means common (Andrey 2006). Some of these fragments, such as from Grandson-Corcelettes, show impressions which could be the result of combat (Andrey 2006: 152-53). The relative abundance of cranial bones compared to other skeletal parts may be the result of 19th century unsystematic 'excavation' and poor identification of human bones (Andrey 2006: 158). Alternatively, this may be the result of prehistoric cultural selection, with specific remains retained or deposited within lake-settlements for social legitimization practices. Human remains could have performed the function of 'heirlooms' as purely symbolic or functional items, creating links to deceased individuals and past identities in the present (cf. Armit 2012; Bonogofsky 2003). However, with a low number of individuals represented (minimum of 201 individuals from Lakes Neuchâtel, Murten, and Biel in the study of Andrey) across the Neolithic and the Bronze Age, if such a practice occurred it can be considered neither common nor widespread.

Burial practices may illustrate an element of conservatism within societies, with retention of familiar materials and objects in the funerary domain. For example, the Hohmichele group of burials, related to the Heuneburg (D) fortified settlement, include no imported ceramic materials, i.e. Attic ware, despite the common occurrence of these in nearby high status settlements (i.e. the Heuneburg) (Guggisberg 2011; Riek 1962; Shefton 2000). The general exclusion of imported objects, for instance Attic ware, from burials of the broader northern Alpine region may not only be a result of maintenance of traditional ceramics for the burial sphere, but also a result of the forms Attic ceramics imported: drinking and feasting vessels (cf. Bradley and Smith 2007; Shefton 2000). The rise of drinking and feasting as a socio-political sphere during the Iron Age generated heightened value and significance for imported feasting equipment in the sphere of the living, removing the equipment from the burial practices – particularly when compared to Late Bronze Age bronze and ceramic cups (cf. Martin 2009). However, the use of imported Etruscan *Schnabelkannen* in Iron Age burials north of the Alps demonstrates that some drinking equipment still held a role in burial practices (Vorlauf 1997), and progressing to the later Iron Age, particularly with female associations (Lüscher and Müller 1999: 256-57), for instance in burials at Wohlen (Koller 1998) and Bonstetten (Drack 1985). Exoticism and 'foreignness' did not automatically convey high status or burial functions on objects; knowledge of the objects intended functions in their 'homelands' also influenced how items were used in new cultural settings.

Burial traditions can also be innovative, as can be seen through the varying dominance of cremation and inhumation traditions over time (Arnold and Langenegger 2012). While the burial traditions in central Europe north of the Alps were generally dominated by inhumation practices during the Iron Age (Arnold 2002), the situation is not so clearly demarcated during the Bronze Age and early Iron Age. Cemetery and burial evidence in the northern Circum-Alpine region from the Middle and Late Bronze Age shows a general trend of development from inhumation burials under tumuli (BzB), through cremation under tumuli and in extended graves (BzC), to the typical Urnfield period cremation with remains contained in an urn without burial mound (BzD and later (Fischer, C 1997)). However, Vidy-Chavannes (Kaenel and Klausener 1990; Moinat and David-Elbiali 2003), Le Landeron-Les Carougets (Hofmann Rognon and Doswald 2005), and Le Boiron (Beeching 1977) show that cremation and inhumation practices were used simultaneously during the Late Bronze Age (Table 6.1). Furthermore, the early Iron Age does not demonstrate the universal adoption of inhumation burial practices, but rather the continuation of cremation burials from the Late Bronze Age, though some differences occur between eastern and western Switzerland (Lüscher and Müller 1999: 250-53). What is notable, however, is that more burials are observable than compared to the Late Bronze Age, particularly in the former lake-dwelling regions, and the re-adoption of burial mound construction made burials – and continues to make them, leading to higher excavation rates – more visible in the environment.

In a comparative study of early Iron Age burials, Lüscher (1993: 109-11), noted differences in the predominant burial tradition between eastern and western Switzerland, with cremation popular in the former and inhumation in the latter. Interestingly, there appears to be limited overlap of use between the Late Bronze Age and early Iron Age in any of the cemeteries studied (Lüscher 1993: 111, 43). Such a lack of Bronze Age to Iron Age continuity is illustrated by the establishment of new cemeteries during the HaC period, many of which remained in use throughout the Iron Age. Furthermore, while some flat burials are recorded from the early Iron Age (e.g. Cressier-Balastiere) a trend towards increasing the visibility of burials is evident, with a return to the Middle Bronze Age tradition of using small tumuli to mark graves (e.g. Gals-Jolimont). In fact, ancient (Middle Bronze Age) tumuli were even re-used as burial locations (e.g. Cressier-La Baraque (Arnold 2002; Dunning and Rychner 1994: 83; Lüscher 1993)). This return to 'visible' burials, which may have begun during the latter stages of the Late Bronze

Age at sites such as Ossingen-Im Speck and Rafz-Im Fallentor (Fischer, C 1998b: 320), should be seen as both a formative factor in, and a consequence of, changing social conditions which led to increasingly hierarchical burial practices in the Iron Age, finally culminating in the richly furnished wagon burials and *Fürstengraben* associated with the *Fürstensitze* fortified settlements (Dunning and Rychner 1994: 83).

Visible burials may not only have been used as a method of signifying social identity and heritage, through the re-use of familial or ancestral places (whether actual or manufactured through placement association (cf. Thomas, J 2013: 94)), but may also have been used to signify the social status of the buried individuals. The construction of tumuli would have required a large amount of labour procured from the wider community, for example the creation of a 30m diameter tumuli may have required the movement of 2000 m^3 of material (Spindler 1996). The construction of tumuli can thus be seen as an instance of visual consumption and representative of an individual's ability to organise and control significant labour resources. However, the communal aspect would also create a time and memory mark for the wider society, which is somewhat reminiscent of the communal aspect of Late Bronze Age hoard deposition (see below), but it is also clear that the general emphasis if burial mounds is on that of the entombed individual. Limited representation of community ideals may also be observed in the multiple inhumations found in tumuli, for instance a minimum of 23 burials in the probable late Hallstatt D tumuli at Pratteln (Lüscher 1985) or the nine burials in the tumulus at Thunstetten (Hennig, Heinz 1992). Such repeated or 'community' use does not necessarily detract from the original emphasis placed on the burial of the primary interment through the construction of the mound, but may represent repeated and prolonged use of a place mark to access associations of status, heritage, and legitimization created during the primary construction of the mounds.

Indications of status representation, social symbolism and inter-regional contact can be seen in equipment deposited in burials. For instance, from the early stages of the Late Bronze Age (BzD-HaA) high status wagon burials, of the *Hart an der Alz* type, in which the wagon was cremated along with the entombed individual, are recorded in the northern Circum-Alpine region (Pare 1992: 23-28). Such practices apparently fell out of fashion during the later Urnfield (HaA-HaB) period in the region, though numerous pieces of possible wagon fittings (the *Egemose* type) are known from sites around Lake Neuchâtel and also at Zurich-Wollishofen-Haumesser (Pare 1992: 28-30). A decreasing frequency of wagon burials in Europe north of the Alps during the early Iron Age has been seen as a reflection of increasing elite control and restriction of access to, and use of, wagon symbolism (Pare 1992: 202-05). There are, however, a number of exceptional burials within Switzerland which employ wagons as a part of the burial assemblage – namely those at Ins where a number of wagons are recorded, and even two in the same burial mound (David-Elbiali and Dunning 2004; Drack 1958; Lüscher and Müller 1999: 258-59) – and their association with other high status objects, such as gold jewellery, and bronze vessels, suggests that their use constituted a part of social status display.

The early Iron Age burials also show a development over their Late Bronze Age predecessors in the quantity and forms of object included as burial goods (see Chapter 4). Although there is considerable variation between different regions in Switzerland in the number and form of ceramics included in burials (Lüscher 1993), the range of metal goods is somewhat increased from the previous era. Arm-rings, knives, toilet equipment, and razors represent personal equipment in the burials, but differentiation occurred between the use of materials in male and female burials, for instance iron and bronze arm-rings respectively (Lüscher and Müller 1999: 255). Such differentiation of objects and materials continued through the Iron Age with respective use of fibula, for example, reflecting male or female identity (Primas 1970; Schmid-Sikimić 1995). Thus, general social identities are displayed through the deposition of specific objects, which could then be elaborated through the use of specific higher status materials of the construction of substantial burial mounds.

6.2 Artefact deposition practices

In addition to the ritual deposition of human remains it is well documented that metalwork was deposited in ritualized practices, either as collective hoard assemblages or isolated objects (Bradley 2005). Although it is possible that numerous reasons lie behind the social choices to place metalwork in hoard assemblages, general consensus accepts that most hoards reflect, at least partially, a ritualistic aspect (Bradley 2005; Falkenstein 2011; Görmer 2006; Harding 2000: 354). Whether deposited as a collection or as single items, the social benefits of placing items irretrievably out of reach (with the possible exception of so-called 'founders hoards' (cf. Harding 2000)) outweighed the expenditure required to produce or acquire the object(s) (Falkenstein 2011).

6.2.1 Hoards

Within the lake-dwelling region of the northern Alpine forelands hoard assemblages are a relatively uncommon occurrence (cf. Dunning and Rychner 1994: 71; Ebersbach *et al.* 2010; Fischer, V 2012) – this may well be related to the previously discussed influence of excavation and research (see section 1.3). There are however, a number of hoards known from both inland locations, such as at Basel-Elisabethenschanze and Kerzers (Primas 1977), within the lake-margin, such as at Sursee-Landzunge (Rigert 1997; Weidmann 1983), and within lake-settlements, for example at Auvernier-Nord (Rychner 1987). The deposition of metalwork hoards within lake-settlements is comparable to the deposition of hoards within hilltop settlements throughout Switzerland and central Europe (Berger, L and Brogli 1980; Falkenstein 2011; Hagl 2008; Kubach 1994; Möslein 1998/99; Steinhauser-Zimmermann 1989). It has also been suggested by Fischer (2011, 2012: 143-44) that the placement of hoards within lake-settlements is a result of the condensation of social activities which would in an inland environment be dispersed between smaller settlements.

The placement of hoards within lake-dwellings has similar variability to those in hilltop settlements, with some placed along the settlement perimeter, for instance at Wasserburg-Buchau, (Kimmig, W 1992), and others within the settlement area, such as at Auvernier-Nord and Zurich-Alpenquai (Mäder 2001: 69-73). It is also evident that both fragmentary and complete objects were selected for deposition, occasionally together, as at Auvernier-Nord.

The low representation of hoard assemblages in the Late Bronze Age lake-dwelling region of Switzerland is followed by their almost complete absence during the early Iron Age. Instead, greater numbers of artefacts were placed in burial assemblages during this period, a situation which is replicated across wider central Europe, and can be highlighted by the treatment of specific objects, for example swords (Fontijn 2002: 221; Görmer 2006: 292; Kristiansen 1998a: 76; Kubach 1994: 70; Primas 2004; Roymans 1991; Torbrügge 1959).

6.2.2 Single item depositions

The deposition of single items in certain locations – often wetlands – is well recognized across central Europe during the Bronze Age, and is generally taken to represent sacrificial votive offerings with the objects removed from social circulation and placed permanently out of reach (Bradley 1990, 2005; Görmer 2006: 293). It has also been suggested, however, that in lakeshore regions such individual depositions would be visible and recoverable – if social conditions permitted such action (Rychner 2001). Of course, in this sense 'visible' is a relative term, with the act of deposition potentially witnessed by many individuals, be it of single items, collective hoard assemblages, or burials (Larsson 2001: 169) – and it was social practice and convention which effectively rendered the objects irrecoverable. Thus, the act of object deposition created social memories of objects and participation in events, but also permitted the forgetting-while-remembering of items and events (cf. Jones, A 2007a).

In fact, the act of single – and collective – object deposition would have created, or enhanced existing, places in the landscape, and generated significant levels of social memory concerning those locations (cf. Chapman 2000: 183-90). Such aspects can be seen in the many objects recorded from certain locations along the lakeshore; for example at Zurich-Wollishofen-Haumesser a large assemblage of jewellery pins spanning a broad typological seriation have been recovered (Bauer, S 2002). The identification of such instances of prolonged accumulative deposition in specific locations has led to the suggestion that these were significant 'ritual' or 'sacred' places in the landscape which were subsequently occupied as settlement locations (Baumeister 2011).

While it remains possible that some of these objects represent lost objects or items left behind at the time of abandonment, there are a number of factors, in addition to the extensive evidence of object deposition in wetland locations, suggesting that neither of these situations account for the majority of finds. Firstly, the typological sequencing and dating of finds compared to settlements suggests that some pre-date the construction of settlement. Secondly, if objects were dropped in wetland settlements during their use it is highly likely that they would have been readily recoverable, particularly in settlements constructed in humid locations but not above deep standing water. Finally, the typology and dating spread, and quantity of artefacts recovered from specific areas has been used as an argument against the sudden abandonment of lake-settlements during flooding events (Müller 1993: 86). The case of Ürschhausen-Horn may provide a direct example of this, with exceptionally few pieces of metalwork recovered from the settlement (Nagy 1999), it appears as though most objects were removed prior to site abandonment, a process which also finds support in ethnographic survey (e.g. Deal 1985).

The occurrence of 'old' objects, for example Early Bronze Age needles in Late Bronze Age contexts, in wetland assemblages also raises the possibility that items were curated over extended periods as cultural heirlooms (Fischer, V 2011: 1301-02). It is, however, also possible that such items were encountered during Late Bronze Age activities, for instance agricultural processes, and thereby retained as curiosities (cf. Hingley 2009). If retained as heirlooms such objects may have been used as identifiers of legitimacy to reside in certain locations, or if encountered in the local environment may have provided indications to settle specific sites (see section 2.3). In either situation, the social choice to terminally deposit the objects demonstrates a continuation of traditional practices within the lake-settlements.

Further interpretation can be garnered from the condition in which objects were deposited. For example the deliberate destruction of swords has been seen as a method of ritually 'killing' items in order that they can be included as burial goods, mimicking the destruction of the deceased while also irrevocably removing the object from functional circulation (e.g. Fontijn 2002: 235; Nebelsick 2000). The damage observable on Late Bronze Age swords included in burials, a process which continued into the Iron Age, are in contrast to the almost universally intact examples chosen for isolated deposition in wetland environments (cf. Falkenstein 2005; Krämer 1985; Quillfeldt 1995; Schauer 1971). Late Bronze Age swords from Switzerland, predominantly known from lake-dwelling sites, do not show such a distinct variance, with approximately equal numbers of damaged and intact swords (Jennings 2014b: 170). Thus, it is possible that the deposition of swords, and likely other objects, in the lake-dwellings represent a combination of burial and hoard or isolated deposition activities, as has been proposed by Fischer through the suggestion that the damaged objects are intended to mimic the cremation process (Fischer, V 2011: 1303) and a condensation of cultural activities into the settlement sites.

As with hoard depositions, there are significantly fewer isolated depositions recorded from the early Iron Age in the former lake-dwelling regions, though it is well known that certain places continued to be used as sacred locations, for example at La Tène (Dunning 1991), Port (Lüscher and Müller 1999: 274; Müller and König 1990; Wyss 1955), and bridge locations (Wiemann and Scherer 2008, 2011), and objects were still offered into the water – particularly during the La Tène period. In fact, with reference to the Hallstatt period daggers from the Swiss midlands, mainly relating to Hallstatt D, a significant proportion are known from wetland contexts (Sievers 1982). Thus, object deposition trends show some

	Context					
	Lake-dwelling	**Wetland**	**Burial**	**Hoard**	**Single find**	**No context detail**
Late Bronze Age	36	11	-	3	7	6
Early Iron Age	-	8	21	-	3	1

Table 6.2: Comparison of sword finds contexts between the Bronze and Iron Age. There is a clear reorganisation in the deposition practices adopted for swords and dagger between the Late Bronze Age (HaB) and early Iron Age (HaC-HaD) in Switzerland (data from Krämer 1985; Schauer 1971; Sievers 1982).

continuation from the Late Bronze Age, but also a gradual break with traditional practices including the diversion of objects into new spheres and roles in burial practices (Table 6.2).

6.2.3 Purposes of object deposition

It is clear that the Late Bronze Age settlements were not significantly different to their inland counterparts with regard to the deposition of items, only that the activities occurred in a greatly condensed spatial setting (Fischer, V 2012: 143-44). Thus, the act of deposition would have conveyed the same social functions in communities residing in both dry- and wetland locations. One of the most basic functions of deposition was to create *places* in the landscape, and populate the environment with cultural settings (e.g. Ballmer 2010a, b; Chapman 2000).

Furthermore, the act of deposition should be seen as a communal act, involving multiple members as either participants or observers, but also incorporating multiple identities and individuals in the objects deposited (cf. Fredengren 2011). Such a plurality may be seen in the composition of the small hoard from Wasserburg-Buchau, comprising objects of both male and female nature, and potentially representing the equipment of three (or more) people (Nebelsick 2000). Thus, the hoard assemblages, while disposing of significant objects, do so in a manner which replicates social identities and binds communities together through the construction of significant places and memory. In a similar manner, the repetitive deposition of isolated objects in persistent places, while not reflecting multiple identities, ties the act of deposition to a cultural tradition, re-enforcing the community. The loose spread of inland settlements and hoards also raises the possibility that a number of different communities were co-using the same deposition locations, further widening the cultural significance of such locations (see Fischer, V 2012).

Such representations of community during the Late Bronze Age through the deposition of objects do not appear to be continued into the early Iron. With the revival of the inhumation and burial mound tradition and corresponding gradual increase in the quantities and standard of material included in the burial assemblage, the emphasis of deposition for individuals can be seen. Even though multiple individuals and large sections of a community may have been involved in preparations for burials, the final monument and deposition was concerned with emphasising the status and identity of the entombed rather than the community as a whole.

6.3 'Ritual' material culture

Objects of purportedly ritualistic and symbolic nature were, however, not only confined to burial practices. For example, *Stangentrichter* have been discussed as unusual and enigmatic objects of uncertain function (Mäder 2001: 41-45). These items are particularly prevalent in the Carpathian Basin, upper Danube valley, and lake-dwellings of the northern Alpine region (Figure 6.2). Clear differences in deposition are recorded between the regions, with preference for hoards in the Carpathian Basin and burials in the Danube valley (Mäder 2001: 44), and their distribution is indicative of communication links between the three regions, with movement of either objects or concepts with subsequent local manufacture possible. Various functions for these items have been proposed, including funnels, needles, jewellery, and as parts of horse or wagon equipment (Mäder 2001: 41-43). The rarity of objects indicates that they may have held specific symbolism related

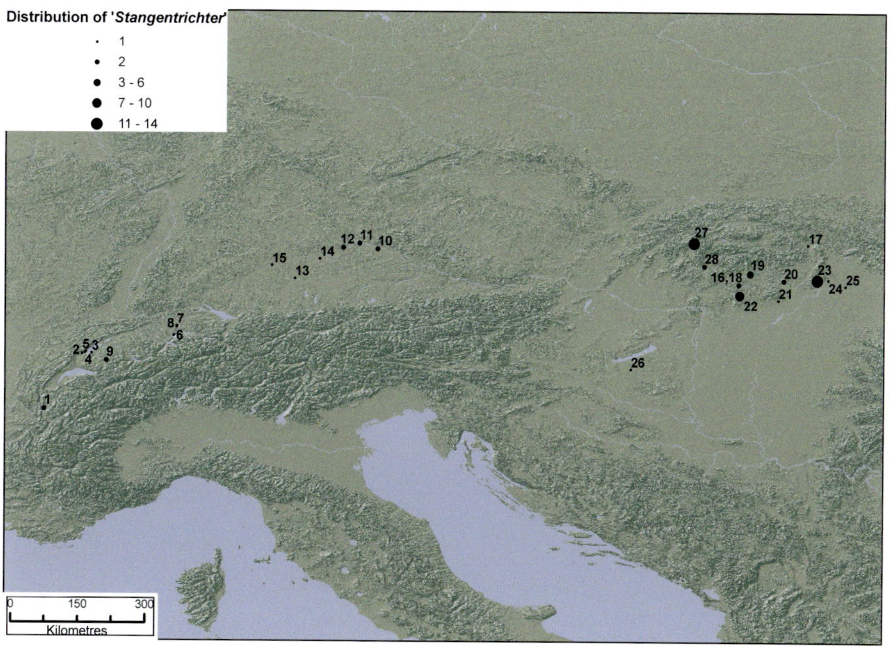

Figure 6.2: European distribution of Stangentrichter. Sites: 1) Grésine, 2 items; 2) Grandson-Corcelettes, 1; 3) Font, 1; 4) Onnens, 1; 5) Concise, 1; 6) Zug-Sumpf, 1; 7) Zürich-Alpenquai, 1; 8) Zürich-Wollishofen, 1; 9) West Switzerland, 2; 10) Straubing-Kagers, 2; 11) Barbing, 2; 12) Kelheim, 2; 13) Haunstetten, 1; 14) Ingolstadt-Zuchering, 1; 15) Lauingen, 1; 16) Radzovce, 2; 17) Presov, 1; 18) Radzovce, 1 mould; 19) Dražice, 6; 20) Edelény, 2; 21) Tibolddaróc, 1; 22) Kisterenye, 10; 23) Erdohorváti, 13; 24) Vajdácska, 1; 25) Rétközberencs, 1; 26) Pamuk, 1; 27) Žabokreky, 14; 28) Zvolen, 2 (data from Mäder 2001).

to a small section of the society, either through status as elites (possibly as horse riders if a bridal function is accepted) or through symbolic status and position (assuming a 'ritual' function).

While the *Stangentrichter* are enigmatic items, other objects have a potentially more recognisable function, though occur in forms and contexts which suggest that they were not purely practical equipment, for example firedogs and zoomorphic drinking vessels.

6.3.1 Firedogs or 'moon idols'?

Firedogs (*Feuerböcke*) or 'moon idols' (*Mondhorn*) (see Primas *et al.* 1989: 126-48) are known from many Late Bronze Age settlements in the central Europe and the northern Circum-Alpine region (Figure 6.3), and during the early Iron Age from burials in various areas of central Europe (Matzerath 2011). The Late Bronze Age objects have been interpreted as functional items, cultic pieces, and instruments for recording lunar and solar calendars (Kerner 2001, 2004, 2007; Primas *et al.* 1989: 132-33), while the Iron Age examples appear to have developed into specific facets and indicators of religious identity (Matzerath 2012). Evidence in support of a calendric function has been identified by Kerner (2001) on examples from Zurich-Alpenquai and -Wollishofen-Haumesser, which apparently

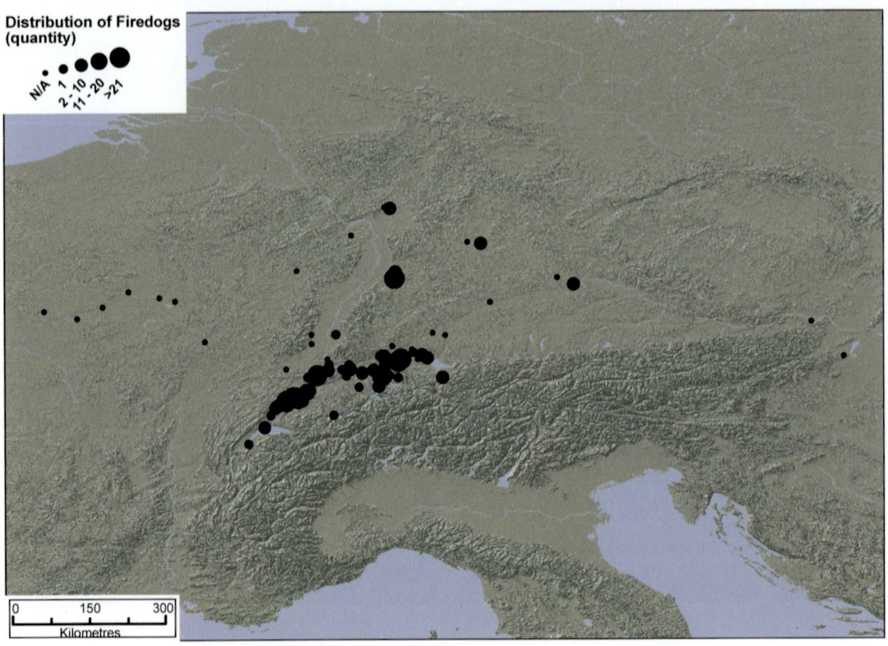

Figure 6.3: Distribution of moon idols / firedogs in Late Bronze Age contexts. (Data compiled from Arnold and Langenegger 2012; Baumeister 1995; Baumstein 1994; Blösch and Wieland 2002; Demaez et al. 2013; Diemer 1995; Fischer, C 1998a; Grimmer 1982; Holstein 2003; Huber 2005; Jacob-Friesen 2013; Kerner 2001; Lüning and von Kaenel 2006; Maise and Enderle 2000; Nagy 1999; Poncet Schmid et al. 2013; Primas et al. 1989)

demonstrate good alignment to lunar cycles. Lunar and solar cycles would have held significance for prehistoric communities; not only concerning agricultural practices, but also for 'religious' functions (Kerner 2001: 108). Although the role of longer term (monthly and annual) solar / lunar cycles are uncertain (but one only has to consider the large monuments across northern Europe with alignment to solstice events to suggest that they held some significance), the role of daily solar cycles in religious systems of the Late Bronze Age is best exemplified by the sun-bird-ship symbolism (see Kaul 1998, 2004).

Decoration of the firedogs, or the various markings used to form the lunar calendar, typically symmetrical along the centreline of the piece and only on one side (Kerner 2001: 132; Matzerath 2011), may provide indications that these were not intended as calendric systems. If they were to be used as calendar, time, or position markers, then it may be reasonable to expect a repetition of design systems or styles – focussed around the same basic principles such as number of markings – but this is not the case. The number of these objects found in single sites may also argue against such a function – especially if it is assumed that the ability to record calendar events would represent an element of social status. For example, a minimum of 36 are known from Eschenz-Insel Werd (Primas *et al.* 1989: 127-28), at least 50 from Ürschhausen-Horn (Nagy 1999: 76), and an impressive 192 from Hauterive-Champréveyres (Anastasiu and Bachmann 1991). Considering the potential population of 300 individuals at Ürschhausen-Horn (Gollnisch-Moos 1999), this suggests a ratio of 6:1 (people : 'moon idols'), and although the potential population of Hauterive-Champréveyres remains un-calculated, the number of identified structures – 59 – spread between c. 1050 and 871 BC (see Benkert 1993; and Böhringer and Honegger in preparation cited by Pillonel 2007: 18, Fig. 19), indicate that the settlement may have been home to quite a large population, which is matched by a similarly large number of 'moon idols'. If all of these objects were in use at the same time then a relatively high proportion of the community may have been able to record calendar cycles; thereby negating any prestige or individualization that could have been obtained from such practices. Furthermore, the manufacture of the firedogs was evidently rather careless, without thorough processing of the clay before moulding into shape (Primas *et al.* 1989: 128). This suggests a potentially hurried and non-specialized, possibly household, manufacture, which may be at odds with a specialized function of the finished object.

A functional use of the firedogs may account for their typical fragmentary condition. In light of their low quality manufacture, exposure to high temperatures in hearths may have caused the object to fracture due to airspaces in the clay. Intended use of the objects in hearths could have influenced decisions to manufacture the objects in relatively poor quality, but the decoration applied to the pieces clearly demonstrates that they were to be viewed and observed, and also that they were not manufactured entirely without care. Although few of the Late Bronze Age firedog fragments recovered from archaeological contexts are from within hearths (e.g. two from Eschenz-Insel Werd) most of them are known from settlement pits and areas, and occasionally in burials (Primas *et al.* 1989: 133). Clearly these objects were more than just functional, though the symbolism associated with them, other than possible calendric functions, remains unknown.

6.3.2 Drinking vessels

Zoomorphic and double-ended drinking vessels (*vase a libations*) or infant drinking bottles (*Sauggefässe*) are known from several settlements within the northern Circum-Alpine region (Table 6.3). These vessels may show some influence from the bird shaped vessels (*Vogelgefäss*) typical of the Carpathian Basin and eastern central Europe, but are less obviously zoomorphic and more stylized, showing greater similarity to vessels from central Germany, Austria and the Czech Republic (Eibner 1973). Findings of these vessels in child burials, e.g. at Wien-XI-Simmering (Grave 1, AT (Eibner 1973: 176-78)) and Gundersheim (D, Kubach 1973: no. 1407), supports their use as infant feeding/drinking vessels, though they are also known from adult burials and settlements (Eibner 1973: 178-82). Iconographic and written evidence from the middle ages provides further evidence of ceramic vessels, similar in design to the Bronze Age examples, being used as child's drinking utensils (Eibner 1973: 190-93). Examples from the northern Circum-Alpine region are from predominantly from lake- and inland settlements.

Site	Qty	Context	References
Auvernier	1	Lake-Dwelling	Eibner, 1973
Grandson-Corcelettes	1	Lake-Dwelling	Wyss, 1972
Grésine	2	Lake-Dwelling	Eibner, 1973
Insel Werd	2	Lake-Dwelling	Primas et al, 1989
Lake Bourget	1	Lake	Eibner, 1973
Montilier	1	Lake-Dwelling	Eibner, 1973
Ossingen	1	Cremation burial	Ruoff, 1974
Saint-Prex La Moraine	1	Lake-Dwelling	Moinat and David-Elbiali, 2003
Üetliberg	1	Hilltop settlement	Bauer et al, 1992
Ürschhausen-Horn	2	Lake-Dwelling	Nagy, 1999
Wasserburg Buchau	5	Lake-Dwelling	Eibner, 1973
Zug-Sumpf	1	Lake-Dwelling	Ruoff, 1974
Zürich-Alpenquai	1	Lake-Dwelling	Ruoff, 1974
Zürich-Grosser-Hafner	1	Lake-Dwelling	Wyss, 1972, Eibner, 1973
Zürich-Wollishofen	1	Lake-Dwelling	Wyss, 1972

Table 6.3: Lake-dwellings in the northern Circum-Alpine region with bird-shaped or double ended vessels.

Decoration on these vessels includes linear grooves around the base of the neck, linear grooves on the body, and often circles or half circles surrounding the protruding ends or 'nozzles'. In light of its decoration and form, the vessel from Üetliberg was described as having a "realistically modelled breast" (Bauer, I *et al.* 1991: 132). However, the occurrence of circular bumps and protuberances surrounded by concentric circles is not only confined to these 'drinking vessels' but appears on other ceramics during the Late Bronze Age, as '*Buckelverzierung*' (e.g. Fischer, C 1997: Figs. 46.173, 47.78, 50.211; Kimmig, W 2000a: Figs. 19.311-19.15, 21.31; Seifert 1997: Figs. 36.626, 37.62; Unz 1973). The same design and symbolism principles can even be seen in the *Pfahlbauperlen* (see section 4.1.1), and in two-dimensional form as the circular 'eye' decoration on many forms of arm-/leg-ring jewellery and knives. Whether these vessels were utilized as children's drinking or libation vessels is still unclear (Primas 2008: 187), though in the case of the former it must be noted that these objects are rather uncommon when compared to other vessel types. They must have held some form of social significance for their inclusion in burials, though what this significance is remains unclear.

6.3.3 Symbolism

During the Late Bronze Age, the sun-bird-boat symbolism became widespread across central Europe, and was represented frequently on bronzework, for example razors, buckets and amphorae (Jung and Maraszek 2005; Kaul 1998; Tomedi 2002). Such representations are however relatively uncommon in the lake-dwelling communities of the northern Circum-Alpine region. Although the boss decoration (*Buckelverzierung*) on ceramics (e.g. BzD period Neftenbach-Steinmori, Fischer, C 1997: Tab. 40.110, 42.24; and BzD period Vuadens, Rychner 1998b: Fig. 23) and concentric circular/semi-circular designs on many HaB period bronze objects (e.g. knives, pins, and ring jewellery – see Figure 4.5) may represent small solar symbols, bird representations are uncommon. Exceptional examples include the tin bird model from Hauterive-Champréveyres (Schweizerisches Landesmuseum 2004: Fig. 111), the ceramic bird vessel with plant inlay decoration from Zurich-Alpenquai (Schweizerisches Landesmuseum 2004: Fig. 68), and the birds/ducks modelled on the handles of keys from Zurich-Alpenquai and -Grosser Hafner (see section 4.2.1). The rarity of these objects and decoration indicates that they fulfilled a specific role in society for use in certain circumstances and occasions. It is possible that one of the reasons for the scarcity of waterbird symbolism, with associations to both life and death and the afterlife (Kaul 1998, 2004; Tomedi 2002), in the lake-dwelling communities of the northern Circum-Alpine region is related to their close connection to the lake and wetland environments. The communities were effectively residing in the habitat of the waterbird (and therefore of life/death), possibly making incorporation of such symbolism into social practices more difficult. As effective trade and social centres the lake-settlements may, therefore, have largely inhibited the translation, importation, and influence of the bird symbolism in the wider northern Alpine forelands (see section 2.4).

6.4 Comprehending 'ritual' aspects in the northern Circum-Alpine lake-dwelling region

The distribution of early Iron Age burials in the northern Circum-Alpine region clearly indicates that the lake regions were not totally abandoned with the decline of the lake-dwelling tradition (Boisaubert *et al.* 2008; Dunning and Rychner 1994: 78; Lüscher 1993). Burials and cemeteries throughout the Late Bronze and Iron Age were used to create social spaces in the landscape, in order to construct identities and display the status and power of individuals and communities. However, the surviving evidence suggests that the lake-dwelling communities had, to some extent, disposed of the need to create specific places in the landscape for burial practices. Circumvention of this requirement may, partly, have been achieved through the retention of some human remains within settlements (Andrey 2006), while the remainder was disposed of in an unknown location – perhaps even within the lake after possible cremation (cf. Menotti 2012: 194-98).

The occurrence of human remains within settlement contexts, even small bone fragments, should not be considered as casual disposal, but symbolically charged acts (Chapman 2000: 140). Utilization of cemeteries further inland from the lakeshore and -settlements, possibly in conjunction with inland settlements, would have provided a separate place for burial practices, but would not have created a visible link between settlement and location, thus lacking some of the resonance of permanence, tradition, ancestry, stability, and legitimacy that could have been provided by burial grounds located in close proximity to the utilizing community(ies) (see e.g. Chapman 2000: 188 ff; Thomas, J 2013). A return to visible burials, although not necessarily in prominent locations within the landscape (Lüscher and Müller 1999: 259), and use of them over several centuries (e.g. Unterlunkhofen (CH, Lüscher 1993)) may have been a social method to create structural links between individuals and communities as well as between the environment and landscape of settlements. The transition from Urnfield burials to tumulus burials between the Late Bronze Age and early Iron Age not only created visible and permanent monuments in, and social ties to, the landscape, but also required control of communal labour to construct the mounds (cf. Eggert 1988). This would have demonstrated the status and ability of emerging elites to control, organize, and support labour resources required to create such monuments (Lüscher and Müller 1999: 250).

The few wagon burials from the northern Alpine forelands show that these practices were indigenous developments in central Europe, directly imported from neither the Carpathian Basin nor the Italian peninsula. Such burials do, however, illustrate levels of social stratification, with rich assemblages for the social elites, particularly during the Iron Age. The apparent disappearance of such practices during the Late Bronze Age corresponds to the appearance of horse and wagon equipment in the northern Alpine lake-settlements. Such a transition may reflect an increasing presence and less stringent control of horse and wagon equipment in communities, leading to a de-valuation of the objects as symbols of elite status, while outside of the lake-dwelling region they were retained in burial practices and as social indicators.

The various types of unusual material culture from lake-dwellings, e.g. firedogs/moon idols and drinking vessels, may represent either specific ritualistic/cultic practices or profane everyday actions. Both explanations have reasonable archaeological support, though it is clear that the lake-dwelling communities played a significant role in their use and deposition. Drinking vessels may have been used as infant feeding devices or in adult drinking ceremonies, practices which may also have influenced the circulation and deposition of Late Bronze Age metal vessels (cf. Martin 2009). The firedogs could have been used as such (in hearths), but may also have been involved in calculating the passage of time and lunar cycles, which would have held social and cultural significance for agricultural and religious practices; their exact function is, however, difficult to extrapolate. Similarly, *Stangentrichter* fulfilled an unknown function in the Late Bronze Age communities, but their occurrence in the northern Alpine lake-settlements, southern Germany, and the Carpathian Basin demonstrate Late Bronze Age networks of exchange and communication along which either the concept of manufacture and use for *Stangentrichter* themselves travelled.

Waterbird and solar-boat symbolism of the Late Bronze Age is relatively uncommon in the northern Circum-Alpine region, some examples are, however, known from lake-dwellings (e.g. Zurich-Alpenquai and Hauterive-Champréveyres). Designs, possibly representing the solar element of the sun-ship-bird combination, are seen on many objects of the Late Bronze Age (particularly those of the HaB1-B3 period). Whether these circular 'eyes' and half circle designs truly represent a selective adoption of the sun-bird-boat symbolism according to specific cultural settings and domains (within the waterbird environment and regular use of boats), or simply a circular design is open to debate (cf. Blanco-González 2014: 445, Fig. 4-3a). Circular design elements on material culture objects (e.g. ceramics, arm-rings, belt plates) continued into the Iron Age, when they were combined with other geometric elements to create complex and repetitive designs, and drew influence from motifs and emblems used during the Late Bronze Age (Berger, L and Schindler 1999: 229-30; Dunning and Rychner 1994: 86-91; Schmid-Sikimić 1996). It is, however, apparent that the wetland environment maintained a symbolically significant position. The sword remains (and other objects, cf. Bauer, S 2002; Fischer, V 2012: 116) recovered in the vicinity of many lake-settlements, demonstrate that depositions in wetland environments, similar to those observed in central Germany and Austria, were practiced by the lake-dwelling communities (Jennings 2014b: 168; Krämer 1985; Quillfeldt 1995; Schauer 1971).

Chapter 7

Trade as Influence for Cultural Change in the Northern Circum-Alpine Region?

It is abundantly evident that some of the lake-dwelling communities of the northern Circum-Alpine region were incorporated in exchange and communication networks which extended across central Europe and northern Italy. It is also evident that those communities were primarily involved in the manufacture and export of objects to regional settlements and beyond. In contrast, the quantity of imported objects found within lake-settlements is relatively low, with the *Pfahlbauperlen* and *Allumiere* jewellery beads (glass and amber respectively) from Hauterive-Champréveyres (Rychner-Faraggi 1993) representing one of the largest concentration of artefacts from south of the Alps in the northern Alpine lake-dwellings. Otherwise, the indications of 'foreign' material culture are generally rare, with a small number of examples distributed across a range of material culture forms (Jennings 2014b). For example, some jewellery pins from Zurich-Alpenquai and Hauterive-Champréveyres, which show similarities to items found in the Middle Rhine Valley, the Carpathian Basin, and northern Italy (Kubach 1973; Mäder 2001: 26-28; Říhovský 1979: 158, 81-82; Rychner-Faraggi 1993: 47), and a few imported forms of razors and sickles are far outweighed by locally produced objects (Jennings 2014b). Combining all of the evidence for 'foreign' objects in the lake-dwellings, and other contexts, of the northern Circum-Alpine region (see Chapter 4), it is clear that relatively few items were imported to, and utilized by, communities of northern Alpine region. Where such objects do occur, it appears that they were deposited in 'local' practices, indicating that value associations did not necessarily travel with the object. Exceptions to this pattern may indicate instances of individual mobility, for example the *Herrnbaumgarten* razor from Chelin/Lens, and the Nordic style objects from Grandson-Corcelettes (Fischer, V 2005; Jockenhövel 1971; Sprockhoff 1966).

The general rejection of foreign objects, and lack of value transfer, suggests that the primary involvement of the lake-dwelling communities in European short- and long-distance trade and communication networks was on a production and export basis, as opposed to importing objects. In this respect the continuation and development of regional decorative styles throughout the Late Bronze Age and into the early Iron Age (Dunning and Rychner 1994; Ruoff 1974; Vogt 1952), and the continued establishment of lake-settlements during the Late Bronze Age can be interpreted as (either conscious/active or un-conscious/passive) practices designed to maintain the cultural identity of the lake-dwelling communities. However, it is clear that the trade and communication routes also included some elements of acceptance and incorporation – for example the glass beads which became widely circulated throughout central Europe cannot be seen as spread purely through individual mobility. In this respect the lake-dwelling communities may have acted as 'barrier' or 'translation' regions, converting the beads from a foreign, (proto-) Villanovan object, to a culturally acceptable item to Urnfield societies north of the Alps.

However, it is also clear that cultural changes were occurring in the lake-dwelling communities during the Late Bronze Age as a direct result of their involvement in, and possible control of, far reaching exchange and communication networks. The presence of weights at numerous lake-settlements corresponding to systems used in northern Italy during the Middle and Late Bronze Age (see section 4.2.2) is a direct reference to changing social attitudes towards the circulation of materials in the northern Circum-Alpine region. Whilst it is possible that scales could have been used for symbolic purposes, their occurrence in different regions may also indicate the emergence of commodity exchange systems linking those regions and communities. The appearance of such commodity systems in the northern Alpine region at the end of the Bronze Age marks a break with previous patterns of gift exchange and social enchainment that may have dominated the limited inter-regional exchange networks with which the communities were involved, and which resulted in the distribution of, for example, *Brotlaibidole* around Lake Constance (Köninger and Schlichtherle 2001), *Allumiere* beads at Hauterive-Champréveyres and Montlingerberg, and *Pfahlbauperlen* throughout northern Europe. How prevalent commodity exchange practices were is difficult to estimate, but the relative scarcity of weights suggests that they were utilized by a small section of society, possibly retained by specific community members involved in trade systems. In conjunction with weights and scales, the occurrence of sickle fragments as a 'proto-currency' (Primas 1986: 37-41; Sommerfeld 1994) should also be considered. The circulation of sickle fragments of relatively regularized mass could have been used to 'purchase' other items on a commodity basis, or to circulate refined metal stock as ingots and fragments thereof, and may represent another facet of a quasi-commoditized exchange system.

Furthermore, social changes during the Late Bronze Age can also be observed through the occurrence of new objects in the lake-dwelling communities of the northern Circum-Alpine region, specifically keys. Whether these objects were connected to exchange and communication routes is unknown as few Late Bronze Age precedents occur in Europe, though some 'key'-like features can be seen in 'ring grip bars' from Austria (Grossweikersdorf; Schönberg (cf. Říhovský 1979: nos. 1781-83)); and Iron Age examples are recorded from northern Italy (see section 4.2.1). The occurrence of keys in a range of settlement sizes, from the small population Greifensee-Böschen to the large settlements at Estavayer-le-Lac, Zurich-Alpenquai and Wasserburg-Buchau, suggests that their use was not strictly related to population and/or settlement size. It is notable that they also occur at settlements interpreted as significant positions on trade routes – such as Mörigen and Montlingerberg; do they represent a desire to secure valuable imported goods, or the symbolic ability to control access to specific buildings?

Waterbird decoration on several of the lake-dwelling keys has been used to support their interpretation as 'ritual' objects (see Van Willigen 2011), but such decoration only occurs on two of the examples, and symbolic decoration does not necessarily signify 'ritual' use. However, the low quantity of keys recovered from the Late Bronze Age, and the range of settlement sizes from where they are known, suggest that they were used by a minority (elite or 'ritual'?) section of society, and that access to certain areas of communities was becoming more rigidly controlled. Societies and communities, even small ones, were becoming more stratified and controlled, with divisions based around the (in)ability to access specific areas and structures within the village community.

The introduction and early adoption of iron as a decorative (Stage 1 use, after Snodgrass 1980: 336-37), and occasional functional material at several of the lake-dwelling communities (Jennings 2014b), is also indicative of increasing social stratification. Even on objects which were utilized by small sections of society, such as swords and horse gear, iron was used as a decorative material in practices of object singularization between elites. The occurrence of iron inlay on more widely spread items, such as ring and pin jewellery, would have symbolized the elevated status of both the object and wearer, while the use of functional solid iron objects, such as a knife or spear, would have marked individuals (and objects) as significantly different from the rest of the community. The occurrence of many iron objects in lake-dwellings and assemblages in the northern Alpine area from the Late Bronze Age indicates that these communities were amongst the pioneer adopters of the techniques and practices of iron metallurgy in the region. The new routes along which iron travelled, and the techniques required to produce functional iron objects during the early Iron Age, may have threatened the position of the lake-dwellings as regional centres of bronzework production.

During the early Iron Age a reduction, either voluntary or forced, in the level of involvement in inter-regional exchange networks is visible in both the quantity and variety of imported materials found in the northern Circum-Alpine region, and the quantity of locally manufactured materials exported to other areas of Europe. The question here is whether the lake-dwellings were abandoned before the trade routes shifted, i.e. abandonment caused the movement of exchange networks, or occurred after the trade route shift, i.e. abandonment was influenced by the variation. In this respect erosion of some upper settlement layers (e.g. Künzler Wagner 2005; Wiemann *et al.* 2012), and early excavations of some settlements the 19th century (e.g. Mörigen) hinder interpretation and identification of causal sequences. It is clear, however, that the involvement of lake-dwelling communities in inter-regional trade survived some settlement relocations – for example during the Late Bronze Age the alternate flourishing and decline of Hauterive-Champréveyres between 1050 and 870 BC (Rychner-Faraggi 1993), Grandson-Corcelettes, and Mörigen (Bernatzky-Goetze 1987).

The distribution of *Gündlingen* type swords, utilized for a relatively short period of time during the late 9th and early 8th centuries BC, indicates that the former lake-dwelling communities of Switzerland were largely excluded from participation in the use and movement of these weapons, though those in eastern France, around Lake Chalain (FR), may have been involved in the transport routes (Jennings 2014b). The *Gündlingen* swords recorded from Switzerland show a significant reduction in the quantity of swords recorded from the area over the short time period following the circulation of *Mörigen* swords during the Late Bronze Age (HaB2-HaB3). Even the inclusion of HaC and HaD period iron swords – of undefined or '*Hallstatt*' type (Jennings 2014b) – does not significantly increase the quantity of swords known from Switzerland, and retains the image of relative disassociation from the use, exchange, and circulation of these objects.

The circulation of early Iron Age ring jewellery and razors provides further indications of limited, primarily regional, exchange and circulation patterns. With specific regard to razors, some more widespread connections are demonstrated by the distribution of the *Cordast* type, linking the northern Alpine forelands to southern France, though as has been seen for the Late Bronze Age, generally, razors did not travel large distances. The ring jewellery types show a significantly more regional, and 'local', distribution than their Late Bronze Age predecessors (see Schmid-Sikimić 1996), with little sign of the far-reaching inter-regional circulation that can be observed, for example, in the distribution of *Homburg* and *Corcelettes* type rings (Jennings 2014b).

Social changes are evident in the newly emphasized concern with status and celebration of the individual through burial practices. While the funerary activities of the lake-dwelling communities of the Late Bronze Age are largely unknown, those employed by the subsequent Iron Age communities are more identifiable – partly through a return to utilization of burial mounds instead of flat urn burials (cf. Lüscher and Müller 1999). An increase of tumulus size can be observed between the early and later Iron Age, for example from four metres in diameter at Unterlunkhofen (CH), to 20 metres at Thunstetten (CH), but of course there was variability in the size of individual examples (Lüscher and Müller 1999: 250). The use of tumuli instead of flat burials created a visible and perpetual link between communities and their environment and location, while also permitting expression of status and prestige through their physical size. Objects included in burials, as in earlier periods, were utilized to show both the identity of the entombed individual and display power and status. For example, the later Iron Age *Schnabelkannen* demonstrated the ability of the individuals to control and access trade routes linking Europe north of the Alps to the Italian peninsula (Vorlauf 1997).

Settlement sizes also provide indications of cultural change. From the relatively high population density lake-settlements of the Late Bronze Age, a degradation towards small dispersed communities occurred during the early Iron Age. A true comparison of settlement size is, however, difficult, because relatively few early Iron Age settlements are known when compared to number of Late Bronze Age lake-dwellings (Ebersbach *et al.* 2010), but the quantity of burials indicates that communities were still occupying the former lake-dwelling areas: although they had abandoned the lake-settlements they did not totally leave the area (cf. Bauer, I 1993; Boisaubert *et al.* 2008). If the communities had moved to single, large settlements of similar size to those which they abandoned (e.g. Estavayer-le-Lac La Pianta II (c.30,000 m^2), Hauterive-Champréveyres (c. 9,300 m^2 and 59 structures (Benkert 1993; Pillonel 2007)), Mörigen (c. 11,000 m^2, potential population of c. 300 people (Bernatzky-Goetze 1987: 124)), or Zurich-Alpenquai (c. 28,000 m^2) (site size data from Palafittes 2010)), it would be reasonable to expect that some archaeological indicators of these settlements would have been recovered. Instead, current evidence suggests relatively small and loosely arranged settlements existing in the lake hinterland, such as Frasses-Praz au Doux, extending over an area of up to 10,000 m^2, but with potentially only 12 dwelling structures (Mauvilly *et al.* 1997; Mauvilly and Ruffieux 2008). The current, admittedly sparse, evidence suggests that communities in the lake-dwelling regions, especially eastern Switzerland and southern Germany but also in western Switzerland and eastern France, abandoned an experiment with 'proto-urbanism' (Arnold 1990a) in favour of loosely arranged small settlements, forms of which can be seen in other regions, e.g. Brig-Glis Waldmatte in the Alpine Rhône valley (Curdy *et al.* 1993). Such a transition to small open settlements is even observed during the occupation of lake-dwellings, for example at Conjux-Le Port 3, Lake Bourget, France (Billaud 2011), and also in the open arrangement of some lake-dwellings in eastern Switzerland, such as Ürschhausen-Horn (see section 5.2.1).

In other areas of the northern Alpine region, away from the lake margins but still on transport routes linking the regions north and south of the Alps, settlements were occupied between the Late Bronze Age and early Iron Age without apparent decrease in size, for example Montlingerberg (Steinhauser-Zimmermann 1989), and new, small, villages were established, e.g. Brig-Glis Waldmatte, at up to 2000 m^2 (Curdy *et al.* 1993). Both of these settlements show connections to communities north and south of the Alps, particularly in the range of ceramics utilized in the communities.

The use of hilltop settlements, such as Wittnauer Horn and Baarburg, and later *Fürstensitze*, such as the Üetliberg and Châtillon-sur-Glâne, may have provided larger settlements with higher population density than the surrounding low-lying villages, and also acted as regional trade and manufacturing centres. The *Fürstensitze* in particular were significant in the control and manipulation of wide ranging exchange and communication networks, as evidenced by the recurrent findings of imported Attic pottery, wheel thrown pottery, and objects of Etruscan origin. Contemporary with the habitation of 'highland' settlements and development of *Fürstensitze*, isolated re-occupation of lakes is seen at Ürschhausen-Horn (660-635 BC, Billamboz and Gollnisch 1998) and Oggelshausen-Bruckgraben (c.730-620 BC, Köninger 2001/2002: 51).

However, except Ürschhausen-Horn (where limited preservation and excavation of the early Iron Age structures makes full identification of the settlement function and exploitation difficult, Gollnisch-Moos 1999: 155-57), the occupation of these lakes between the late 8th and late 7th century BC was not for settlement, but resource exploitation – as methods to intensively extract fish on a seasonal basis – particulalrly at Oggelshausen-Bruckgraben. These small resource access points were, in a similar manner to Alpine mines (e.g. Schibler *et al.* 2011), likely supported/temporarily occupied by communities some distance from the lake, possibly up to 30km to the west in the Swabian Alb the case of Oggelshausen (Köninger In Preparation). A clear change of social attitude towards the lake environment occurred between the Late Bronze Age settlement abandonment and Iron Age re-occupation: from potential dwelling zone to non-residential resource extraction environment. Such a change of association, and population/ support of these 'fishing' stations by distant communities may also reflect concepts of 'ownership' of the lakes – with only certain members of society permitted to 'exploit' the lake.

7.1 Narratives of social change in lake-dwelling communities

Combining all of the evidence of trade and exchange relationships, settlement movement and relocation, social changes, and artefact distribution, with the principle of a relational model (see section 2.1) it is possible to suggest a sequence of events relating to the abandonment of lake-settlements at the end of the Late Bronze Age and the limited re-occupation of the lakeshore during the early Iron Age (Figure 7.1):

1. Cyclical movement of settlements as some wax and others wane.
2. Climatic change influencing lake-levels and directly affecting some settlements.
3. Dispersal of lake-dwelling centres of trade and manufacture, and abandonment of 'proto-urbanism' experiment.
4. Establishment of small, self-sufficient settlements with limited inter-regional exchange contacts, and de-centralized production of goods.
5. Reorganization of north-south exchange route flowing along the riverine-lacustrine system, to an arcing route from southern and central Germany to the Rhône valley and southern France.
6. Increased social expression of individual identity and status, and increased concern with visibility in the environment.
7. Establishment of hilltop settlements as new centres of population density, exchange and manufacture.
8. Re-integration of the northern Circum-Alpine region to inter-regional exchange systems.
9. Exploitation of lake-resources by centres of population and manufacture.

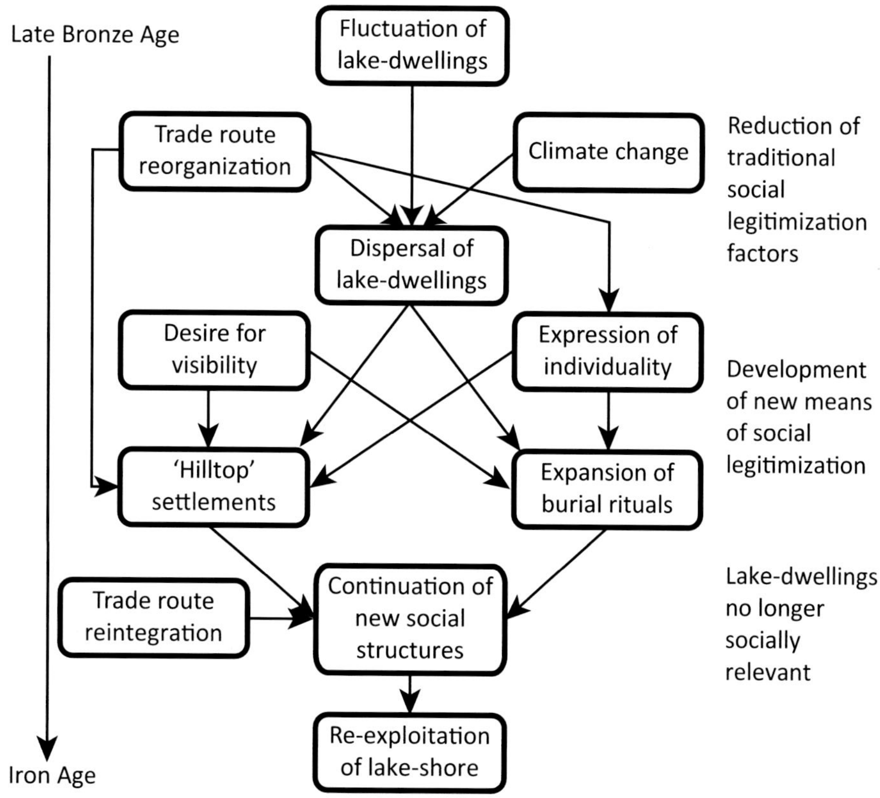

Figure 7.1: Sequential interaction of events leading to the decline of the Lake-Dwelling tradition in the northern Alpine region, and particularly in Switzerland.

1) Cyclical movement of settlements

As previously detailed under the proposal of settlement biography (see section 5.3.3), lake-settlements underwent various stages of waxing and waning, dependent upon social events and life-cycles. This may have accounted for the growth and decline of centres of trade, such as Hauterive-Champréveyres and Mörigen, and Zurich-Wollishofen-Haumesser and -Alpenquai. The role of individual members ('leaders', 'chiefs', 'merchants', 'translators') in the growth, decline, and movement of trade centres could have been highly significant, with those individuals skilled in the politics of exchange able to create a greater role for themselves and their settlement in the system (cf. the Kula exchange system).

2) Climatic change

Climatic change and lake-level rise during the Late Bronze Age is well documented (see section 1.1.1.1), though there are some doubts as to the synchronicity and ubiquity of these events (Bleicher 2013). Such water table changes may have directly influenced some of the lake-dwellings, leading to architectural attempts to combat rising humidity (e.g. Ürschhausen-Horn Gollnisch-Moos 1999; see also Menotti *et al.* 2014), but in other cases direct influence is not readily discernible, e.g. Zurich-Alpenquai (Wiemann *et al.* 2012).

3) Dispersal of population, trade, and manufacturing centres and 4) Establishment of small communities

Due to climatic influence directly impacting settlements or adversely affecting economic productivity, or the beginnings of trade-route circumvention/reorganization (or a combination of all), lake-dwellings were abandoned at the end of the 9th century BC, and the communities dispersed into the lake hinterland – either joining existing settlements or establishing new ones. Through either a lack of strong social leadership or insufficient economic productivity in the hinterland, the high-density settlements capable of supporting a high level of manufacturing output and manipulation of inter-regional exchange routes dissolved. In their place arose small communities, largely self-sufficient, with limited regional exchange and circulation of material culture, as typified by the widespread Late Bronze Age distribution of ring jewellery compared to small scale distribution in the early Iron Age.

5) Reorganization of trade routes

The distribution of early Iron Age swords, particularly the *Gündlingen* type, and other material objects, indicates that a reorganization of trade routes flowing through the northern Circum-Alpine region was essentially contemporary with the decline of the lake-dwelling manufacturing centres. Instead of the three lakes region of western Switzerland region, i.e. the area of Lake Neuchâtel/Lake Biel/Lake Murten, being a leading manufacturing centre through which multiple exchange routes flowed, the area was now on the periphery of an exchange route linking central Europe to southern France via the Rhône, Doubs, and Rhine Valley. This route did not develop during the Iron Age after the decline of the lake-dwellings, but was actually one of the routes in which the lake-dwelling communities were involved during the Late Bronze Age, as exemplified by the distribution of *Mörigen* swords.

6) Increased status of the individual

A renewed emphasis on the individual during the Iron Age is evident through the change in burial practices, with burial under tumuli rather than flat burials becoming dominant as tradition in the northern Alpine region (as well as broadly across central Europe). The beginnings of increased emphasis of identity and status may be seen in the Late Bronze Age lake-dwellings with the occurrence of keys in communities, privileging some and constraining others, and the occurrence of iron decoration on objects as a method of demonstrating status. The increased placement of objects (e.g. swords) in burials, as opposed to in wetland contexts or hoards, which began in the final stages of the Late Bronze Age and continued through the early Iron Age, reflects an emphasis on deposition for the individual as opposed to the collective community. Heightened emphasis of the individual rather than the community may also partly explain the abandonment of the 'proto-urban' experiment, with agglomerate communities fracturing to form multiple small communities with local elite groups.

7) Establishment of hilltop settlements

In addition to the increased emphasis of individual status, it became important for settlements to be overtly visible, influencing the use of hilltop settlements with significantly greater presence in the landscape than Late Bronze Age lake-dwellings (see section 5.4), and culminating in the high status *Fürstensitze*. These hilltop sites acted as regional manufacturing and trade centres, as indicated by the occurrence of, for example, wheel thrown pottery and fibulae at many of the sites, and amber shards at Glauberg (D, Balzer 2009; Bauer, I 1992; Kreuz and Schäfer 2008; Lüscher 1991). Such high status materials indicate that the, frequently fortified, hilltop settlements formed the centre of regional social systems, with community elites residing there.

8) Re-integration in exchange networks

During the latter HaC and HaD period the former lake-dwelling regions of the northern Alpine forelands were re-incorporated to the inter-regional exchange systems, as can be seen in the distribution of ring jewellery and daggers. New nodal regions and points on this exchange system occurred further afield at Hallstatt (AT), and in the Rhine Valley around Breisach (D). The occurrence of Hallstatt phase D *Rheinisch* type situla in burials within the region of the Üetliberg and Châtillon-sur-Glâne *Fürstensitze* indicates that these areas were connected to the Rhine Valley and southern Germany (Drack 1977; Jacob 1995). During the late-early Iron Age, the status and role of these hilltop settlements in inter-regional exchange is less clear; imported Etruscan *Schnabelkannen* are unknown from the northern Alpine foreland, but occur in large quantities in the Rhine Valley (Vorlauf 1997), while imported Attic ceramics are known from both regions (Guggisberg 1991), indicating the northern Alpine re-connection, but possibly at the periphery, of the Rhône-Doubs-Rhine route that began to emerge during the Late Bronze Age (see Chapter 4).

9) Exploitation of lacustrine resources

Material culture remains from the limited re-occupation of the lakeshore during the Iron Age for resource exploitation at Oggelshausen-Bruckgraben shows links to the settlements in the region of the Heuneburg (D) (see section 5.2.4). The intensive seasonal exploitation indicated by the fish traps suggests that the resource was being utilized to support a larger population, as potentially vast quantities of fish could be caught within a short period of time. Control of the lake by larger, elite populations is a likely explanation for this site (Köninger In Preparation). This does not preclude smaller communities, along the lake-hinterland, from utilising the lake, but in such settlements it would be plausible to expect that the lake resources were exploited on a smaller scale and continual basis. The small re-occupation at Ürschhausen-Horn may represent just such a small community. Larger re-occupation of the lake did not occur due to irrevocably changed social and economic circumstances: the trade routes which had been controlled by the lake-dwelling manufacturing centres had shifted, and new 'highland' settlements emerged to fill the void left when the lake-settlements were abandoned, while increased concern with overt display of individual status and prestige required greater permanence and presence in the landscape, which was not compatible with the former lake-dwelling system of periodically mobile settlements.

Chapter 8

Final Reflections: Cultural vs. Environmental Change in the Lake-Dwelling Abandonment?

The central theme to this discussion of portable and static material culture from the northern Circum-Alpine region and beyond – *'Did cultural events influence the abandonment of the lake-dwelling tradition in addition to climatic deterioration?'* – has led to an in-depth consideration of Bronze and Iron Age cultural practices in Switzerland, in addition to an extensive comparative study of material from the lake-dwellings and settlements of the northern Alpine forelands, central Europe, and the Italian peninsula (see Jennings 2014b). The consideration of the well documented climatic deterioration and its impact upon lake-dwelling communities of the Neolithic and Middle Bronze Age (see section 1.1.1.1) demonstrated how vulnerable these settlements were to climatic variations. However, a review of some Late Bronze Age settlement evidence has indicated that communities did not leave settlements directly in the face of climatic decline, but took measures to ensure that they could continue inhabiting the lakeshore (e.g. see section 5.2.1).

A combination of Relational Theory (see section 2.1) and the Biography of Objects (see section 2.2) has been applied to various categories of material culture as a method of understanding changing value associations between different regions to infer cultural connections. The production of distribution patterns and Multiple Correspondence Analysis provided further indications of such cultural communication and trade links between the areas, and also indicated that relatively little value transfer occurred between the northern Alpine region and areas of Europe with which they were incorporated in exchange partnerships (Jennings 2014b). Within the northern Alpine region it is relatively clear that while some continuation in the style and typology of material culture occurred between the Late Bronze Age and the Iron Age, there was also a distinct break with many traditions. The restricted distribution of many forms of material culture attest to the realignment of exchange partnerships and networks, while development of new burial methods and development of visible hilltop settlements attest to new social conditions during the Iron Age.

8.1 Cultural influence in the Late Bronze Age lake-dwelling abandonment?

The apparent abandonment of the lakeshore during the Late Bronze Age and early Iron Age transition brought an end to a tradition of lake-settlement and pile-dwelling occupation spanning more than three and a half millennia in the northern Circum-Alpine region. Traditional interpretations for this abandonment have focussed on the role of climatic decline in forcing people to relocate to regions away from the lakeshore (e.g. Magny 2004b), either through direct inundation or economic degradation, but the region-wide synchronicity of events has recently been questioned (Bleicher 2013). Correlations between cultural and environmental change should not be inferred as, or confused for, causality factors (cf. Grattan 2010; Walsh 2014: 4, 91-92), as has been suggested by other researchers, for example Magny (2004b: 75):

> *phases of higher lake-level coincided with an increase in annual precipitation, a decrease in summer temperature and a shortening of the growing season. […] It is noteworthy that changes of culture within the Neolithic and Bronze Age periods mostly occurred during phases of higher lake level, i.e. cooler and wetter climatic conditions, probably inducing a destabilization of the former socio-economic equilibrium.*

Combining the principles of object biographies and the available dating evidence from lake-dwellings, an idealized biography of lake-settlements has been proposed (see section 5.3.3) as a method of incorporating social influences to the relocation and abandonment of settlements (cf. Jennings 2012a). Although the influences proposed are, admittedly, rather vague conceptions (it is after all difficult to observe the death of elite individuals in communities where little burial evidence survives, or to measure the ability of individuals to attract and direct both people and goods), the apparent cyclical re-occupation, renovation, or movement of some settlements (e.g. Wasserburg-Buchau, or around Lake Neuchâtel and Lake Biel, see section 5.3) indicates that factors other than purely climate dictated the mobility of communities and individuals.

Clearly, a fundamental problem exists in trying to interpret cultural change leading to the abandonment of the lake-dwellings, as there are no lake-dwellings recorded from the Iron Age, limiting a direct comparison between the settlement assemblages of the respective periods. However, viewing lake-dwelling occupation in a normative manner (i.e. lake-dwelling occupation was the standard practice in communities, ignoring previous periods of non-occupation), and therefore the abandonment as a novel event, it is possible to compare the contexts from which objects are known during both the Late Bronze Age and the early Iron Age, and subsequently infer potential sources of cultural change. A range of material culture groups (see Chapter 4) suggest that the lake-dwelling communities of the northern Alpine forelands were important regional and inter-regional manufacturing centres during the Late Bronze Age, exporting goods, such as ring jewellery, swords, spears and knives, to communities in the north of Europe, but rarely to regions south of the Alps (Jennings 2014b).

In opposition to the large number of objects manufactured by the lake-dwelling communities and exported to other regions of Europe, there are limited instances of 'imported' objects in these settlements. Some of the 'foreign' objects, such as needles, bronze vessels and axes (e.g. from Zurich-Alpenquai (Mäder 2001) and Hauterive-Champréveyres (Rychner-Faraggi 1993)) indicate links to central Germany and central/eastern Europe, while others, such as glass beads (*Pfahlbauperlen*), amber beads, and razors (e.g. Mörigen, Bernatzky-Goetze 1987; and Hauterive-Champréveyres, Rychner-Faraggi 1993) demonstrate links to the southern Circum-Alpine region and the Po Plain. It is also evident that some of these objects may have arrived as the personal equipment of travelling individuals, for example the *Herrnbaumgarten* razor at Chelin/Lens, and the collection of Nordic objects at Grandson-Corcelettes (Fischer, V 2005; Jockenhövel 1971; Nicolas 2003; Sprockhoff 1966).

Some objects of unusual or 'ritual' nature suggest that the northern Circum-Alpine lake-dwellings were similar-but-different to their neighbouring Urnfield culture communities, and that they shared some ideological references, for example the *Stangentrichter*, 'moon idols'/firedogs, and bird-shaped vessels, which represent links to southern Germany and the Carpathian Basin (e.g. Eibner 1973; Matzerath 2009, 2011, 2012). However, the sun-bird-ship symbolism appears as an uncommon aspect in the northern Alpine lake-dwelling communities, despite its more frequent occurrence across central Europe. This may be a result of the lake-dwelling communities position as regional centres, and therefore 'translator' communities (see Chapter 4), who rejected some of the symbolism due to their close connection to the wetland/lake/water environment. Furthermore, the lake-dwelling communities differ from many other Urnfield societies in that there is currently little evidence for their funerary practices (see section 6.1), but some evidence suggests that they were utilizing marginally inland cemeteries and burial places (e.g. Le Boiron; Vidy-Chavannes) detached from the actual location of settlement. However, such evidence accounts for a minority of the potential population residing in the lake-settlements.

The early Iron Age evidence is in direct contrast to that of the Late Bronze Age; a significant proportion of the material assemblage from the northern Circum-Alpine region is known from burial contexts, while very little is from settlements. Evidence of settlements is, with the exception of some 'highland' and fortified sites, very sparse (e.g. Ebersbach *et al.* 2010), but cemeteries indicate that the former lake-dwelling regions were still being utilized for social practices (see section 5.3.2) and material culture decoration, form, and deposition associations, e.g. ceramics, arm-/leg-rings, show some continuation from the Bronze Age (Dunning and Rychner 1994; Ruoff 1974). Furthermore, instead of being at the centre of exchange networks spreading across central Europe, the region was left at the periphery of the main distribution of swords and arm-rings (see Chapter 4). While it is possible that the lack of catalogue publication for Iron Age metal objects (in contrast to their Bronze Age counterparts) has contributed to this apparent exclusion, the occurrence of few *Gündlingen* type swords in the region compared to their Bronze Age predecessors suggests that the exclusion is not simply a synthetic observation resulting from publication or excavation rates (see Jennings 2014b). That the exclusion from inter-regional circulation routes occurred is further suggested by the apparent re-integration to wider trends during the latter stages of the early Iron Age (late HaC and HaD), with daggers and ring-jewellery found in burials in Switzerland similar to types in Austria and Germany.

With re-integration to the long-distance exchange networks the lakeshores were, for instance at Ürschhausen-Horn and Oggelshausen-Bruckgraben, temporarily re-occupied. However, this re-occupation of the lakes did not last for long, or mark a widespread re-settlement trend. Instead, at least at Oggelshausen, the motivation was for intensive exploitation of lake resources – in this case fish – by communities living further afield (see section 5.2.4). This does not exclude the possibility of small communities occupying the lakeshore, such as that at Ürschhausen-Horn, but such villages were apparently neither common nor long-lived.

A proposed sequence for the abandonment of the lakeshores in the northern Circum-Alpine region at the end of the Late Bronze Age (see Chapter 7) shifts the focus of research from climatically driven models to incorporate social aspects, specifically the involvement in exchange networks and transformation of burial practices and settlement systems during the early Iron Age, and the influence that this may have had on the decline of the lake-dwelling tradition. Whether climatic decline or cultural change (as a result of shifting trade networks) was the driving factor is unclear. Given the low time resolution of typological chronologies and dating of lake-sediments it is unlikely that a definite answer will ever be found, particularly as many of the high lake water events are interpreted through the absence of lake-settlements on lakeshores (see e.g. Bleicher 2013; Magny 2004b). However, it is somewhat clear that lake shorelines – and a lake always must have a shore – would always be suitable, in some locations at least if not necessarily around the entire circumference of the lake, for settlement construction if communities were inclined to do so. Therefore, assuming a normative practice of lake-dwelling, it would be expected that the Late Bronze Age communities would simply shift their settlement within the lake-margin correlating to the raising/lowering of the lake-level, as can be seen on Lake Chalain (see section 5.3.1.4) if climatic change forced them; without cultural change the lake-dwelling tradition would have perpetuated indefinitely. It is clear though, that both climatic decline and the loss of inter-regional exchange contacts would have impacted upon the economic productivity of settlements, agrarian production in the former case and circulation of bronzework and consumables in the latter, resulting in an inability to support large centralized populations and a dispersal of communities into the wider environment.

The cultural changes occurring in the final stages of the Late Bronze Age and beginning of the Iron Age primarily heightened the concern with the celebration of the individual rather than the community, as demonstrated by the increased deposition of objects in burials rather than in hoards (see section 6.2). At the same time, a greater concern with visual consumption in both burial (see section 6.1) and settlement practices (see section 5.4), created a cultural setting in which lake-dwellings were no longer a viable or desirable option. This reduction in the desire to reside in wetland environments may relate to their unsuitability as high status settlements through their relative impermanence, requiring frequent renovation and rebuilding (Bleicher 2009; Ebersbach 2009) and environmental 'invisibility' (see section 5.4), reducing the potential for practices of overt visual consumption (of materials and labour) when compared to hilltop settlements. Such aspects were not relevant to the Late Bronze Age communities, who favoured the lake as their position of dominance of trade and exchange routes running through the region. Certain objects – i.e. keys (see section 4.2.1) – from some of the lastly occupied lake-dwellings attest to changing social structures within the settlements, and a division of the community along the principles of those with (and those without) access to structures or areas, and the ability to control the access of others. The use of iron to adorn a number of objects found within the lake-settlements, and further into Europe (Jennings 2014b; Primas 2008; Speck 1981a), shows a developing segregation of society through, amongst other factors, the display of this novel material on weapons, tools, utensils, and jewellery. This segregation can be seen as another facet of the developing concern with celebration of identity and emphasis of the individual rather than the community during the Iron Age.

Furthermore, the former lake-dwelling communities had little visual connection to their environmental setting; other than possible pile remains in the lake, and social memory (see section 5.3.3), there would have been little to indicate that former settlements had occurred in the area; a factor amplified by the general absence of cemeteries in their vicinity. This is in contrast to a return to tumuli burials during the early Iron Age, which can be seen as a method of legitimizing and supporting settlement in specific regions. Thus, the former lake-dwelling zones, showing little sign of previous occupation, were not legitimate settlement areas, and the lake resources may have been controlled by individuals residing in elite settlements and utilizing such legitimizing practices further afield. The wetland environments did, however, remain socially significant places during the Iron Age, as exemplified by the deposition of metalwork at, for example, La Tène in the later Iron Age (Dunning 1991).

Whether the lake-dwelling communities were aware that their movement away from the lakeshore would bring a tradition of occupation (which had endured for many centuries) to an end is unclear, but they would certainly have recognized that they were breaking away from their recent pattern of settlement and occupation (see section 2.3). It is, however, certain that their decision to move away from the lake was a deliberate action, not solely a passive response to climatic decline. Due to the new cultural emphasis on individual visibility, identity and status, the social changes occurring in the communities made a full return to lake-dwelling an unlikely occurrence.

8.2 Future research directions

Models of cultural variability in the French Jura region (e.g. Vital 1992; Vital 1993: 174-78) have suggested that societies changed from having areas of communal space and communal organization during the Final Bronze Age II (HaA-HaB1) with an increased hierarchy in the Final Bronze Age III (HaB1-B3), to a strictly hierarchical society with burial practices and control of exchange routes used as legitimizing techniques during the early Iron Age (HaC). Such practices required a re-organization to concepts of inheritance and legitimacy, not only with reference to material objects but also to house plots, burial locations, and possibly even trade and exchange contacts (cf. Blanco-González 2011; González-Ruibal 2006). If the rights to dwell in specific areas were lost with the death of individuals, then possible influences for the movement of settlements and deliberate vacation of building plots may be identified. Future research should attempt to recognize principles of inheritance in the lake-dwelling communities to achieve an understanding of how the societies reproduced themselves across generations and identify possible influences in the movement of settlements. How the ability to trade with specific communities was regulated and perpetuated remains unknown, and will be difficult to identify from the archaeological record, but it should be anticipated that as individuals died then specific trade contacts were lost as the relationships in which they participated died with them. However, such decline of specific relationships should be expected over time, and the loss of individual connections may not have impacted significantly upon the general movement of objects, as other relationships would have flourished to fill the void, though not necessarily between the same communities or settlements.

The study of various forms of Late Bronze Age full grip swords has suggested different regimes of circulation: the *Mörigen* swords show a relatively consistent spread from the northern Alpine region to northern Europe, while the *Auvernier* and Antenna type swords show distinct banding in their distribution with increasing distance from the Alps/Lake Neuchâtel, and the quantities of specific sword forms within the Alpine region shows considerable variation (for expanded discussion see Jennings 2014b). The use practices generating this distribution pattern may have involved different valuation levels for specific sword forms, with use of prescribed forms by individuals exhibiting certain status or social identity, as has been proposed for Denmark in the Bronze Age (cf. Kristiansen 2002) and the early Iron Age *Gündlingen* and *Mindelheim* types (e.g. Cowen 1968). Alternatively, the distribution pattern may suggest the method of circulation of swords: either as trade commodity or as gift objects. The locally manufactured *Mörigen* type, with relatively consistent distribution, may have travelled as exchange 'commodities', in contrast to the infrequent *Auvernier* and Antenna swords, which may have travelled as 'gifts' between elite members at nodal regions on the long-distance exchange routes as symbols of their ability to participate in such practices or as objects presented at the beginning or conclusion of exchange events. Further study of other sword forms occurring in the northern Alpine region dating to the entire Bronze Age, and particularly Late Bronze Age composite handle swords, their associated distribution in Europe, and patterns of separation between sites, may suggest further forms of valuation schemes relating to these objects and internal structuring of society.

Other areas of research interest should focus on the influences and social choices which led communities to settle in specific locations of the environment, both wetland and inland. It is well recognized in other areas of Europe that landscape features, both natural and built, played a significant role in the placement and alignment of settlements and other structures. The prevalence of 'moon idols' in the northern Circum-Alpine region suggests the possible social significance of marking calendar events or calculating lunar or solar positions (Kerner 2001, 2007), which could have been used to align buildings or other structures. Furthermore, the influence of inheritance practices and social 'rights' to settle or occupy specific areas during not only the Bronze Age and Iron Age, but also the Neolithic, should be addressed, particularly given the well discussed *Hausplatz* and *Siedlungsplatz* concepts (Ebersbach 2013, see section 5.3). An understanding of such practices may be highlighted through a study of the location of lake-settlements, and also inland settlements, in relation to earlier human landscape features – particularly burials and cemeteries. Studies of Neolithic and Bronze Age ceramics have often proposed small-scale household production of pottery and have even identified individual potter's work (e.g. Greifensee-Böschen (Eberschweiler *et al.* 2007) and Zug-Sumpf (Bauer, I *et al.* 2004)), but few inter-site comparative studies have been undertaken. Although time consuming, an examination of the ceramic assemblage from several contemporary or sequential lake-dwellings from the same region (e.g. Lake Feder (see section 5.3.1.1)) may identify the same pottery producers at several sites. If household rather than specialized pottery production and exchange of ceramics is accepted, then this would confirm suggestions of household mobility and the possible identification of individuals acting in several settlements.

With regard to the issue of visibility, and the role that the need for visually prominent settlements may have played in the choice to move away from the lakeshores, recent developments combining GIS and methods from Social Network Analysis may suggest significant routes to follow (Brughmans In press; Brughmans *et al.* 2014). The use of Exponential Random Graph Models to test hypotheses of built landscape evolution offers a way to examine whether settlements were sited to ensure that they could see or be seen by others, but of course there needs to be a relatively substantial dataset of sites to conduct both GIS visibility analysis and create the ERGM. As previously detailed, there is a relative dearth of information regarding Late Bronze Age and early Iron Age inland settlement sites in Switzerland, particularly when compared to the lakeshore sites. However, such analysis should be an aimed for in the future, and it would also be interesting to insert cemeteries and burial sites into the model.

Such future studies may offer great potential for enhancing the comprehension of social structures in the prehistoric communities occupying inland and lakeshore settlements in the Alpine region. Yet, with regard to the issue of the decline of the lake-dwelling tradition, the presented research has highlighted a number of key issues.

Many types of material culture from the northern Alpine region relating to the Late Bronze Age and early Iron Age demonstrate a continuation of form and decorative styles between the epochs, despite the terminal decline of a long-established lake-dwelling tradition (see Dunning and Rychner 1994; Ruoff 1974). Although material culture groups show continuation of style across the two periods, the social practices of their use and deposition show a defined re-organization; deposition of objects in hoards was common in the former, while burial deposition became the norm in the latter. This change in deposition practice is a direct reflection of socio-cultural changes related to the emphasis of individuality and status at the expense of communal and collective identities. Changes to the inter-regional exchange and communication networks, roughly contemporaneous with these social developments, resulted in the (former) lake-dwelling region being marginalized and causing both a diminution of the role of the area as an important manufacturing and exchange node linking northern Europe to the central Mediterranean and changes to practices of social legitimization. Without entirely discounting the possible influence of climatic change on the lake-dwelling communities, it is clear that significant social and cultural changes were occurring at the same time as the lake-settlements were being abandoned, and climatically deterministic models do not reflect the whole situation. These cultural changes were so fundamental and significant to the composition of society that a full return to occupation of the lakeshore became impossible, even during periods of 'favourable' climatic conditions. Although climate may have been one of a number of triggers, it was, however, a series of cultural variables which determined communities' decision to break with the long standing lake-dwelling tradition.

Appendix 1

List of sites for Figure 5.11

No.	Site name	Site type	References	LBA	IA
1	Allschwil-Vogelgärten	Settlement	(Deschler-Erb 1989; Lüscher 1986)		X
2	Alt-Thierstein	Settlement	(Deschler-Erb 1989)	X	
3	Avenches - En Chaplix	Settlement	(Doiteau 1989; Dunning and Rychner 1994)	X	X
4	Balsthal-Holzfluh	Settlement	(Deschler-Erb 1989)		X
5	Bannwil	Settlement-Cemetery	(Deschler-Erb 1989; Dunning 1992)		X
6	Banzenreuthe	Settlement	(Hopert *et al.* 1998)	X	
7	Basel-Martinskirchplatz	Settlement	(Deschler-Erb 1989)	X	
8	Basel-Utengasse	Settlement	(Matt 2012)	X	
9	Bischofsstein	Settlement	(Deschler-Erb 1989)	X	
10	Bönistein	Settlement	(Deschler-Erb 1989)		X
11	Bülach-Schwerzgrueb	Settlement-activity area	(Drack 1980; Hagen *et al.* 1986)	X	
12	Dettingen-Weiherried	Settlement	(Hopert *et al.* 1998)	X	X
13	Dingelsdorf-Bussensee	Settlement	(Hopert *et al.* 1998)	X	
14	Fällanden-Fröschbach	Settlement-activity area	(Fischer, C 1996, 1997)	X	X
15	Faoug - Derriere le Chaney	Settlement	(Doiteau 1991, 1992; Dunning and Rychner 1994)		X
16	Friedrichshafen-Waggershausen	Settlement	(Hopert *et al.* 1998)	X	
17	Frohburg	Settlement	(Deschler-Erb 1989)	X	
18	Isteiner Klotz	Settlement	(Deschler-Erb 1989)	X	
19	Kestenberg	Settlement	(Deschler-Erb 1989)		X
20	Lausanne - Vidy Basilique	Settlement	(Moinat and David-Elbiali 2003)		X
21	Le Landeron-Les Carougets	Settlement-Cemetery	(Hofmann 1991; Hofmann Rognon and Doswald 2005)		X
22	Courfaivre, Les Esserts-Est	Settlement	(Pousaz *et al.* 1994)	X	
23	Litzelstetten "Burren"	Settlement-Cemetery	(Hopert *et al.* 1998)	X	X
24	Marin - Les Bourgignones	Settlement	(Arnold 1992)		X
25	Möggingen-Mindelsee	Settlement	(Hopert *et al.* 1998)	X	
26	Mont Terri	Settlement	(Deschler-Erb 1989)	X	
27	Murten - Löwenberg	Settlement	(Bouyer and Boisaubert 1992)		X
28	Neunkirch-Tobeläcker	Settlement	(Gutzwiller 1994; Ruckstuhl 1989)		X
29	Oensingen-Lehnfluh	Settlement	(Deschler-Erb 1989)		X
30	Oensingen-Ravellenfluh	Settlement	(Deschler-Erb 1989)	X	

No.	Site name	Site type	References	LBA	IA
31	Olten-Wartenberg	Settlement	(Deschler-Erb 1989)		X
32	Roc de Courroux	Settlement	(Deschler-Erb 1989)	X	
33	Säckingen	Settlement	(Deschler-Erb 1989)	X	
34	Schafrain	Settlement	(Deschler-Erb 1989)		X
35	Schalberg	Settlement	(Deschler-Erb 1989)	X	
36	Stahringen-"Oberes Weidfeld"	Settlement	(Hopert *et al.* 1998)		X
37	Zurzach-Rainen	Settlement	(Gutzwiller 1994)		X
38	Châbles-Les Biolleyres	Settlement-Cemetery	(Vigneau and Boisaubert 2008)	X	X
39	Bussy-Pré de Fond	Settlement	(Boisaubert *et al.* 2008)		X
40	Attiswil-Wybrunne	Settlement	(Ramstein 2010)		X
41	Frasses - Praz-au-Doux	Settlement	(Mauvilly *et al.* 1997; Mauvilly and Ruffieux 2008)		X
42	Birg-Glis Waldmatte	Settlement	(Curdy *et al.* 1993)		X
43	Flüeli-Amsteg	Settlement	(Primas *et al.* 1992)	X	X
44	Bavois-En Raillon	Settlement	(Vital and Voruz 1984)	X	
45	Onnens Clos Dessous	Settlement	(Poncet Schmid *et al.* 2013)	X	
46	Onnens Le-Motti	Settlement	(Poncet Schmid *et al.* 2013)	X	
47	Tschugg-Steiacher	Settlement	(Glauser *et al.* 1996)	X	
48	Pieterlen-Under Siedebrunne 3	Settlement	(ADB - Abteiling Ur- und Frühgeschichte 1999)	X	X
49	Boltigen-I de Tröglene	Cave	(Tschumi, 1953)	X	
50	Ipsach-Räberain / Oberdörfli	Settlement?	(ADB - Abteiling Ur- und Frühgeschichte 1998, 2006b; Ramstein 2005a)	X	X
51	Erlach-Winzerweg	Settlement	(ADB - Abteiling Ur- und Frühgeschichte 2006a; Erziehungsdirektion des Kantons Bern 2008a)	X	
52	Ipsach-Moosstrasse	Settlement	(Dénervaud 2012; Ramstein 2005a)	X	

Appendix 2

List of sites for Figure 5.12

References are not intended to be exhaustive, but provide an introductory point to the sites.

No.	Site	References
1	Allensbach-Langenrain "Hals"	(Hopert *et al.* 1998)
2	Alt-Thierstein	(Hopert *et al.* 1998)
3	Berg am Irchel	(Biel 1987)
4	Bleibeskopf (Bad Homburg)	(Jockenhövel 1974)
5	Bogenberg	(Hopert *et al.* 1998)
6	Bönistein	(Biel 1987)
7	Bösenburg	(Jockenhövel 1974)
8	Dommelberg	(Jockenhövel 1974)
9	Dotternhausen-Plettenberg	(Biel 1987)
10	Eisenberg	(Jockenhövel 1974)
11	Felsburg	(Jockenhövel 1974)
12	Fridingen-Lehenbühl	(Biel 1987)
13	Glauberg	(Jockenhövel 1974)
14	Gomadingen-Hackberg	(Biel 1987)
15	Gönningen-Roßberg	(Biel 1987)
16	Hausen am Tann, Lochenstein	(Biel 1987)
17	Hausen am Tann, Schafberg	(Biel 1987)
18	Heidenschanze-Coschütz	(Jockenhövel 1974)
19	Heinrichsberg	(Jockenhövel 1974)
20	Hesselberg	(Jockenhövel 1974)
21	Heunischenburg	(Jockenhövel 1974)
22	Hoffstetten-Chöpfli	(Biel 1987)
23	Holderbank-Alt Bechburg	(Biel 1987)
24	Kestenberg	(Biel 1987)
25	Kiebingen-Bergvorsprung am Rammert	(Biel 1987)
26	Kirchberg-Iddaburg	(Biel 1987)
27	Kratzeburg	(Jockenhövel 1974)
28	Laufen an der Eyach, Schalksburg	(Biel 1987)

No.	Site	References
29	Mels-Castels	(Biel 1987)
30	Montlingerberg	(Biel 1987)
31	Nagold, Schloßberg	(Biel 1987)
32	Offingen-Bussen	(Biel 1987)
33	Radisch	(Jockenhövel 1974)
34	Ramosch-Mottata	(Biel 1987)
35	Reusten-Kirchberg	(Biel 1987)
36	Roc de Courroux	(Biel 1987)
37	Römerschanze	(Jockenhövel 1974)
38	Runden Bergs bei Urach	(Biel 1987)
39	Schafberg	(Jockenhövel 1974)
40	Schalberg	(Biel 1987)
41	Seinsheim Bullenheimer Berg	(Jockenhövel 1974)
42	Siblingen-Schönägertli	(Biel 1987)
43	Spaichingen-Dreifaltigkeitsberg	(Biel 1987)
44	Stahringen-"Oberes Weidfeld"	(Aufdermauer and Dieckmann 1985; Köninger and Schöbel 2010)
45	Talheim-Farrenberg	(Biel 1987)
46	Talheim-Lupfen	(Biel 1987)
47	Tübingen-Burgholz	(Biel 1987)
48	Üetliberg	(Biel 1987)
49	Wittnau Horn	(Biel 1987)
50	Würtingen-Stettenrain	(Biel 1987)
51	Rhinsberg	(Bigler 2005)
52	Schlossberg-Rudolfingen	(Bigler 2005)
53	Rheinau	(Bigler 2005; Frascoli 1991)
54	Frauenberg	(Rind 1999)
55	Heidenburg, Seegräben-Aathal	(Altorfer 2010)
56	Spiez-Spiezberg	(Sarbach 1959; Tschumi 1953)
57	Spiez-Bürg	(Sarbach 1959; Tschumi 1937, 1953; Wenzler 2001)
58	Bolligen-Stockeren / Flugbrunnen	(Keller-Tarnuzzer 1937a; Tschumi 1934, 1953)
59	Niederbipp-Erlinsburg	(Frei, B 1955a; Gutscher 2008; Gutzwiller 2004)
60	Oberburg-Waldbrueder	(Guyan 1962; Schwab 1961)
61	Schwarzenburg-Grasburg-Schlössli	(Sarbach 1966)

Appendix 3

List of sites for Figure 6.1

Unless stated references from Lüscher 1993.

No.	Site name	LBA	IA	References
1	Aarwangen-Moosbergwald; -Zopfen		X	
2	Bannwil-Bännli; -Moosbahn; -Rüchihölzli		X	
3	Bäriswil-Kriegsholz		X	
4	Bonstetten-Im Gibel		X	
5	Châbles-Les Biolleyres	X		(Vigneau and Boisaubert 2008)
6	Cortaillod-Aux Murgiers	X		(Hapka 1995)
7	Delémont-En La Pran	X		(Pousaz *et al.* 2000)
8	Dietikon-Im Hohneret		X	
9	Dinhard-Rietmühle		X	
10	Dörflingen-Gailingerberg		X	
11	Eich-Schenkon		X	
12	Elgg-Breiti	X		(Mäder 2002)
13	Elgg-Ettenbühl	X		(Mäder 2002)
14	Ermatingen-Wolfsberg		X	
15	Eschenbach-Balmenrain		X	
16	Grüningen-Strangenholz		X	
17	Hemishofen-Im Sankert		X	
18	Jegenstorf-Kirchgasse; -Im Hurst		X	(Erziehungsdirektion des Kantons Bern 2008b)
19	Kernenried, Oberholz		X	(Ramstein 2012)
20	Kloten-Homberg		X	
21	Kreuzlingen-Geissberg		X	
22	Le Boiron	X		(Beeching 1977)
23	Lenzburg-Lindwald		X	
24	Lyssach-Birchiwald		X	
25	Möhlin-Niederriburg	X		(Maier 1986)
26	Morat-Lowenburg		X	(Boisaubert and Bugnon 2008; Bouyer and Boisaubert 1992)
27	Muttenz-In den hinteren Bitzenen; -Im Lutzert	X	X	(Lüscher 1993)
28	Neftenbach-Steinmöri		X	
29	Neunforn-Mönchhof		X	
30	Niederweningen-Erlenmoos		X	

No.	Site name	LBA	IA	References
31	Obergösgen-Hard		X	
32	Ossingen-Im Speck	X	X	(Lüscher 1993; Ruoff 1974)
33	Pratteln-Neueinschlag		X	
34	Rafz-Im Kirchtürmli; -im Fallentor	X	X	(Lüscher 1993; Ruoff 1974)
35	Reinach-Einschlag		X	
36	Rüschlikon-Feldimoos		X	
37	Saint-Prex La Moraine; -Gravière Chiavazza	X		(David-Elbiali and Moinat 2005; Reinbold 1957)
38	Schaffhausen-Gaisberg		X	
39	Schaffhausen-Wolfsbuck		X	
40	Schafisheim-In den Muren		X	
41	Schötz-Schleifmatt		X	
42	Schupfart-Tegertli		X	
43	Seon-Fornholz		X	
44	Subingen-Erdbeereinschlag		X	
45	Sursee-Bahnhofstrasse		X	
46	Thunstetten-Tannwäldli		X	
47	Trüllikon-Im freien Kreuzli		X	
48	Unterlunkhofen-Bärhau		X	
49	Urtenen-Buebeloo		X	
50	Wangen-Wieslistein		X	
51	Wil-Egghof		X	
52	Wohlen-Hohbühl		X	
53	Wynigen-Bickigen		X	
54	Zollikon-Fünfbühl		X	
55	Zürich-Burghölzli		X	
56	Koppigen-Usserfeld	X		(Ramstein and Cueni 2005)
57	Lausanne Vidy-Chavannes	X	X	(Moinat and David-Elbiali 2003)
58	Thun -Talacker; -Hofstettenstrasse	X		(Erziehungsdirektion des Kantons Bern 2008c; Tschumi 1953)
59	Wiedlisbach-Wiedlisbach	X		(Mühlethaler 1967)
60	Belp-Aebnit; -Bützacher/Holiebi	X		(David-Elbiali 2000; Primas 1971; Tschumi 1953)
61	Niederösch-Büelen	X		(Keller-Tarnuzzer 1937b; Tschumi 1953)
62	Kiesen-Dorf	X		
63	Oberbipp-Haserain	X		(Osterwalder 1982)
64	Pully-Chamblandes	X		(Moinat and David-Elbiali 2003)
65	Muri-Lindenhof/Siiloah	X		(Tschumi 1953)

No.	Site name	LBA	IA	References
66	Pieterlen-Vorem Holz 3	X		(Ramstein 2005b)
67	Frauenkappelen-Spilwald	X		(Tschumi 1935, 1953)
68	Wangen an der Aare-Galgenrain	X		(Mühlethaler 1967)
69	Le Landeron-Les Carougets	X		(Hofmann 1991)
70	Lausanne Vidy-Musée Romain; -Vernand de Blonay	X	X	(Kaenel 1990; Moinat and David-Elbiali 2003)
71	Sutz-Lattrigen	X		(Heireli 1911; Wiedmer-Stern 1909)
72	Sion-Rue De Lausanne; -Maison Solioz; -Maison de Torrenté; -Maison Cocatrix; -l'Hôtel de la Poste	X		(Gallay and Kaenel 1986)
73	Zurzach-Schlosspark	X		(Gutzwiller 1994)
74	Beringen-Unterer Stieg	X		(Höneisen 1984)
75	Vuadens-Le Briez	X		(Schwab 1982)
76	Saint-Sulpice-En Pétoleyres	X		(Kaenel 1990)
77	Andelfingen-Im Ländli	X		(Ruoff 1974)
78	Regensdorf-Adlikon	X		(Bauer, I *et al.* 1992)

Bibliography

ADB - ABTEILING UR- UND FRÜHGESCHICHTE (1998) Ipsach BE, Räberain, *Jahrbuch der Schweizerischen Gesellschaft für Ur- und Frühgeschichte* 81, 272.

ADB - ABTEILING UR- UND FRÜHGESCHICHTE (1999) Pieterlen, BE Under-Siedebrunne 1, *Jahrbuch der Schweizerischen Gesellschaft für Ur- und Frühgeschichte* 82, 266.

ADB - ABTEILING UR- UND FRÜHGESCHICHTE (2006a) Erlach BE, Winzerweg, *Jahrbuch Archäologie Schweiz* 2006, 226.

ADB - ABTEILING UR- UND FRÜHGESCHICHTE (2006b) Ipsach BE, Räberain, *Jahrbuch Archäologie Schweiz* 89, 227-28.

AESCHIMANN, D. & GUISAN, A. (1995) Introduction to the Alps, in A. GUISAN, J. I. HOLTEN, R. SPICHIGER & L. TESSIER (Eds.) *Potential ecological impacts of climate change in the Alps and Fennoscandian mountains*, Genève: Conservatoire et Jardin botaniques. 81-85.

ALBORE LIVADIE, C., BARTOLI, C., BOENZI, G., CICIRELLI, C. & GUZZO, P. G. (2005) The Poggiomarino river settlement in the Longola area, in P. A. J. ATTEMA, A. NIJBOER & A. ZIFFERERO (Eds.) *Papers in Italian archaeology VI : communities and settlements from the Neolithic to the early Medieval period*, Oxford: Archaeopress. 699-705.

ALTORFER, K. (2004a) Die Pfahlbauten — Ein neues Fenster in die Vergangenheit, in ANTIQUARISCHE GESELLSCHAFT IN ZÜRICH (Ed.) *Pfahlbaufieber: Von Antiquaren, Pfahlbaufischern, Altertümerhändlern und Pfahlbaumythen*, Zürich: Chronos Verlag. 60-90.

ALTORFER, K. (2004b) Pfahlbautourismus und Pfahlbauentdeckungen im Ausland, in ANTIQUARISCHE GESELLSCHAFT IN ZÜRICH (Ed.) *Pfahlbaufieber: Von Antiquaren, Pfahlbaufischern, Altertümerhändlern und Pfahlbaumythen*, Zürich: Chronos Verlag. 91-101.

ALTORFER, K. (2010) *Die prähistorischen Feuchtbodensiedlungen am Südrand des Pfäffikersees : Eine archäologische Bestandesaufnahme der Stationen Wetzikon-Robenhausen und Wetzikon-Himmerich*, Monographien der Kantonsarchäologie Zürich 41, Zürich / Egg: FO-Fotorotar.

AMBROSE, W., ALLEN, C., O'CONNOR, S., SPRIGGS, M., OLIVEIRA, N. V. & REEPMEYER, C. (2009) Possible obsidian sources for artifacts from Timor: narrowing the options using chemical data, *Journal of Archaeological Science* 36 (3), 607-15.

AMT FÜR ARCHÄOLOGIE THURGAU (2010) *Archäologie im Thurgau*, Frauenfeld: Huber.

ANASTASIU, R. & BACHMANN, F. (1991) *Hauterive-Champréveyres 5. Les terres cuites du Bronze final, témoins de la vie quotidienne et religieuse*, Archéologie neuchâloise 11, Saint-Blaise: Editions du Ruau.

ANDREY, S. (2006) Les ossements humains épars des stations littorales de la région des Trois-Lacs, *Cahiers d'Archéologie Fribourgeoise* 8, 146-61.

ANGELINI, I., ARTIOLI, G., BELLINTANI, P., DIELLA, V., GEMMI, M., POLLA, A. & ROSSI, A. (2004) Chemical analyses of Bronze Age glasses from Frattesina di Rovigo, Northern Italy, *Journal of Archaeological Science* 31 (8), 1175-84.

ANGELINI, I., ARTIOLI, G., BELLINTANI, P. & POLLA, A. (2005) Protohistoric Vitreous Material of Italy: from Early Faience to Final Bronze Age Glasses, in ASSOCIATION INTERNATIONALE POUR L'HISTOIRE DU VERRE (Ed.) *16e Congrès de l'Association Internationale pour l'Histoire du Verre*, Nottingham: AIHV. 32-36.

ANGELINI, I. & BELLINTANI, P. (2005) Archaeological ambers from Northern Italy: An FTIR-Drift study of provenance by comparison with the Geological Amber Database, *Archaeometry* 47 (2), 441-54.

ANGELINI, I., POLLA, A., GIUSSANI, B., BELLINTANI, P. & ARTIOLI, G. (2009) Final Bronze-Age glass in Northern and Central Italy: is Frattesina the only glass production centre?, in J.-F. MOREAU, R. AUGER, J. CHABOT & A. HERZOG (Eds.) *Proceedings of the 36th International Symposium on Archaeometry*, Quebec: CELAT. 329-37.

APPADURAI, A. (1986) Introduction: Commodities and the politics of value, in A. APPADURAI (Ed.) *The social life of things : commodities in cultural perspective*, Cambridge: Cambridge University Press. 3-63.

ARBOGAST, R.-M., JACOMET, S., MAGNY, M. & SCHIBLER, J. (2006) The significance of climate fluctuations for lake level changes and shifts in subsistence economy during the late Neolithic (4300–2400 b.c.) in central Europe, *Vegetation History and Archaeobotany* 15 (4), 403-18.

ARENSTAM GIBBONS, S. J. & NICHOLLS, R. J. (2006) Island abandonment and sea-level rise: An historical analog from the Chesapeake Bay, USA, *Global Environmental Change* 16 (1), 40-47.

ARLETTI, R., MAIORANO, C., FERRARI, D., VEZZALINI, G. & QUARTIERI, S. (2010) The first archaeometric data on polychrome Iron Age glass from sites located in northern Italy, *Journal of Archaeological Science* 37 (4), 703-12.

ARMIT, I. (2012) *Headhunting and the body in Iron Age Europe*, Cambridge: Cambridge University Press.

ARNOLD, B. (1983) Les 24 maisons d' Auvernier-Nord (Bronze final), *Jahrbuch der Schweizerischen Gesellschaft für Ur- und Frühgeschichte* 66, 87-104.

ARNOLD, B. (1986) *Fouille subaquatique et photographie aérienne*, Saint-Blaise: Editions du Ruau.

ARNOLD, B. (1990a) *Cortaillod-Est et les villages du lac de Neuchâtel au Bronze final : structure de l'habitat et proto-urbanisme*, Saint-Blaise: Editions du Ruau.

ARNOLD, B. (1990b) Villages du Bronze Final sur les rives du lac de Neuchâtel, in C. MORDANT & A. RICHARD (Eds.) *L'habitat et l'occupation du sol à l'âge du bronze en Europe*, Paris: Editions du Comité des travaux historiques et scientifiques. 303-12.

ARNOLD, B. (1992) Le site hallstattien et l'enceinte quadrangulaire laténienne de Marin-Les Bourguignonnes (canton de Neuchâtel), in G. KAENEL & P. CURDY (Eds.) *L'âge du Fer dans le Jura : actes du 15e colloque de l'Association française pour l'étude sur l'âge du Fer, Pontarlier (France) et Yverdon-les-Bains (Suisse), 9-12 mai 1991*, Lausanne: Bibliothèque historique vaudoise. 309-15.

ARNOLD, B. (1995) *Pirogues monoxyles d'Europe centrale : construction, typologie, évolution,* Neuchâtel: Musée cantonal d'archéologie.

ARNOLD, B. (2002) A Landscape of Ancestors: The Space and Place of Death in Iron Age West-Central Europe, in H. SILVERMAN & D. B. SMALL (Eds.) *The Space and Place of Death*, Arlington: Archaeological Papers of the American Anthropological Association. 129-43.

ARNOLD, B. (2010) Eventful Archaeology, the Heuneburg Mudbrick Wall, and the Early Iron Age of Southwest Germany, in D. J. BOLENDER (Ed.) *Eventful archaeologies : new approaches to social transformation in the archaeological record,* Albany: State University of New York Press. 100-14.

ARNOLD, B. & LANGENEGGER, F. (2012) *Plateau de Bevaix, 8. Bevaix Sud: plongée dans le passé, fouille subaquatique d'un village du Bronze final,* Neuchâtel: Office et Musée cantonal d'archéologie de Neuchâtel.

ARNOLDUSSEN, S. (2013) Life history approaches and wetland habitation: a later prehistoric case study from the Dutch delta, in F. MENOTTI & A. O'SULLIVAN (Eds.) *The Oxford Handbook of Wetland Archaeology*, Oxford: Oxford University Press. 733-48.

ARTURSSON, M. & NICOLIS, F. (2007) Cultural relations between the Mediterranean and the Baltic Seas during the Bronze Age? The evidence from northern Italy and southern Scandinavia, in I. GALANAKI, H. TOMAS, Y. GALANAKIS & R. LAFFINEUR (Eds.) *Between the Aegean and Baltic seas : prehistory across borders*, Liège: Université de Liège. 331-42.

ASLAN, C. (2006) Individual, Household, and Community Space in Early Bronze Age Western Anatolia and the Nearby Islands, in E. C. ROBERTSON, J. D. SEIBERT, D. C. FERNANDEZ & M. U. ZENDER (Eds.) *Space and spatial analysis in archaeology*, Calgary: University of Calgary Press. 133-40.

AUFDERMAUER, J. & DIECKMANN, B. (1985) Eine bronze- und eisenzeitliche Siedlung in Stahringen, Kreis Konstanz, *Archäologische Ausgrabungen in Baden-Württemberg* 1984, 51.

BABIĆ, S. (2007) "Translation Zones" or gateway communities revisited: the case of Trebenište and Sindos, in I. GALANAKI, H. TOMAS, Y. GALANAKIS & R. LAFFINEUR (Eds.) *Between the Aegean and Baltic seas : prehistory across borders*, Liège: Université de Liège. 57-61.

BALASSONE, G., BONI, M., DI MAIO, G. & VILLA, I. M. (2009) Characterization of metallic artefacts from the Iron Age culture in Campania (Italy): a multi-analytical study, *Periodico di Mineralogia* 78 (1), 45-63.

BALISTA, C. & BELLINTANI, P. (Eds.) (1998) *Canàr di San Pietro Polesine. Ricerche archeo-ambientali sul sito palafitticolo*, Rovigo: Padusa.

BALLMER, A. (2010a) Measuring the Mental - A Quantitative Approach to Mental Landscape Concepts in Prehistory, in UNIVERSITÄT KIEL. GRADUIERTENSCHULE "HUMAN DEVELOPMENT IN LANDSCAPES" (Ed.) *Landscapes and human development: the contribution of European archaeology : proceedings of the International Workshop "Socio-Environmental Dynamics over the Last 12'000 Years: The Creation of Landscapes (1st-4th April)"*, Bonn: Dr. Rudolf Habelt. 193-202.

BALLMER, A. (2010b) Zur Topologie des bronzezeitlichen Deponierens von der Handlungstheorie zur Raumanalyse, *Prähistorische Zeitschrift* 85, 120-31.

BALZER, I. (2009) *Chronologisch-chorologische Untersuchung des späthallstatt- und frühlatènezeitlichen "Fürstensitzes" auf dem Münsterberg von Breisach (Grabungen 1980-1986),* Stuttgart: Konrad Theiss Verlag.

BANDI, G. (1974) Über den Usprung und die historische Beziehungen der Tonstempel der bronzezeitlichen Gruppen: Madarovče und Polada, *Preistoria Alpina* 10, 237-52.

BARFIELD, L. H. (1991) Wessex with and without Mycenae: new evidence from Switzerland, *Antiquity* 65 (246), 102-07.

BARFIELD, L. H. (1994) The Bronze Age of Northern Italy: Recent Work and Social Interpretation, in S. STODDART & C. MATHERS (Eds.) *Development and decline in the Mediterranean Bronze Age*, Sheffield: J. R. Collis Publications. 129-44.

BARON, J. & LASAK, I. (Eds.) (2007) *Long Distance Trade in the Bronze Age and Early Iron Age*, Wrocław: Wydawnictwo Uniwersytetu Wrocławskiego.

BARRETT, J. C. (2000) A thesis on agency, in M.-A. DOBRES & J. E. ROBB (Eds.) *Agency in archaeology*, London: Routledge. 61-68.

BAUER, A. A. (2008) Import, Imitation, or Communication? Pottery style, technology, and coastal contact in the Early Bronze Age Black Sea, in P. F. BIEHL & Y. Y. RASSAMAKIN (Eds.) *Import and imitation in archaeology*, Langenweissbach: Beier & Beran. 89-104.

BAUER, I. (1985) Neolithische und bronzezeitliche Befunde am Rietspitz bei Fällanden, *Jahrbuch der Schweizerischen Gesellschaft für Ur- und Frühgeschichte* 68, 41-64.

BAUER, I. (1992) Frühe scheibengedrehte Keramik von der Baarburg, Kanton Zug, *Jahrbuch der Schweizerischen Gesellschaft für Ur- und Frühgeschichte* 75, 155-63.

BAUER, I. (1993) Ein hallstattzeitlicher Fundkomplex aus der Zuger Altstadt, *Jahrbuch der Schweizerischen Gesellschaft für Ur- und Frühgeschichte* 76, 93-112.

BAUER, I., FORT-LINKSFEILER, D., RUCKSTUHL, B., HASENFRATZ, A., HAUSER, C. & MATTER, A. (1992) *Bronzezeitliche Landsiedlungen und Gräber,* Egg: Komm. Fotorotar.

BAUER, I., FRASCOLI, L., PANTLI, H., SIEGFRIED, A., WEIDMANN, T. & WINDLER, R. (1991) *Üetliberg, Uto-Kulm : Ausgrabungen 1980-1989,* Zürich: Komm. Orell Füssli.

BAUER, I. & NORTHOVER, P. J. (1998) Zug-Sumpf: an extensive approach to the analysis of a single site and the development of samping strategies for other sites, in C. MORDANT, M. PERNOT & V. RYCHNER (Eds.) *L'Atelier du bronzier en Europe du XXe au VIIIe siècle avant notre ère : actes du colloque international "Bronze 96". I : Production, circulation et consomation du bronze*, Paris: Editions du Comité des Travaux Historiques et Scientifiques. 175-89.

BAUER, I., RUCKSTUHL, B. & SPECK, J. (2004) *Zug-Sumpf: Die Funde der Grabungen 1923-37,* Zug: Kantonales Museum für Urgeschichte.

BAUER, S. (2002) Verloren, verwahrt oder geweiht? Nadeln aus Pfahlbauten des Zürichsees, in L. ZEMMER-PLANK (Ed.) *Kult der Vorzeit in den Alpen : Opfergaben - Opferplätze - Opferbrauchtum*, Bozen: Athesia. 1047-85.

BAUMEISTER, R. (1995) Aussergewöhnliche Funde der Urnenfelderzeit aus Knittlingen, Enzkreis. Bemerkungen zu Kult und Kulgerät der Spätbronzezeit, *Fundberichte aus Baden-Württemberg* 20, 377-448.

BAUMEISTER, R. (Ed.) (2009) *Mord im Moor?*, Bad Schussenried: Federsee Museum Bad Buchau.

BAUMEISTER, R. (2011) Nadeln im Moor, in R. BAUMEISTER (Ed.) *Glaubenssachen. Kult und Kunst der Bronzezeit. Begleitband zur Sonderausstellung 15. Mai bis 1. November 2011*, Bad Buchau: Verein für Altertumskunde und Heimatpflege with Federseemuseum. 32-33.

BAUMSTEIN, R. (1994) Bretten, *Fundberichte aus Baden-Württemberg* 19 (2), 42-44.

BÉARAT, H. & BAUER, I. (1994) Früheisenzeitliche Keramik von Baarburg ZG und Üetliberg ZH: Eine mineralogisch-petrographische und chemische Untersuchung zur Frage der Herstellungsorte scheibengedrehter Keramik in der ausgehenden Hallstattzeit, *Germania* 72 (1), 67-93.

BECH, J.-H. (1997) Bronze Age settlements on raised sea-beds at Bjerre, Thy, NW-Jutland, in J. J. ASSENDORP (Ed.) *Forschungen zur bronzezeitlichen Besiedlung in Nord- und Mitteleuropa*, Espelkamp: Verlag Marie Leidorf. 3-15.

BECH, J.-H. (2003) The Thy Archaeological Project - Results and Reflections from a Multinational Archaeological Project, in H. THRANE (Ed.) *Diachronic settlement studies in the metal ages : report on the ESF workshop, Moesgård, Denmark, 14-18 october 2000*, Højbjerg: Jutland Archaeological Society. 45-60.

BECK, C. W., HARTNETT, H. E. & PHOCAS, J. G. (1993) The origin of amber found at Hauterive-Champréveyres, Switzerland, in A.-M. RYCHNER-FARAGGI (Ed.) *Hauterive-Champréveyres 9: Métal et parure au Bronze final*, Neuchâtel: Musée cantonal d'archéologie : Service cantonal de la conservation des monuments et des sites. 119-21.

BECK, C. W. & SHENNAN, S. J. (1991) *Amber in prehistoric Britain,* Oxford: Oxbow Monograph.

BECK, C. W. & STOUT, E. C. (2000) The Origin of the Prehistoric Amber Finds in Southern Switzerland, in R. C. DE MARINIS & S. B. SIMONA (Eds.) *I Leponti tra mito e realtà : raccolta di saggi in occasione della mostra*, Vol. 2, Locarno: Armando Dadò Editore. 41-61.

BEECHING, A. (1977) *Le Boiron : une nécropole du bronze final près de Morges (Vaud, Suisse),* Lausanne: Musée d'archéologie et d'histoire.

BELLINTANI, P. (1997) Frattesina: l'ambra e la produzione vitrea nel contesto delle relazioni transalpina, in L. ENDRIZZI & F. MARZATICO (Eds.) *Ori delle Alpi*, Trento: Servizio beni culturali Provinica autonoma di Trento. 117-29.

BELLINTANI, P. & RESIDORI, G. (2003) Quali e quante conterie: perle ed altri materiali vetrosi dell'italia settentrionale nel quadro dell'età del bronzo europea, in I. I. D. P. E. PROTOSTORIA (Ed.) *Atti Della XXXV Riunione Scientifica*, Firenze: Istituto Italiano di Preistoria e Protostoria. 483-98.

BELLINTANI, P. & STEFAN, L. (2009) Nuovi dati sul primo vetro Europeo: il caso di Frattesina, in A. MAGNA (Ed.) *Atti del primo convegino interdiciplinare sul vetro nei beni culturali e nell'arte di ieri e di oggi*, Parma: 71-86.

BENDER, B. (2002) Time and Landscape, *Current Anthropology* 43 (s4), S103-S12.

BENKERT, A. (1993) *Hauterive-Champréveyres 8: Les structures de l'habitat au Bronze final : zone A,* Neuchâtel: Musée cantonal d'archéologie.

BENKERT, A., CARAZZETTI, R., GOLLNISCH, H., RAGETH, J. & SEIFERT, M. (1998) Siedlungswesen, in S. HOCHULI, U. NIFFELER & V. RYCHNER (Eds.) *SPM III Bronzezeit: Die Schweiz vom Paläolithikum bis zum frühen Mittelalter*, Basel: Verlag Schweizerische Gesellschaft für Ur- und Frühgeschichte. 193-229.

BENKERT, A. & EGGER, H. (1986) Dendrochronologie d'un site du Bronze final, Hauterive-Champréveyres (Suisse), *Bulletin de la Société préhistorique française*, 486-502.

BENTLEY, R. A., HAHN, M. W. & SHENNAN, S. J. (2004) Random drift and culture change, *Proceedings of the Royal Society of London. Series B: Biological Sciences* 271 (1547), 1443-50.

BERGER, D. (2011) *Bronzezeitliche Färbetechniken an Metallobjekten nördlich der Alpen*, unpublished thesis for Doktor der Naturwissenschaften, (Eberhard-Karls-Universität Tübingen).

BERGER, L. & BROGLI, W. (1980) *Wittnauer Horn und Umgebung,* Basel: Schweiz Gesellschaft für Ur- und Frühgeschichte.

BERGER, L. & SCHINDLER, M. P. (1999) Kunst und Kunstgewerbe, in F. MÜLLER, G. KAENEL & G. LÜSCHER (Eds.) *SPM IV Eisenzeit: Die Schweiz vom Paläolithikum bis zum frühen Mittelalter*, Basel: Verlag Schweizerische Gesellschaft für Ur- und Frühgeschichte. 229-42.

BERGFJORD, C., MANNERING, U., FREI, K. M., GLEBA, M., SCHARFF, A. B., SKALS, I., HEINEMEIER, J., NOSCH, M. L. & HOLST, B. (2012) Nettle as a distinct Bronze Age textile plant, *Scientific Reports* 2 (664).

BERNATZKY-GOETZE, M. (1987) *Mörigen : die spätbronzezeitlichen Funde,* Basel: Verlag Schweizerische Gesellschaft für Ur- und Frühgeschichte.

BERSU, G. (1945) *Das Wittnauer Horn im Kanton Aargau : seine ur- und frühgeschichtlichen Befestigungsanlagen,* Basel: Verlag Birkhäuser & CIE.

BERTSCH, K. (1931) *Paläobotanische Monographie des Federseerieds,* Stuttgart: E. Schweizerbart'sche Verlagsbuchhandlung.

BETZLER, P. (1974) *Die Fibeln in Süddeutschland, Österreich und der Schweiz I : (urnenfelderzeitliche Typen)*, Prähistorische Bronzefunde 14 / 3, München: Beck.

BIANCO PERONI, V. (1976) *Die Messer in Italien*, Prähistorische Bronzefunde 7 / 2, München: Beck.

BIANCO PERONI, V. (1979) *I rasoi nell'Italia continentale*, Prähistorische Bronzefunde 8 / 2, München: Beck.

BIEHL, P. F. & RASSAMAKIN, Y. Y. (Eds.) (2008) *Import and imitation in archaeology*, Langenweissbach: Beier & Beran.

BIEL, J. (1987) *Vorgeschichtliche Höhensiedlungen in Südwürttemberg-Hohenzollern*, Stuttgart: Konrad Theiss.

BIETTI SESTIERI, A. M. (1984) L'abitato di Frattesina, *Padusa* 20, 413-27.

BIETTI SESTIERI, A. M. (1988) The 'Mycenean connection' and its impact on the central Mediterranean societies, *Dialoghi di Archeologia (series 3)* 6 (1), 23-51.

BIETTI SESTIERI, A. M. (1997) Italy in Europe in the Early Iron Age, *Proceedings of the Prehistoric Society* 63, 371-402.

BIGLER, B. (2005) Der Rhinsberg bei Eglisau, Kanton Zürich, *Jahrbuch der Schweizerischen Gesellschaft für Ur- und Frühgeschichte* 88, 169-200.

BILLAMBOZ, A. (1998) Zur dendrochronologischen Datierung der Bohlenwege an der Wuhrstraße westlich von Bad Buchau, Kreis Biberach, *Archäologische Ausgrabungen in Baden-Württemberg* 1997, 50-52.

BILLAMBOZ, A. (2003) Tree rings and wetland occupation in Southwest Germany between 2000 and 500 BC: dendroarchaeology beyond dating in tribute to F. H. Schweingruber, *Tree-ring Research* 59 (1), 37-49.

BILLAMBOZ, A. (2006a) Dendroarchäologische Untersuchungen in den neolithischen Ufersiedlungen von Hornstaadt-Hörnle, in LANDESAMT FÜR DENKMALPFLEGE (Ed.) *Siedlungsarchäologie im Alpenvorland IX. Forschungen und Berichte zur Vor- und Frühgeschichte in Baden-Württemberg 98*, Stuttgart: Konrad Theiss Verlag. 297-414.

BILLAMBOZ, A. (2006b) Die Wasserburg Buchau im Jahrringkalender, *Plattform* 13/14, 97-105.

BILLAMBOZ, A. (2009) The absolute dating of Wasserburg-Buchau, in S. W. MANNING & M. J. BRUCE (Eds.) *Tree-rings, kings and old world archaeology and environment papers presented in honor of Peter Ian Kuniholm*, Oxford: Oxbow Books. 33-40.

BILLAMBOZ, A. & GOLLNISCH, H. (1998) Die Dendrodatierung der Siedlungsphasen von Uerschhausen-Horn (CH Thurgau) in der Spätbronzezeit und frühen Eisenzeit, *Plattform* 5/6, 102-03.

BILLAMBOZ, A. & KÖNINGER, J. (2008) Dendroarchäologische Untersuchungen zur Besiedlungs- und Landschaftsentwicklung im Neolithikum des westlichen Bodenseegebietes, in W. DÖRFLER & J. MÜLLER (Eds.) *Umwelt - Wirtschaft - Siedlungen im dritten vorchristlichen Jahrtausend Mitteleuropas und Südskandinaviens*, Neumünster: Wachholtz. 317-34.

BILLAUD, Y. (2006) L'organisation architecturale des stations Bronze final du lac du Bourget (Savoie): résultats récents à Conjux/le Port 3, *Bulletin de la Société préhistorique française* 103 (1), 167-71.

BILLAUD, Y. (2008) Les stations littorales de l'âge du Bronze final: Perception et évaluation d'un patrimoine subaquatique, in S. JACOMET, I. DOMAIZON, J. POULENARD & F. ARNAUD (Eds.) *Autour du Lac du Bourget. Actes du colloque pluridisiplinaire*, Thonon-les-Bains: Les Editions de la Page Blanche. 49-54.

BILLAUD, Y. (2011) Récupération de bois d'œuvre et réemploi sur une station littorale de la fin du Bronze final: Conjux / Le Port 3, lac du Bourget, Savoie, in I. SÉNÉPART, T. PERRIN, É. THIRAULT & S. BONNARDIN (Eds.) *Marges, frontières et transgressions. Actualité de la recherche.*, Toulouse: Archives d'Écologie Préhistorique. 475-80.

BILLAUD, Y. & MARGUET, A. (2005) Habitats lacustres du Néolithique et de l'âge du Bronze dans les lacs alpins fran?ais: bilan des connaissances et perspectives, in P. DELLA CASA & M. TRACHSEL (Eds.) *WES'04 - Wetland Economies and Societies*, Zurich: Chronos. 169-78.

BILLAUD, Y., MARGUET, A. & SIMONIN, O. (1992) Chindrieux, Châtillon (Lac du Bourget, Savoie) Ultime Occupation des Lacs Alpins Français à l'âge du Bronze?, in COMITÉ DES TRAVAUX HISTORIQUES ET SCIENTIFIQUES (Ed.) *Archéologie et environnements des milieux aquatiques: actes du 116e congrès national des sociétés savantes*, Paris: Editions du Comité des travaux historiques et scientifiques. 277-310.

BINSBERGEN, W. M. J. V. (2005) Commodification: Things, agency, and identities: Introduction, in W. M. J. V. BINSBERGEN & P. GESCHIERE (Eds.) *Commodification : Things, Agency, and Identities : (The Social Life of Things Revisited)*, Münster: Lit. 9-51.

BLANCO-GONZÁLEZ, A. (2011) From Huts to 'The House': the shift in perceiving home between the Bronze Age and the Early Iron Age in Central Iberia (Spain), *Oxford Journal of Archaeology* 30 (4), 393-410.

BLANCO-GONZÁLEZ, A. (2014) Tracking the social lives of things: biographical insights into Bronze Age pottery in Spain, *Antiquity* 88 (340), 441-55.

BLEICHER, N. (2009) *Altes Holz in neuem Licht: Archäologische und dendrochronologische Untersuchungen an spätneolithischen Feuchtbodensiedlungen in Oberschwaben,* Stuttgart: Konrad Theiss Verlag.

BLEICHER, N. (2013) Summed radiocarbon probability density functions cannot prove solar forcing of Central European lake-level changes, *The Holocene* 23 (5), 755-65.

BLEICHER, N., MÄDER, A., MOTSCHI, A., RIETHMANN, P. & SCHWÖRER, P. (2011) Die Rettungsgrabung Parkhaus Opéra, *Archäologie Schweiz* 34 (3), 16-23.

BLÖSCH, W. & WIELAND, G. (2002) Kraithtal - Menzingen, *Fundberichte aus Baden-Württemberg* 26, 112-13.

BOAS, F. (1982) The Aims of Ethnology, in F. BOAS *Race language and culture*, Chicago: University of Chicago Press. 626-38.

BOGAARD, A. (2011) Farming practice and society in the Central European Neolilthic and Bronze Age: an archaeobotanical response to the secondary products revolution model, in A. HADJIKOUMIS, E. ROBINSON & S. VINER (Eds.) *The Dynamics of Neolithisation in Europe. Studies in honour of Andrew Sherratt*, Oxford: Oxbow Books. 266-83.

BÖHRINGER, S. & HONEGGER, M. (in preparation) *Hauterive-Champréveyres. Dendrochronologie du village Bronze Final,* Neuchâtel: Office et musée cantonal d'archéologie.

BOISAUBERT, J.-L. & BUGNON, D. (2008) Morat/Löwenberg, in J.-L. BOISAUBERT, D. BUGNON & M. MAUVILLY (Eds.) *Archéologie et autoroute A1, destins croisés : 25 années de fouilles en terres fribourgeoises, premier bilan (1975-2000),* Fribourg: Service archéologique de l'Etat de Fribourg. 64-79.

BOISAUBERT, J.-L., BUGNON, D. & MAUVILLY, M. (2008) *Archéologie et autoroute A1, destins croisés : 25 années de fouilles en terres fribourgeoises, premier bilan (1975-2000),* Fribourg: Service archéologique de l'Etat de Fribourg.

BÖNISCH, E. (2005) Begrabene Häuser? Brandschutt mit bronzezeitlichem Hausinventar, in B. HÄNSEL & B. HOREJS (Eds.) *Interpretationsraum Bronzezeit : Bernhard Hänsel von seinen Schülern gewidmet,* Bonn: Rudolf Habelt. 445-62.

BONOGOFSKY, M. (2003) Neolithic Plastered Skulls and Railroading Epistemologies, *Bulletin of the American Schools of Oriental Research* (331), 1-10.

BORIĆ, D. (Ed.) (2009) *Archaeology and memory*, Oxford: Oxbow.

BOUYER, M. & BOISAUBERT, J.-L. (1992) La nécropole de l'âge du Bronze de Murten/Löwenberg, *Archäologie der Schweiz* 15 (2), 68-73.

BOUZEK, J. (1993) The shifts of the amber route, in C. W. BECK, J. BOUZEK & D. DRESLEROVÁ (Eds.) *Amber in archaeology : proceedings of the Second International Conference on Amber in Archaeology, Liblice 1990*, Praha, Czech Republic: Institute of Archaeology, Czech Academy of Sciences. 141-46.

BOUZEK, J. (1994) Late Bronze Age Greece and the Balkans: a review of the present picture, *The Annual of the British School at Athens* 89, 217-34.

BOUZEK, J. (1997) *Greece, Anatolia and Europe: cultural interrelations during the Early Iron Age,* Jonsered: Paul Åströms Förlag.

BOYD, R. & RICHERSON, P. J. (2005) *The origin and evolution of cultures,* Oxford: Oxford University Press.

BRADLEY, R. (1990) *The passage of arms : an archaeological analysis of prehistoric hoards and votive deposits,* Cambridge: Cambridge University Press.

BRADLEY, R. (2005) *Ritual and domestic life in prehistoric Europe,* (Reprinted edition), London: Routledge.

BRADLEY, R. & SMITH, A. C. (2007) Questions of Context: A Greek Cup from the River Thames, in C. GOSDEN, H. HAMEROW, P. DE JERSEY & G. LOCK (Eds.) *Communities and connections : essays in honour of Barry Cunliffe,* Oxford: Oxford University Press. 30-42.

BRADLEY, R. & WILLIAMS, H. (Eds.) (1998) The Past in the Past: the re-use of ancient monuments, *World archaeology*, 30 (1).

BREM, H., BOLLIGER SCHREYER, S. & PRIMAS, M. (1987) *Eschenz, Insel Werd: Die römische und spätbronzezeitliche Besiedlung,* Zürich: Abt. Ur- und Frühgeschichte der Universität Zürich.

BRESTRICH, W. & WAHL, J. (1998) *Die mittel- und spätbronzezeitlichen Grabfunde auf der Nordstadtterrasse von Singen am Hohentwiel,* Stuttgart: Komm. Konrad Theiss Verlag.

BROMBACHER, C. & KLEE, M. (2009) Vestiges carpologiques non carbonisées et carbonisés des dépôts protohistoriques de Délemont - En La Pran, in N. POUSAZ, M. GUÉLAT, L. FREI PAROZ & V. PIUZ LOUBIER (Eds.) *Delémont - En La Pran 1 (Jura, Suisse). Environnement alluvial et premières installations humaines entre Mésolithique réecent at âge du Bronze*, Porrentruy: Office de la culture : Société jurassienne d'émulation. 77-90.

BROODBANK, C. (1993) Ulysses without Sails: Trade, Distance, Knowledge and Power in the Early Cyclades, *World archaeology* 24 (3), 315-31.

BRÜCK, J. (1999) Houses, lifecycles and deposition on Middle Bronze Age settlements in southern England, *Proceedings of the Prehistoric Society* 65, 145-66.

BRUGHMANS, T. (In press) Understading inter-settlement visibility in Iron Age and Roman Southern Spain with exponential random graph models for visibility networks, *Journal of Archaeological Method and Theory.*

BRUGHMANS, T., KEAY, S. & EARL, G. (2014) Introducing exponential random graph models for visibility networks, *Journal of Archaeological Science* 49, 442-54.

BRUN, P. (1992) La place du Jura franco-suisse dans l'économie-monde méditerranéenne au Premier âge du Fer: essai de modélisation, in G. KAENEL & P. CURDY (Eds.) *L'âge du Fer dans le Jura : actes du 15e colloque de l'Association française pour l'étude sur l'âge du Fer, Pontarlier (France) et Yverdon-les-Bains (Suisse), 9-12 mai 1991*, Lausanne: Bibliothèque historique vaudoise. 189-205.

BUCHLI, V. A. (2004) Material Culture: Current Problems, in L. MESKELL & R. W. PREUCEL (Eds.) *A companion to social archaeology*, Oxford: Blackwell. 179-94.

BUKOWSKI, Z. (1988) Critically about the so-called Amber Route in the Odra and Vistula river basins in the Early Iron Age, *Archaeologia Polona* 28, 71-122.

BURGA, C. A. (1988) Swiss Vegetation History during the Last 18 000 Years, *New Phytologist* 110 (4), 581-602.

BURGA, C. A. (1991) Vegetation History and Palaeoclimatology of the Middle Holocene: Pollen Analysis of Alpine Peat Bog Sediments, Covered Formerly by the Rutor Glacier, 2510 m (Aosta Valley, Italy), *Global Ecology and Biogeography Letters* 1 (5), 143-50.

BUSBY, C. (1997) Permeable and Partible Persons: a comparative analysis of gender and body in South India and Melanesia, *Journal of the Royal Anthropological Institute* 3 (2), 261-78.

CAMPBELL, S. F. (1983) Attaining rank: a classification of kula shell valuables, in J. W. LEACH & E. LEACH (Eds.) *The Kula : new perspectives on Massim exchange*, Cambridge: Cambridge University Press. 229-48.

CHADWICK, A. M. & GIBSON, C. D. (Eds.) (2013) *Memory, myth and long-term landscape inhabitation*, Oxford: Oxbow Books.

CHAPMAN, J. (1998) Ojectification, embodiment and the value of places and things, in D. W. BAILEY (Ed.) *The archaeology of value : essays on prestige and the processes of valuation*, Oxford: Hedges. 106-30.

CHAPMAN, J. (2000) *Fragmentation in archaeology : people, places and broken objects in the prehistory of South Eastern Europe,* London: Routledge.

CHAPMAN, J. (2008) Approaches to Trade and Exchange in Earlier Prehistory (Late Mesolithic-Early Bronze Age), in A. JONES (Ed.) *Prehistoric Europe : theory and practice*, Chichester: Wiley-Blackwell. 333-55.

CHAPMAN, J. & GAYDARSKA, B. (2007) *Parts and wholes : fragmentation in prehistoric context,* Oxford: Oxbow Books.

CHESSON, M. S. (2003) Households, Houses, Neighbourhoods and Corporate Villages: Modeling the Early Bronze Age as a House Society, *Journal of Mediterranean Archaeology* 16 (1), 79-102.

CHILDE, V. G. (2003 original publication 1936) *Man makes himself,* (4th reprint edition), London: Spokesman.

CLELAND, H. F. (1927) Commerce and Trade Routes in Prehistoric Europe, *Economic Geography* 3 (2), 232-38.

CLINE, E. H. (1994) *Sailing the wine-dark sea : international trade and the Late Bronze Age Aegean,* Oxford: Tempus Reparatum.

COLES, B. & COLES, J. (1992) The wetland revolution: a natural event, in B. COLES (Ed.) *The Wetland revolution in prehistory*, Exeter: Department of History and Archaeology University of Exeter. 147-53.

COLOMB, A. & MUYDEN, B. V. (1896) *Antiquités lacustres : album,* Lausanne: G. Bridel.

CONNERTON, P. (1989) *How societies remember,* Cambridge: Cambridge University Press.

CONOLLY, J. & LANE, M. (2006) *Geographical information systems in archaeology,* (Reprinted edition), Cambridge: Cambridge University Press.

CONSCIENCE, A.-C. (2001) Frühbronzezeitliche Uferdörfer aus Zürich-Mozartstrasse - eine folgenreiche Neudatierung, *Jahrbuch der Schweizerischen Gesellschaft für Ur- und Frühgeschichte* 84, 147-57.

CORNAGGIA CASTIGLIONI, O. (1976) I "talismani a tavoletta" del Bronzo europeo. Esegesi della problematica ed inventario dei repertie italiani, *Natura* 67 (3-4), 135-70.

COWEN, J. D. (1968) The Hallstatt Sword of Bronze: on the Continent and in Britain, *Proceedings of the Prehistoric Society* 33 (1967), 377-454.

CREWE, L. (2007) *Early Enkomi : regionalism, trade and society at the beginning of the Late Bronze Age on Cyprus,* Oxford: Archaeopress.

CURDY, P. (2007) Prehistoric settlement in middle and high altitudes in the Upper Rhone Valley (Valais-Vaud, Switzerland): A summary of twenty years of research, *Preistoria Alpina* 42, 99-108.

CURDY, P., MANUEL MOTTET, NICOUD, C., BAUDAIS, D., LUNDSTRÖM-BAUDAIS, K. & MOULIN, B. (1993) Brig-Glis/Waldmatte, un habitat alpin de l'âge du Fer Fouills archéologiques N9 en Valais, *Archäologie Schweiz* 16 (4), 138-51.

DAMON, F. H. (1983) What moves the kula: opening and closing gifts on Woodlark Island, in J. W. LEACH & E. LEACH (Eds.) *The Kula : new perspectives on Massim exchange*, Cambridge: Cambridge University Press. 309-42.

DAVID-ELBIALI, M. (2000) *La Suisse occidentale au IIe millénaire av. J.-C. : chronologie, culture, intégration européenne,* Lausanne: Cahiers d'archéologie romande.

DAVID-ELBIALI, M. & DUNNING, C. (2004) Le cadre chronologique relatif et absolu au nord-ouest des Alpes entre 1060 et 600 av. J.-C, in G. E. D. F. BARTOLONI (Ed.) *Oriente e Occidente : metodi e discipline a confronto : riflessioni sulla cronologia dell'età del ferro italiana*, Pisa-Roma: Istituti editoriale poligrafici internazionali. 145-95.

DAVID-ELBIALI, M. & MOINAT, P. (2005) Saint-Prex (Vaud) à l'âge du Bronze: le cas d'une commune lémanique, *Jahrbuch der Schweizerischen Gesellschaft für Ur- und Frühgeschichte* 88, 119-68.

DE CAPITANI, A., DESCHLER-ERB, S., LEUZINGER, U., MARTI-GRÄDEL, E. & SCHIBLER, J. (Eds.) (2002) *Die jungsteinzeitliche Seeufersiedlung Arbon, Bleiche 3 : Funde*, Frauenfeld: Departement für Erziehung und Kultur des Kantons Thurgau, Amt für Archäologie.

DE MARINIS, R. C. (2009) Continuity and discontinuity in Northen Italy from the Recent to the Final Bronze Age: a view from North-Western Italy, in A. CARDARELLI, A. CAZZELLA, M. FRANGIPANE & R. PERONI (Eds.) *Scienze dell'Antichità 15: Atti del convegno internazionale "Le ragioni del cambiamento/Reasons for change*, Rome: Edizioni Quasar. 535-45.

DE NAVARRO, J. M. (1925) Prehistoric Routes between Northern Europe and Italy Defined by the Amber Trade, *The Geographical Journal* 66 (6), 481-503.

DEAL, M. (1985) Household Pottery Disposal in the Maya Highlands: An Ethnoarchaeological Interpretation, *Journal of Anthropological Archaeology* 4, 243-91.

DELLA CASA, P. (2001) Natural and cultural landscapes: models of utilization of the Alpine area in the Non Valley (I), Mittelbünden (CH) and Maurienne (F), *Preistoria Alpina* 35, 125-40.

DELLA CASA, P. (2002) *Landschaften, Siedlungen, Ressourcen : Langzeitszenarien menschlicher Aktivität in ausgewählten alpinen Gebieten der Schweiz, Italiens und Frankreichs,* Montagnac: Monique Mergoil.

DELLA CASA, P. (2007) Transalpine pass routes in the Swiss Central Alps and the strategic use of topographic resources, *Preistoria Alpina* 42, 109-18.

DELLA CASA, P. (2013) Switzerland and the Central Alps, in H. FOKKENS & A. F. HARDING (Eds.) *The Oxford handbook of the European Bronze Age*, Oxford: Oxford University Press. 706-22.

DELLA CASA, P., BASS, B. & FEDELE, F. (1999) The Grisons Alpine Valleys survey 1995-97: Methods, results and prospects of an interdisciplinary research program, in P. DELLA CASA (Ed.) *Prehistoric alpine environment, society, and economy*, Universitätsforschungen zur prähistorischen Archäologie. 151-72.

DEMAEZ, J.-D., GAUMER, I. & GUÉLAT, M. (2013) Nouvelles Données sur les Occupations de l'âge du Bronze, de le tène et de l'epoque romaine à Boécourt Ju-les Montoyes, *Jahrbuch Archäologie Schweiz* 96, 59-92.

DÉNERVAUD, S. (2012) Ipsach, Moosstrasse 1a/b. Prähistorische Siedlungsspuren im Hinterland, *Archäologie Bern* 2012, 60-61.

DESCHLER-ERB, S. (1989) Die prähistorischen Funde der Holzfluh bei Balsthal SO, *Archäologie des Kantons Solothurn* 6, 7-100.

DIEMER, G. (1995) *Der Bullenheimer Berg und seine Stellung im Siedlungsgefüge der urnenfelderkultur Mainfrankens,* Kallmünz/Opf: Michael Lassleben.

DIETRICH-WEIBEL, B., LÜSCHER, G. & KILKA, T. (1998) *Posieux/Châtillon-sur-Glâne : Keramik : (6.-5. Jh. v. Chr.),* Fribourg: Editions universitaires.

DOBRES, M.-A. & ROBB, J. E. (2000) Agency in archaeology: paradigm or platitude?, in M.-A. DOBRES & J. E. ROBB (Eds.) *Agency in archaeology*, London: Routledge.

DOITEAU, S. (1989) Le site pré-protohistorique "En Chaplix" (Avenches VD), *Jahrbuch der Schweizerischen Gesellschaft für Ur- und Frühgeschichte* 72, 245-52.

DOITEAU, S. (1991) Faoug VD, Derrière Le Chaney, *Jahrbuch der Schweizerischen Gesellschaft für Ur- und Frühgeschichte* 74, 244-46.

DOITEAU, S. (1992) Nouvelles données sur l'habitat et le Premier Age du Fer en Suisse occidentale, in C. MORDANT & A. RICHARD (Eds.) *L'habitat et l'occupation du sol a l'âge du bronze en Europe*, Paris: Editions du Comité des travaux historiques et scientifiques. 313-25.

DOONAN, O. P. & BAUER, A. A. (2010) Buying a Table in Erfelek: socialities of contact and community in the Black Sea region, in A. A. BAUER & A. S. AGBE-DAVIES (Eds.) *Social Archaeologies of Trade and Exchange: Exploring Relationships among People, Places, and Things*, California: West Cost Press. 183-206.

DOPPLER, T. (2013) *Archäozoologie als zugang zur sozialgeschichte in der feuchtbodenarchäologie. Forschungsperspektiven am Fallbeispiel der neolithischen Seeufersidelung Arbon Bleiche 3 (Schweiz)*, unpublished thesis for Doctoral degree in Archaeology, (Universität Basel).

DOPPLER, T., PILCHER, S., JACOMET, S., SCHIBLER, J. & RÖDER, B. (2010) Archäobiologie als sozialgeschichtliche Informationsquelle : ein bislang vernachlässigtes Forschungspotential, in E. CLAßEN, T. DOPPLER & B. RAMMINGER (Eds.) *Familie - Verwandtschaft - Sozialstrukturen: Sozialarchäologische Forschungen zu neolithischen Befunden*, Kerpen-Loogh: Welt und Erde. 119-39.

DRACK, W. (1958) Wagengräber und Wagenbestandteile aus Hallstattgrabhügeln der Schweiz, *Zeitschrift für Schweizerische Archäologie und Kunstgeschichte* 18, 1-67.

DRACK, W. (1973) Waffen und Messer der Hallstattzeit aus dem Schweizerischen Mitteland und Jura, *Jahrbuch der Schweizerischen Gesellschaft für Ur- und Frühgeschichte* 57, 119-68.

DRACK, W. (1977) Die Bronzegefässe der Hallstattzeit aus dem schweizerischen Mittelland und Jura, *Jahrbuch der Schweizerischen Gesellschaft für Ur- und Frühgeschichte* 60, 103-20.

DRACK, W. (1980) Schwerzgrueb, Kantonsschul-Areal, *Zürcher Denkmalpflege* 8 (1975-1976), 38.

DRACK, W. (1985) Drei hallstattzeitliche Grabhügel bei Bonstetten, Kanton Zürich, *Jahrbuch der Schweizerischen Gesellschaft für Ur- und Frühgeschichte* 68, 123-72.

DU GARDIN, C. (1993) The Circulation of Amber in Prehistoric Europe, in C. SCARRE & F. HEALY (Eds.) *Trade and exchange in Prehistoric Europe : proceedings of a conference held at the University of Bristol, April 1992*, Oxford: Oxbow Books in association with the Prehistoric Society and the Société Préhistorique Française. 131-33.

DUNNING, C. (1991) La Tène, in S. MOSCATI (Ed.) *The Celts*, London: Thames and Hudson. 366-68.

DUNNING, C. (1992) Époque charnière dans un carrefour d'influences: le VIII siècle av. J.-C. a l'ouest du plateau Suisse, in C. MORDANT & A. RICHARD (Eds.) *L'habitat et l'occupation du sol à l'âge du bronze en Europe*, Editions du Comité des travaux historiques et scientifiques. 327-47.

DUNNING, C. & RYCHNER, V. (1994) Archäologische Untersuchungen zum Übergang von der Bronze- zur Eisenzeit in der Westschweiz, in P. SCHAUER (Ed.) *Archäologische Untersuchungen zum Übergang von der Bronze- zur Eisenzeit zwischen Nordsee und Kaukasus*, Bonn: Universitätsverlag Regensburg / Rudolf Habelt. 63-97.

EARLE, T. K. (2002) The Bronze Age Economy of Thy: Finance in a Networked Chiefdom, in T. K. EARLE *Bronze Age economics : the first political economies*, Boulder (Colorado): Westview. 293-324.

EARLE, T. K., BECH, J.-H., KRISTIANSEN, K., APERLO, P., KELERTAS, K. & STEINBERG, J. (1998) The Political Economy of Late Neolithic and Early Bronze Age Society: the Thy Archaeological Project, *Norwegian archaeological review* 31 (1), 1-28.

EARLE, T. K. & KRISTIANSEN, K. (Eds.) (2010) *Organizing Bronze age societies : the Mediterranean, Central Europe, and Scandinavia compared*, Cambridge: Cambridge University Press.

EBERLI, U. (2010) *Die horgenzeitliche Siedlung Pfäffikon-Burg*, Zürich: Baudirektion Kanton Zürich.

EBERSBACH, R. (2009) Gachnang-Niederwil TG-Egelsee: Neuinterpretation der Baubefunde, *Jahrbuch Archäologie Schweiz* 92, 97-116.

EBERSBACH, R. (2013) Houses, households and settlements: architecture and living spaces, in F. MENOTTI & A. O'SULLIVAN (Eds.) *The Oxford Handbook of Wetland Archaeology*, Oxford: Oxford University Press. 283-301.

EBERSBACH, R., HOYER, W. & ZAHND, E. (2010) Ein "Repräsentatives Inventar" für den Kanton Bern, *Archäologie Bern* 2010, 249-71.

EBERSCHWEILER, B. (1990a) Blockbauten im spätbronzezeitlichen Dorf von Greifensee-Böschen, in M. HÖNEISEN (Ed.) *Die ersten Bauern : Pfahlbaufunde Europas*, Vol. 1, Zürich: Schweizerisches Landesmuseum. 193-200.

EBERSCHWEILER, B. (1990b) Die Türe von Robenhausen, in M. HÖNEISEN (Ed.) *Die ersten Bauern : Pfahlbaufunde Europas*, Vol. 1, Zürich: Schweizerisches Landesmuseum. 191-92.

EBERSCHWEILER, B. (2004) *Bronzezeitliches Schwemmgut vom "Chollerpark" in Steinhausen (Kanton Zug) : bemerkenswerte Holzfunde vom nördlichen Zugersee sowie weitere bronzezeitliche Hölzer von Fundplätzen an Gewässern der Zentral- und Ostschweiz*, Basel: Schweizerische Gesellschaft für Ur- und Frühgeschichte.

EBERSCHWEILER, B., RIETHMANN, P. & RUOFF, U. (2007) *Das spätbronzezeitliche Dorf von Greifensee-Böschen : Dorfgeschichte, Hausstrukturen und Fundmaterial*, Zürich: Neue Medien.

EGGERT, M. K. H. (1988) Riesentumuli und Sozialorganisation. Vergleichende Betrachtungen zu den sogenannten "Fürstenhügeln" der späten Hallstattzeit, *Archäologisches Korrespondenzblatt* 18 (3), 263-74.

EIBNER, C. (1973) Die urnenfelderzeitlichen Sauggefässe. Ein Beitrag zur morphologischen und ergologischen Umschreibung, *Prähistorische Zeitschrift* 48, 144-99.

ELES MASI, P. V. (1986) *Le fibule dell'Italia settentrionale*, Prähistorische Bronzefunde 14 / 5, München: C. H. Beck.

ERZIEHUNGSDIREKTION DES KANTONS BERN (2008a) Fundberichte: 23 Erlach Winzerweg 8, *Archäologie Bern* 2008, 32.

ERZIEHUNGSDIREKTION DES KANTONS BERN (2008b) Fundberichte: 35 Jegenstorf Kirchgasse, *Archäologie Bern* 2008, 33.

ERZIEHUNGSDIREKTION DES KANTONS BERN (2008c) Fundberichte: 85 Thun Hofstettenstrasse, *Archäologie Bern* 2008, 39.

FALKENSTEIN, F. (2005) Zu den Gewässerfunden der älteren Urnenfelderzeit in Süddeutschland, in B. HÄNSEL & B. HOREJS (Eds.) *Interpretationsraum Bronzezeit : Bernhard Hänsel von seinen Schülern gewidmet*, Bonn: Rudolf Habelt. 491-504.

FALKENSTEIN, F. (2011) Zu Struktur und Deutung älterurnenfelderzeitlicher Hortfunde im nordalpinen Raum, in U. L. DIETZ & A. JOCKENHÖVEL (Eds.) *Bronzen im Spannungsfeld zwischen praktischer Nutzung und symbolischer Bedeutung : Beiträge zum internationalen Kolloquium am 9. und 10. Oktober 2008 in Münster*, Stuttgart: Steiner. 71-105.

FISCHER, C. (1996) Ein Siedlungsplatz der Ürnenfelder-, Hallstatt- und Latènezeit in Fällanden-Fröschbach, *Archäologie im Kanton Zürich* 1993-1994, 55-100.

FISCHER, C. (1997) *Innovation und Tradition in der Mittel- und Spätbronzezeit : Gräber und Siedlungen in Neftenbach, Fällanden, Dietikon, Pfäffikon und Erlenbach*, Zürich: Fotorotar AG/Druck Kommunikation Verlag.

FISCHER, C. (1998a) Die spätbronzezeitlichen Kindergräber von Reinach-Alte Brauerei, in J. EWALD & J. TAUBER (Eds.) *Tatort Vergangenheit : Ergebnisse aus der Archäologie heute*, Basel: Wiese Verlag. 165-80.

FISCHER, C. (1998b) Symbolische Handlungen und Bestattungsbräuche in der Bronzezeit, in S. HOCHULI, U. NIFFELER & V. RYCHNER (Eds.) *SPM III Bronzezeit: Die Schweiz vom Paläolithikum bis zum frühen Mittelalter*, Basel: Verlag Schweizerische Gesellschaft für Ur- und Frühgeschichte. 309-25.

FISCHER, V. (2005) La Station de Grandson-Corcelettes a l'Age du Bronze Final, *Revue historique vadoise* 113, 153-67.

FISCHER, V. (2011) The deposition of bronzes at Swiss lakeshore settlements: new investigations, *Antiquity* 85 (330), 1298-311.

FISCHER, V. (2012) *Les bronzes en contexte palafittique sur les rives du Léman et des Trois-Lacs (Suisse occidentale),* Lausanne: Musée cantonal d'archéologie et d'histoire.

FISHER, P., FARRELLY, C., MADDOCKS, A. & RUGGLES, C. (1997) Spatial Analysis of Visible Areas from the Bronze Age Cairns of Mull, *Journal of Archaeological Science* 24 (7), 581-92.

FOGEL, J. & LANGER, J. L. (1999) Europejskie "Idole chlebkowate" z wczesnej epoki brązu. Próba nowej interpretacji trésci metodami matematycznymi, *Folia Praehistorica Posnaniensia* 9, 79-133.

FONTIJN, D. R. (2002) *Sacrificial landscapes : cultural biographies of persons, objects and 'natural' places in the Bronze Age of the southern Netherlands, c. 2300-600 B.C.*, Leiden: University of Leiden.

FONTIJN, D. R. (2009) Land at the other end of the sea? Metalwork circulation, geographical knowledge and the significance of British/Irish imports in the Bronze Age of the Low Countries, in P. CLARK (Ed.) *Bronze Age connections : cultural contact in prehistoric Europe*, Oxford: Oxbow Books. 129-48.

FONTIJN, D. R. (2010) *Living near the dead : the barrow excavations of Rhenen-Elst: two millennia of burial and habitation on the Utrechtse Heuvelrug,* Leiden: Sidestone.

FORD, D., GOODWIN, J., BOOTHROYD, N., ABBY, R., COOK, B. & YOUNGS, S. (1998) A prehistoric Excalibur and other artefacts of diverse dates: a catalogue of selected finds from Staffordshire recovered through metal detecting, *West Midlands Archaeology* 41, 36-48.

FOWLER, C. (2004) *The archaeology of personhood : an anthropological approach,* London: Routledge.

FRASCOLI, L. (1991) Der "Keltenwall" von Rheinau, Kt. Zürich - Die Grabung von 1989, *Jahrbuch der Schweizerischen Gesellschaft für Ur- und Frühgeschichte* 74, 7-42.

FREDENGREN, C. (2011) Where Wandering Water Gushes - the Depositional Landscape of the Mälaren Valley in the Late Bronze Age and Earliest Iron Age of Scandinavia, *Journal of Wetland Archaeology* 10, 109-35.

FREI, B. (1955a) Niederbipp, *Jahrbuch der Schweizerischen Gesellschaft für Ur- und Frühgeschichte* 44, 145-46.

FREI, B. (1955b) Zur Datierung der Melauner Keramik, *Zeitschrift für Schweizerische Archäologie und Kunstgeschichte* 15, 129-73.

FREI, K. M., FREI, R., MANNERING, U., GLEBA, M., NOSCH, M. L. & LYNGSTRØM, H. (2009) Provenance of ancient textiles - a pilot study evaluating the strontium isotope system in wool, *Archaeometry* 51 (2), 252-76.

FREY, O.-H. & ROTH, H. (Eds.) (1983) *Glasperlen der vorrömischen Eisenzeit I*, Mainz am Rhein: Philipp von Zabern.

FREY, O.-H., ROTH, H. & DOBIAT, C. (Eds.) (1987) *Glasperlen der vorrömischen Eisenzeit II: Ringaugenperlen und verwandte Perlengruppen*, Mainz am Rhein: Philipp von Zabern.

FRIEMAN, C. J. (2010) Imitation, identity and communication: The presence and problems of skeuomorphs in the Metal Ages, in B. V. ERIKSEN (Ed.) *Lithic technology in metal using societies*, Højbjerg: Jutland Archaeological Society. 33-44.

FRIEMAN, C. J. (2012a) Going to pieces at the funeral: Completeness and complexity in early Bronze Age jet 'necklace' assemblages, *Journal of Social Archaeology* 12 (3), 334-55.

FRIEMAN, C. J. (2012b) *Innovation and imitation : stone skeuomorphs of metal from 4th-2nd millennia BC northwest Europe,* Oxford: Archaeopress.

GALANAKI, I., TOMAS, H., GALANAKIS, Y. & LAFFINEUR, R. (Eds.) (2007) *Between the Aegean and Baltic seas : prehistory across borders : proceedings of the International Conference "Bronze and early iron age interconnections and contemporary developments between the Aegean and the regions of the Balkan Peninsula, Central and Northern Europe", University of Zagreb, 11-14 April 2005*, Liège: Université de Liège.

GALLAY, A. & KAENEL, G. (1986) Sion aux âges du Bronze et du Fer, in A. GALLAY (Ed.) *Le Valais avant l'histoire 14'000 av. J.-C. - 47 apr. J.-C. : Expostition Musées cantonaux Sion*, Sion: Musées cantonaux. 254-65.

GAMBARI, F. M. (2004) I signori del commercio sulle vie d'acqua. Il ruolo degli scambi nella cultura di Golasecca, in F. MARZATICO & P. GLEIRSCHER (Eds.) *Guerrieri, principi ed eroi fra il Danubio e il Po dalla Preistoria all'Alto Medioevo*, Trento: Castello del Buonconsiglio. 304-13.

GAMPER, M. (1981) Heutige Solifluktionsbeträge von Erdströmen und klimamorphologische Interpretation fossiler Böden, *Ergebnisse der wissenschaftlichen Untersuchungen im Schweizerischen Nationalpark*, Zürich: Geographisches Institut. 355-443.

GELL, A. (1998) *Art and agency : an anthropological theory,* Oxford: Clarendon Press.

GEORGIADIS, M. & GALLOU, C. (Eds.) (2009) *The past in the past : the significance of memory and tradition in the transmission of culture*, Oxford: Archaeopress.

GERDSEN, H. (1986) *Studien zu den Schwertgräbern der älteren Hallstattzeit,* Mainz am Rhein: Philipp von Zabern.

GERRITSEN, F. (1999) To Build and to Abandon. The Cultural Biography of Late Prehistoric Houses and Farmsteads in the Southern Netherlands, *Archaeological dialogues : Dutch perspectives on current issues in archaeology* 6 (2), 78-114.

GERRITSEN, F. (2003) Local identities : landscape and community in the late prehistoric Meuse-Demer-Scheldt region, *Amsterdam archaeological studies 9*, Amsterdam: Amsterdam University Press.

GERRITSEN, F. (2008) Domestic Times: Houses and Temporalities in Late Prehistoric Europe, in A. JONES (Ed.) *Prehistoric Europe : theory and practice*, Chichester: Wiley-Blackwell. 143-61.

GERSBACH, E. (1995) *Baubefunde der Perioden IVc-IVa der Heuneburg : Text und Tafeln,* Mainz am Rhein: Verlag Philipp von Zabern.

GLAUSER, K., RAMSTEIN, M. & BACHER, R. (1996) *Tschugg-Steiacher: prähistorische Fundschichten und römischer Gutshof,* Bern: Berner Lehrmittel- und Medienverlag.

GOLLNISCH-MOOS, H. (1999) *Haus- und Siedlungsstrukturen der spätestbronzezeitlichen Siedlung,* Frauenfeld: Departement für Erziehung und Kultur des Kantons Thurgau.

GONZÁLEZ-RUIBAL, A. (2006) House societies vs. kinship-based societies: An archaeological case from Iron Age Europe, *Journal of Anthropological Archaeology* 25 (1), 144-73.

GÖRMER, G. (2006) Bronzezeitliche Depots in Mitteleuropa und ihre Deutung, *Ethnographisch-Archäologische Zeitschrift* 47 (3), 289-98.

GÓRSKI, J. & MAKAROWICZ, P. (2007) Reception of Transcarpathian influence in Trzciniec cultural circle as a sign of long-distance exchange contacts, in J. BARON & I. LASAK (Eds.) *Lond Distance Trade in the Bronze Age and Early Iron Age*, Wrocław: Wydawnictwo Uniwersytetu Wrocławskiego. 101-16.

GOSDEN, C. (1985) Gifts and Kin in Early Iron Age Europe, *Man* 20 (3), 475-93.

GOSDEN, C. (2005) What Do Objects Want?, *Journal of Archaeological Method and Theory* 12 (3), 193-211.

GOSDEN, C. & LOCK, G. (1998) Prehistoric Histories, *World archaeology* 30 (1), 2-12.

GOSDEN, C. & MARSHALL, Y. (1999) The cultural biography of objects, in C. GOSDEN & Y. MARSHALL (Eds.) *The Cultural Biography of Objects*, World Archaeology Vol. 31.2, London: Routledge. 169-78.

GRATTAN, J. P. (2010) Testing Eventful Archaeologies: Eventful Archaeology and Volcanic "Disasters", in D. J. BOLENDER (Ed.) *Eventful archaeologies : new approaches to social transformation in the archaeological record*, Albany: State University of New York Press. 179-88.

GREEN, D., HASELGROVE, C. & SPRIGGS, M. (1978) *Social organisation and settlement : contributions from anthropology, archaeology and geography,* Oxford: British Archaeological Reports.

GRIMMER, B. (1982) Ein "Feuerbock" oder "Mondidol" aus Ton von Bötzingen, *Archäologische Nachrichten aus Baden* 29, 3-6.

GROSS-KLEE, E. & SCHIBLER, J. (1995) Fäll- und Behaubeile, in W. E. STÖCKLI, U. NIFFELER & E. GROSS-KLEE (Eds.) *SPM II Neolithikum: Die Schweiz vom Paläolithikum bis zum frühen Mittelalter*, Basel: Verlag Schweizerische Gesellschaft für Ur- und Frühgeschichte. 159-68.

GROSS, E., BROMBACHER, C., DICK, M., DIGGELMANN, K., HARDMEYER, B., JAGHER, R., RITZMANN, C., RUCKSTUHL, B., RUOFF, U., SCHIBLER, J., VAUGHAN, P. C. & WYPRÄCHTIGER, K. (1987) *Zürich "Mozartstrasse" : neolithische und bronzezeitliche Ufersiedlungen,* Zürich: Orell Füssli.

GROSS, E. & RITZMANN, C. (1990) Die neolithischen und bronzezeitlichen Siedlungen im Zürcher Seefeld, in M. HÖNEISEN (Ed.) *Die ersten Bauern : Pfahlbaufunde Europas*, Vol. 1, Zürich: Schweizerisches Landesmuseum. 161-76.

GUGGISBERG, M. (1991) Die Kontakte zwischen der frühkeltischen Schweiz und dem Süden: Eine Bestandesaufnahme, *Archäologie der Schweiz* 14 (1), 75-88.

GUGGISBERG, M. (2011) La ceramica greca a nord delle Alpi. Contesto e fuzione, in F. MARZATICO, R. GEBHARD & P. GLEIRSCHER (Eds.) *Le grandi vie delle civiltà : relazioni e scambi fra Mediterraneo e il centro Europa dalla preistoria alla romanità*, Trento: Castello del Buonconsiglio, Monumenti e collezioni provinciali. 227-28.

GUREVICH, A. Y. (1968) Wealth and Gift-Bestowal among the Ancient Scandinavians, *Scandinavica : an international journal of Scandinavian studies* 7, 126-38.

GUTSCHER, D. (2008) Lehnfluh und Erlinsburgen bei Niederbipp / Oensingen, *Archäologie Bern* 2008, 125-31.

GUTZWILLER, P. (1994) Die vörromische Besiedlung des Fleckens Zurzach, *Jahrbuch der Schweizerischen Gesellschaft für Ur- und Frühgeschichte* 77, 7-33.

GUTZWILLER, P. (2004) *Die Bronze- und Hallstattzeitlichen Fundstellen des Kantons Solothurn : ein Beitrag zur metallzeitlichen Siedlungsgeschichte der Nordwestschweiz,* Basel: Schweizerische Geschellschaft für Ur- und Frühgeschichte.

GUYAN, W. U. (1962) Oberburg, *Jahrbuch der Schweizerischen Gesellschaft für Urgeschichte* 49, 98.

HAEVERNICK, T. E. (1975) Hallstatt Glasringe und Hagenauer Perlen, *Trierer Zeitschrift* 38, 63-73.

HAEVERNICK, T. E. (1978) Urnenfelderzeitliche Glasperlen, *Zeitschrift für Schweizerische Archäologie und Kunstgeschichte* 35, 145-57.

HAFNER, A. (2005) Biel-Vingelz, Insel, *Archäologie im Kanton Bern* 6 (A), 62-66.

HAFNER, A. & SUTER, P. J. (2000) *-3400 : die Entwicklung der Bauerngesellschaften im 4. Jahrtausend v.Chr. am Bielersee aufgrund der Rettungsgrabungen von Nidau und Sutz-Lattrigen,* Bern: Berner Lehrmittel- und Medienverlag.

HAFNER, A. & SUTER, P. J. (2004) *5000 Jahre abgetaucht - aufgetaucht 1984-2004,* Bern: Archäologischer Dienst des Kantons Bern.

HAGEN, C., KUNZ, C., MÜLLER, T. & ZÜRCHER, A. (1986) Bülach-Schwerzgrueb, *Zürcher Denkmalpflege* 10 (1), 22.

HAGL, M. (2008) *Ein urnenfelderzeitlicher Depotfund vom Bullenheimer Berg in Franken (Hort F),* München: Verlag C.H. Beck.

HAHN, H. P. & WEISS, E. (2013) Introduction: biographies, travels and itineraries of things, in H. P. HAHN & E. WEISS (Eds.) *Mobility, meaning and transformation of things*, Oxford: Oxbow. 1-14.

HÄNSEL, B. (2007) Ägäische Siedlungsstrukturen in Monkodonja/Istrien?, in I. GALANAKI, H. TOMAS, Y. GALANAKIS & R. LAFFINEUR (Eds.) *Between the Aegean and Baltic seas : prehistory across borders*, Liège: Université de Liège. 149-55.

HÄNSEL, B. & TERŽAN, B. (2000) Ein bronzezeitliches Kuppelgrab ausserhalb der mykenischen Welt im Norden der Adria, *Praehistorische Zeitschrift* 75 (2), 161-83.

HAPKA, R. (1995) Deux tombes à incinération du Bronze final à Cortaillod NE-Aux Murgiers, *Jahrbuch der Schweizerischen Gesellschaft für Ur- und Frühgeschichte* 78, 160-62.

HARDING, A. F. (1984) *The Mycenaeans and Europe,* London: Academic Press.

HARDING, A. F. (2000) *European societies in the Bronze Age,* Cambridge: Cambridge University Press.

HARDING, A. F. (2006) Enclosing and excluding in Bronze Age Europe, in A. F. HARDING, S. SIEVERS & N. VENCLOVÁ (Eds.) *Enclosing the past: inside and outside in prehistory*, Sheffield: J.R. Collis. 97-115.

HARDING, A. F. (2013) World Systems, Cores, and Peripheries in Prehistoric Europe, *European Journal of Archaeology* 16 (3), 378-400.

HÄRKE, H. (1979) *Settlement types and settlement patterns in the West Hallstatt province : an evaluation of evidence from excavated sites,* Oxford: British Archaeological Reports.

HÄRKE, H. (1989) Transformation or Collapse? Bronze Age to Iron Age Settlement in West Central Europe, in M. L. S. SØRENSEN & R. THOMAS (Eds.) *The Bronze Age-Iron Age transition in Europe : aspects of continuity and change in European societies, c. 1200 to 500 B.C*, Vol. 1, Oxford: B.A.R. 184-203.

HARRIS, O. J. T. (2013) Relational communities in prehistoric Britain, in C. WATTS (Ed.) *Relational Archaeologies: humans, animals, things*, Abingdon: Routledge. 173-89.

HASENFRATZ, A. & CASPARIE, W. A. (2006) *Niederwil, eine Siedlung der Pfyner Kultur: anorganische Funde, Palynologie, und Synthese,* Frauenfeld: Departement für Erziehung und Kultur des Kantons Thurgau.

HASENFRATZ, A. & SCHNYDER, M. (1998) *Das Seebachtal : eine archäologische und paläoökologische Bestandesaufnahme,* Frauenfeld: Departement für Erziehung und Kultur des Kantons Thurgau.

HASTORF, C. A. & JOHANNESSEN, S. (1991) Understanding Changing People/Plant Relationships in the Prehispanic Andes, in R. W. PREUCEL (Ed.) *Processual and postprocessual archaeologies : multiple ways of knowing the past*, Carbondale: Center for Archaeological Investigations. 140-55.

HAUGHEY, F. (2007) Glimpsing the water, in SWAP (Ed.) *Archaeology from the wetlands : recent perspectives : proceedings of the 11th WARP conference, Edinburgh 2005*, Edinburgh: Society of Antiquaries of Scotland. 119-25.

HAUGHEY, F. (2013) Rivers and lakes: a network of wetland highways, in F. MENOTTI & A. O'SULLIVAN (Eds.) *The Oxford Handbook of Wetland Archaeology*, Oxford: Oxford University Press. 385-97.

HAWKES, C. (1954) Wenner-Gren Foundation Supper Conference: Archeological Theory and Method: Some Suggestions from the Old World, *American Anthropologist* 56 (2), 155-68.

HAYDEN, B. & CANNON, A. (1983) Where the Garbage Goes: Refuse Disposal in the Maya Highlands, *Journal of Anthropological Archaeology* 2, 117-63.

HEIRELI, J. (1911) Lattrigen bei Sutz, *Jahresbericht der Schweizerischen Gesellschaft für Urgeschichte* 3, 72.

HELMS, M. W. (1988) *Ulysses' sail : an ethnographic odyssey of power, knowledge, and geographical distance,* Princeton: Princeton University Press.

HENNIG, H. (1986) Einige Bemerkungen zu den Urnenfeldern im Regensburger Raum, *Archäologisches Korrespondenzblatt* 16 (3), 289-301.

HENNIG, H. (1992) *Zwei halstattzeitliche Grabhügel aus dem Berner Mittelland: Thunstetten-Tannwäldi und Urtenen-Buebeloo/Chrache,* Bern: Staatlicher Lehrmittelverlag.

HERBICH, I. & DIETLER, M. (2009) Domestic Space, Social Life and Settlement Biography: Theoretical Reflections from the Ethnography of a Rural African Landscape, in M. C. BELARTE (Ed.) *L'espai domèstic i l'organizatió de la societat a la protohistòria de la Mediterrània occidental (ler mil.lenni aC). Actes de la IV Reunió Internacional d'Arqueologia de Calafell,* Barcelona: Institut Català d'Arqueologia Clàssica. 11-23.

HESKE, I. (2009) Siedlung, Waren und Wege - Eine Fallstudie aus dem östlichen Braunschweiger Land, in M. BARTELHEIM & H. STÄUBLE (Eds.) *Die wirtschaftlichen Grundlagen der Bronzezeit Europas,* Rahden/Westf.: Verlag Marie Leidorf GmbH. 321-37.

HINGLEY, R. (2009) Esoteric Knowledge? Ancient Bronze Artefacts from Iron Age Contexts, *Proceedings of the Prehistoric Society* 75, 143-65.

HOCHULI, S., NIFFELER, U. & RYCHNER, V. (Eds.) (1998) *SPM III Bronzezeit: Die Schweiz vom Paläolithikum bis zum frühen Mittelalter,* Basel: Verlag Schweizerische Gesellschaft für Ur- und Frühgeschichte.

HODDER, I. (1984) Archaeology in 1984, *Antiquity* 58 (222), 25-32.

HODDER, I. (1985) Postprocessual Archaeology, in M. B. SCHIFFER (Ed.) *Advances in Archaeological Method and Theory,* Vol. 8, New York: Academic Press. 1-26.

HODDER, I. (1986) *Reading the past : current approaches to interpretation in archaeology,* Cambridge: Cambridge University Press.

HODDER, I. (1991) Interpretive Archaeology and Its Role, *American Antiquity* 56 (1), 7-18.

HODDER, I. & LANE, P. (1982) A Contextual Examination of Neolithic Axe Distribution in Britain, in J. E. ERICSON & T. K. EARLE (Eds.) *Contexts for prehistoric exchange,* New York: Academic Press. 213-35.

HODDER, I. & ORTON, C. (1976) *Spatial analysis in archaeology,* Cambridge: Cambridge University Press.

HOFMANN, P. (1991) Le Landeron NE, Les Carougets, *Jahrbuch der Schweizerischen Gesellschaft für Ur- und Frühgeschichte* 74, 240-41.

HOFMANN ROGNON, P. & DOSWALD, C. (2005) *Le Landeron - Les Carougets : vestiges protohistoriques, villa romaine, tombes et habitat médiévaux,* Hauterive: Service et musée cantonal d'archéologie de Neuchâtel.

HOHLBEIN, M. (2008) *Die spätbronze- und urnenfelderzeitlichen Bronzemesser im mittleren und südlichen Westdeutschland I,* unpublished thesis for Doctor of Philosophy, Alte Geschichte, Archäologie, (Westfälische Wilhelms-Universität zu Münster (Westf.)).

HOLE, F., FLANNERY, K. V. & NEELY, J. A. (1969) *Prehistory and human ecology of the Deh Luran plain : an early village sequence form Khuzistan, Iran,* Ann Arbor: University of Michigan Museum of Anthropology.

HOLSTEIN, D. (2003) *Der Kestenberg bei Möriken (AG) : Auswertung der Ausgrabungen 1950-1953 in der bronze- und eisenzeitlichen Höhensiedlung,* Basel: D. Holstein.

HOLZHAUSER, H., MAGNY, M. & ZUMBUÜHL, H. J. (2005) Glacier and lake-level variations in west-central Europe over the last 3500 years, *The Holocene* 15 (6), 789-801.

HÖNEISEN, M. (1984) Beringen-Unterer Stieg, *Jahrbuch der Schweizerischen Gesellschaft für Ur- und Frühgeschichte* 67, 188.

HOPERT, S., SCHLICHTERLE, H., SCHÖBEL, G., SPATZ, H. & WALTER, P. (1998) Der "Hals" bei Bodman. Eine Höhensiedlung auf dem Bodanrück und ihr Verhältnis zu den Ufersiedlung des Bodensees, in H. KÜSTER, A. LANG & P. SCHAUER (Eds.) *Archäologische Forschungen in urgeschichtlichen Siedlungslandschaften : Festschrift für Georg Kossack zum 75. Geburtstag,* Regensburg: Universitätsverlag. 91-154.

HORDEN, P. & PURCELL, N. (2000) *The corrupting sea : a study of Mediterranean history,* Oxford: Blackwell Publishers.

HORMES, A., MÜLLER, B. U. & SCHLÜCHTER, C. (2001) The Alps with little ice: evidence for eight Holocene phases of reduced glacier extent in the Central Swiss Alps, *The Holocene* 11 (3), 255-65.

HOSKINS, J. (1998) *Biographical objects : how things tell the stories of people's lives,* New York: Routledge.

HUBER, A. (2005) *Zürich-Alpenquai IX : keramische Kleinfunde und Sonderformen,* Zürich: Kantonsarchäologie.

HURCOMBE, L. (2008) Organics from inorganics: using experimental archaeology as a research tool for studying perishable material culture, *World archaeology* 40 (1), 83-115.

ISMAIL-MEYER, K. & RENTZEL, P. (2004) Mikromorphologische Untersuchung der Schichtabfolge, in S. JACOMET, U. LEUZINGER, J. SCHIBLER & F. BOUCHET *Die jungsteinzeitliche Seeufersiedlung Arbon, Bleiche 3 : Umwelt und Wirtschaft,* Frauenfeld: Amt für Archäologie. 66-80.

JACKSON, C. M. & NICHOLSON, P. T. (2010) The provenance of some glass ingots from the Uluburun shipwreck, *Journal of Archaeological Science* 37 (2), 295-301.

JACOB-FRIESEN, G. (1967) *Bronzezeitliche Lanzenspitzen Norddeutschlands und Skandinaviens,* Hildesheim: August Lax.

JACOB-FRIESEN, G. (2013) Zum Altfund eines "Mondhorns" oder "Feuerbocks" aus dem Neuenburger See, *Jahrbuch Archäologie Schweiz* 96, 143-45.

JACOB, C. (1995) *Metallgefässe der Bronze- und Hallstattzeit in Nordwest-, West- und Süddeutschland*, Prähistorische Bronzefunde 2 / 9, Stuttgart: Franz Steiner Verlag.

JACOMET, S. & BROMBACHER, C. (2009) Geschichte der Flora in der Regio Basiliensis seit 7500 Jahren: Ergebnisse von Untersuchungen pflanzlicher Makroreste aus archäologischen Ausgrabungen, *Mitteilungen der Naturforschenden Gesellschaften beider Basel* 11, 27-106.

JACOMET, S., JACQUAT, C., WINTER, M. & WICK, L. (1999) Umwelt, Ackerbau und Sammelwirtschaft, in F. MÜLLER, G. KAENEL & G. LÜSCHER (Eds.) *SPM IV Eisenzeit: Die Schweiz vom Paläolithikum bis zum frühen Mittelalter*, Basel: Verlag Schweizerische Gesellschaft für Ur- und Frühgeschichte. 98-115.

JACOMET, S., LEUZINGER, U., SCHIBLER, J. & BOUCHET, F. (2004) *Die jungsteinzeitliche Seeufersiedlung Arbon, Bleiche 3 : Umwelt und Wirtschaft*, Archäologie in Thurgau 12, Frauenfeld: Amt für Archäologie.

JENNINGS, B. (2012a) Settling and moving: a biographical approach to interpreting patterns of occupation in LBA Circum-Alpine lake-dwellings, *Journal of Wetland Archaeology* 12, 1-21.

JENNINGS, B. (2012b) When the Going Gets Tough...? Climatic or Cultural Influences for the LBA Abandonment of Circum-Alpine Lake-Dwellings, in J. KNIESEL, W. KIRLEIS, M. DAL CORSO, N. TAYLOR & V. TIEDTKE (Eds.) *Collapse or Continuity? Environment and Development of Bronze Age Human Landscapes. Proceedings of the International Workshop "Socio-Environmental Dynamics over the Last 12,000 Years: The Creation of Landscapes II"*, Kiel: Rudolf Habelt. 85-99.

JENNINGS, B. (2014a) Repair, Recycle or Re-use? Creating mnemonic devices through the modification of object biographies, *Cambridge Archaeological Journal* 24 (1), 163-76.

JENNINGS, B. (2014b) *Travelling Objects : Changing Values. The role of northern Alpine lake-dwelling communities in exchange and communication networks during the Late Bronze Age*, Oxford: Archaeopress.

JIRÁŇ, L. (2002) *Die Messer in Böhmen*, Prähistorische Bronzefunde 7 / 5, Stuttgart: Franz Steiner Verlag.

JOCKENHÖVEL, A. (1971) *Die Rasiermesser in Mitteleuropa (Süddeutschland, Tschechoslowakei, Österreich, Schweiz)*, Prähistorische Bronzefunde 8 / 1, München: C. H. Beck'sche Verlagsbuchhandlung.

JOCKENHÖVEL, A. (1974) Zu befestigten Siedlungen der Urnenfelderzeit aus Süddeutschland, *Fundberichte aus Hessen* 14, 19-62.

JOCKENHÖVEL, A. (1985) Bronzezeitlicher Burgenbau in Mitteleuropa. Untersuchungen zur Struktur frühmetallzeitlicher Gesellschaften, in T. BADER (Ed.) *Orientalisch-ägäische Einflüsse in der europäischen Bronzezeit*, Bonn: Rudolf Habelt. 209-28.

JOHNSON, M. (1989) Conceptions of agency in archaeological interpretation, *Journal of Anthropological Archaeology* 8 (2), 189-211.

JONES, A. (2002) *Archaeological theory and scientific practice,* Cambridge: Cambridge University Press.

JONES, A. (2007a) *Memory and material culture,* Cambridge: Cambridge University Press.

JONES, M. R. (2007b) *Oxhide ingots, copper production, and the Mediterranean trade in copper and other metals in the Bronze Age*, unpublished thesis for Master of Arts, Anthropology, (Texas A&M).

JONES, R. E., LEVI, S. T. & BETTELLI, M. (2005) Mycenaean Pottery in the Central Mediterranean: imports, imitations and derivatives, in R. LAFFINEUR & E. GRECO (Eds.) *Emporia : Aegeans in the Central and Eastern Mediterranean*, Liège: Université de Liège. 539-45.

JONES, R. E., LEVI, S. T. & VAGNETTI, L. (2002) Connections between the Aegean and Italy in the Later Bronze Age: the ceramic evidence, in V. KILIKOGLOU, A. HEIN & Y. MANIATIS (Eds.) *Modern trends in scientific studies on ancient ceramics : papers presented at the 5th European Meeting on Ancient Ceramics*, Oxford: Archaeopress. 171-84.

JOY, J. (2009) Reinvigorating object biography: reproducing the drama of object lives, *World archaeology* 41 (4), 540-56.

JOY, J. (2010) *Iron age mirrors : a biographical approach,* Oxford: Archaeopress.

JUNG, R. & MARASZEK, R. (2005) The European Bronze Age from a Greek perspective?, in R. LAFFINEUR (Ed.) *L'âge du bronze en Europe et en Méditerranée : sessions générales et posters / The bronze age in Europe and the Mediterranean : general sessions and posters. Actes du XIVème Congrès UISPP*, Oxford: Archaeopress. 115-18.

JURIŠIĆ, M. (2000) *Ancient shipwrecks of the Adriatic : maritime transport during the first and second centuries AD,* Oxford: Archaeopress.

KAENEL, G. (1990) *Recherches sur la période de La Tène en Suisse occidentale : analyse des sépultures,* Lausanne: Bibliothèque historique vaudoise.

KAENEL, G. & KLAUSENER, M. (1990) Quelques tombes à incinération du Bronze final (Xe siècle av. J.-C.) à Vidy (Lausanne VD), *Jahrbuch der Schweizerischen Gesellschaft für Ur- und Frühgeschichte* 73 (51-82)

KAESER, M.-A. (2013) Wetland archaeology in the media and popular literature: loosening the scholarly taboos of the 20th century, in F. MENOTTI & A. O'SULLIVAN (Eds.) *The Oxford Handbook of Wetland Archaeology*, Oxford: Oxford University Press. 829-43.

KAUL, F. (1998) *Ships on bronzes : a study in bronze age religion and iconography,* Copenhagen: National Museum.

KAUL, F. (2004) Social and religious perceptions of the ship in Bronze Age Northern Europe, in P. CLARK (Ed.) *The Dover Bronze Age Boat in Context: Society and water transport in Prehistoric Europe*, Oxford: Oxbow Books. 122-37.

KELLER-TARNUZZER, K. (1937a) Bolligen, *Jahresbericht der Schweizerischen Gesellschaft für Urgeschichte* 9, 45-46.

KELLER-TARNUZZER, K. (1937b) IV. Bronzezeit: Niederösch, *Jahresbericht der Schweizerischen Gesellschaft für Urgeschichte* 29, 65.

KELLER, F. (1854) Die keltischen Pfahlbauten in den Schweizerseen, *Mitteilungen der Antiquarischen Gesellschaft in Zürich* 1, 65-100.

KELLY, K. G. (2010) Arenas of Action: Trade as Power, Trade as Identity, in A. A. BAUER & A. S. AGBE-DAVIES (Eds.) *Social Archaeologies of Trade and Exchange: Exploring Relationships among People, Places, and Things*, California: West Cost Press. 99-117.

KERNER, M. (2001) Mondhörner. Urgeschichtliche Messgeräte, *Helvetia Archaeologica* 32 (127/128), 82-136.

KERNER, M. (2004) Frühe astro-geodätische Messgeräte (II), *Geomatik Schweiz* 2004 (2), 67-75.

KERNER, M. (2007) Das Mondhorn vom Alpenquai Zürich, *Geomatik Schweiz* 2007 (2), 65-69.

KIMMIG, P. (1975) Early Celts on the upper Danube: the excavations at the Heuneburg, in R. L. S. BRUCE-MITFORD (Ed.) *Recent archaeological excavations in Europe*, London: Routledge & Kegan Paul. 32-64.

KIMMIG, W. (1992) *Die "Wasserburg Buchau" : eine spätbronzezeitliche Siedlung,* Stuttgart: Konrad Theiss.

KIMMIG, W. (2000a) *Die "Wasserburg Buchau" : Keramikfunde,* Stuttgart: Konrad Theiss.

KIMMIG, W. (Ed.) (2000b) *Importe und mediterrane Einflüsse auf der Heuneburg*, Mainz am Rhein: Philipp von Zabern.

KNAPPETT, C. (2002) Photographs, Skeuomorphs and Marionettes, *Journal of Material Culture* 7 (1), 97-117.

KOHL, P. L. (1981) Materialist Approaches in Prehistory, *Annual Review of Anthropology* 10 (1), 89-118.

KOLLER, H. (1998) Die Gräber der Späthallstattzeit im Freiamt (Kt. Aargau), *Jahrbuch der Schweizerischen Gesellschaft für Ur- und Frühgeschichte* 81, 119-70.

KÖNINGER, J. (1997) Gemusterte Tonobjekte aus der Ufersiedlung Bodman-Schachen I - Zur Verbreitung und Chronologie der sogenannten "Oggetti enigmatici", in B. FRITSCH (Ed.) *Tradition und Innovation : prähistorische Archäologie als historische Wissenschaft : Festschrift für Christian Strahm*, Rahden/Westf.: Verlag Marie Leidorf. 429-68.

KÖNINGER, J. (1998) Oggelshausen "Bruckgraben" - Eine hallstattzeitliche Siedlung im südlichen Federseemoor, Gemeinde Oggelshausen, Kreis Biberach, *Archäologische Ausgrabungen in Baden-Württemberg* 1997, 59-61.

KÖNINGER, J. (1999) Zum Fortgang der Untersuchungen in den hallstattzeitlichen Fundstellen im "Bruckgraben", Gemeinde Oggelshausen, Kreis Biberach, im südlichen Federseeried, *Archäologische Ausgrabungen in Baden-Württemberg* 1998, 95-99.

KÖNINGER, J. (2000) Von Fischen, Fallen und Faschinen. Neues aus den hallstattzeitlichen Fundstellen von Oggelshausen-Bruckgraben, Kreis Biberach, *Archäologische Ausgrabungen in Baden-Württemberg* 1999, 59-64.

KÖNINGER, J. (2001) Zum vorläufigen Abschluss der Sondagen in der eisenzeitlichen Fischfanganlage bei Oggelshausen-Bruckgraben, Kreis Biberach, *Archäologische Ausgrabungen in Baden-Württemberg* 2000, 59-62.

KÖNINGER, J. (2001/2002) Oggelshausen-Bruckgraben - Fund und Befunde aus einer eisenzeitlichen Fischfanganlage im südlichen Federseeried, Gde. Oggelshausen, Krs Biberach, *Heimat- und Altertumsverein Heidenheim an der Brenz e.V.* 2001/2002, 34-56.

KÖNINGER, J. (2006) *Die frühbronzezeitlichen Ufersiedlungen von Bodman-Schachen I : Befunde und Funde aus den Tauchsondagen 1982-1984 und 1986,* Stuttgart: Konrad Theiss.

KÖNINGER, J. (In Preparation) *Oggelshausen-Bruckgraben – eisenzeitliche Fischfanganlage im südlichen Federseeried. Befunde und Funde der Sondierungen und Rettungsgrabungen 1994 bis 2000,* Freiburg: Janus Verlag.

KÖNINGER, J. & SCHLICHTHERLE, H. (2001) Foreign Elements in South-West German Lake Dwellings: transalpine Relations in the Late Neolithic and Early Bronze Ages, *Preistoria Alpina* 35 (1999), 43-53.

KÖNINGER, J. & SCHÖBEL, G. (2010) Bronzeitliche Fundstellen zwischen Bodensee un Oberschwaben, in I. MATUSCHIK & C. STRAHM (Eds.) *Vernetzungen : Aspekte siedlungsarchäologischer Forschung : Festschrift für Helmut Schlichtherle zum 60. Geburtstag, Freiburg im Breisgau: Lavori.* 385-440.

KOPYTOFF, I. (1986) The Cultural biography of things: commoditization as process, in A. APPADURAI (Ed.) *The social life of things : commodities in cultural perspective,* Cambridge: Cambridge University Press. 64-91.

KOTTAK, C. P. (2009) *Window on humanity : a concise introduction to anthropology,* (4th edition), New York: McGraw Hill.

KRÄMER, W. (1985) *Die Vollgriffschwerter in Österreich und der Schweiz,* Prähistorische Bronzefunde 4 / 10, München: C. H. Beck.

KRAUSE, R. (2005) Bronzezeitliche Burgen in den Alpen. Befestigte Siedlungen der frühen bis mittleren Bronzezeit, in B. HÄNSEL & B. HOREJS (Eds.) *Interpretationsraum Bronzezeit : Bernhard Hänsel von seinen Schülern gewidmet,* Bonn: Rudolf Habelt. 389-413.

KRAUSE, R., EULER, D. & FUHRMANN, K. (2008) Der frühkeltische Fürstensitz auf dem Ipf bei Bopfingen im Nördlinger Ries (Ostalbkreis, Baden-Württemberg), in D. KRAUSSE (Ed.) *Frühe Zentralisierungs- und Urbanisierungsprozesse : zur Genese und Entwicklung frühkeltischer Fürstensitze und ihres territorialen Umlandes,* Stuttgart: Kommissionsverlag - Konrad Theiss Verlag. 249-79.

KREUZ, A. & SCHÄFER, E. (2008) Archäobotanische Ergebnisse zur Bronze- und Eisenzeit in Hessen, in D. KRAUSSE (Ed.) *Frühe Zentralisierungs- und Urbanisierungsprozesse : zur Genese und Entwicklung frühkeltischer Fürstensitze und ihres territorialen Umlandes. Kolloquium des DFG-Schwerpunktprogramms 1171,* Stuttgart: Kommissionsverlag - Konrad Theiss Verlag. 115-41.

KRISTIANSEN, K. (1993) From Villanova to Seddin. The Reconstruction of an Elite Exchange Network during the Eighth Century BC, in C. SCARRE & F. HEALY (Eds.) *Trade and exchange in Prehistoric Europe : proceedings of a conference held at the University of Bristol, April 1992*, Oxford: Oxbow Books in association with the Prehistoric Society and the Société Préhistorique Française. 143-51.

KRISTIANSEN, K. (1998a) *Europe before history*, Cambridge: Cambridge University Press.

KRISTIANSEN, K. (1998b) A theoretical strategy for the interpretation of exchange and interaction, in C. MORDANT, M. PERNOT & V. RYCHNER (Eds.) *L'Atelier du bronzier en Europe du XXe au VIIIe siècle avant notre ère : actes du colloque international "Bronze 96". III : Production, circulation et consomation du bronze*, Paris: Comité des Travaux Historiques et Scientifiques. 333-43.

KRISTIANSEN, K. (2002) The tale of the sword - swords and swordfighters in Bronze Age Europe, *Oxford Journal of Archaeology* 21 (4), 319-32.

KRISTIANSEN, K. & LARSSON, T. B. (2005) *The rise of Bronze Age society : travels, transmissions, and transformations*, Cambridge: Cambridge University Press.

KRISTIANSEN, K. & LARSSON, T. B. (2007) Contacts and travels during the 2nd Millenium BC. Warriors on the move, in I. GALANAKI, H. TOMAS, Y. GALANAKIS & R. LAFFINEUR (Eds.) *Between the Aegean and Baltic seas : prehistory across borders*, Liège: Université de Liège. 25-33.

KUBACH, W. (1973) *Die Nadeln in Hessen und Rheinhessen*, Prähistorische Bronzefunde 13 / 3, München: Beck.

KUBACH, W. (1994) Vergraben, versenkt, verbrannt - Opferfunde und Kultplätze, in A. JOCKENHÖVEL & W. KUBACH (Eds.) *Bronzezeit in Deutschland*, Stuttgart: Konrad Theiss. 65-74.

KÜCHLER, S. (1993) Landscape as Memory: The Mapping of Process and its Representation in a Melanesian Society, in B. BENDER (Ed.) *Landscape: politics and perspectives*, Providence: Berg. 85-106.

KUHLMANN, N. & SEGSCHNEIDER, M. (2004) Häuser, Gehöfte und Siedlungen der Bronzezeit, in T. LEHMANN, H. VON SCHMETTOW & J. P. SCHMIDT (Eds.) *Mythos und Magie: Archäologische Schätze der Bronzezeit aus Mecklenburg-Vorpommern*, Lübstorf: Archäologisches Landesmuseum und Landesamt für Bodendenkmalpflege Mecklenburg-Vorpommern. 68-73.

KUNTER, K. & HAEVERNICK, T. E. (1995) *Schichtaugenperlen*, Marburger Studien zur Vor- und Frühgeschichte 4, Espekamp: Verlag Marie Leidorf.

KÜNZLER WAGNER, N. (2005) *Zürich-Alpenquai V : Tauchgrabungen 1999-2001 : Funde und Befunde*, Zürich: Kantonsarchäologie.

KURZ, S. (2000) *Die Heuneburg-Aussensiedlung : Befunde und Funde*, Stuttgart: Konrad Theiss.

LAFFINEUR, R. & GRECO, E. (Eds.) (2005) *Emporia : Aegeans in the Central and Eastern Mediterranean : proceedings of the 10th International Aegean Conference: Athens, Italian School of Archaeology, 14-18 April 2004*, Liège: Université de Liège.

LAMOTTA, V. M. & SCHIFFER, M. B. (2001) Behavioural Archaeology: towards a new synthesis, in I. HODDER (Ed.) *Archaeological Theory Today*, Cambridge: Polity. 14-64.

LANG, A. & SALAČ, V. (Eds.) (2002) *Fernkontakte in der Eisenzeit*, Praha: Archäologisches Institut der Akademie der Wissenschaften der Tschechischen Republik.

LARSSON, L. (2001) South Scandinavian wetland sites and finds from the Mesolithic and the Neolithic, in B. A. PURDY (Ed.) *Enduring records: The environmental and cultural heritage of wetlands*, Oxford: Oxbow Books. 158-71.

LATOUR, B. (1999) *Pandora's hope : essays on the reality of science studies,* Cambridge (Mass.): Harvard University Press.

LEARY, J. (2009) Perceptions of and responses to the Holocene flooding of the North sea lowlands, *Oxford Journal of Archaeology* 28 (3), 227-37.

LEEMANN, A. & NIESSEN, F. (1994) Holocene glacial activity and climatic variations in the Swiss Alps: reconstructing a continuous record from proglacial lake sediments, *The Holocene* 4 (3), 259-68.

LEUZINGER, U. (2000) *Die jungsteinzeitliche Seeufersiedlung Arbon-Bleiche 3. Befunde,* Frauenfeld: Departement für Erziehung und Kultur des Kantons Thurgau.

LEUZINGER, U. (2001) Seesicht, verbaut... Leben im Pfahlbaudorf Arbon-Bleiche 3 vor 5400 Jahren, *Plattform* 9-10, 94-96.

LEUZINGER, U. (2010) Jungsteinzeit, in AMT FÜR ARCHÄOLOGIE THURGAU (Ed.) *Archäologie im Thurgau*, Frauenfeld: Huber. 85-105.

LÉVI-STRAUSS, C. (1989) *The savage mind,* (5th edition), London: Weidenfeld & Nicolson.

LI PUMA, E. (1998) Modernity and forms of personhood in Melanesia, in M. LAMBEK & A. STRATHERN (Eds.) *Bodies and persons : comparative perspectives from Africa and Melanesia,* Cambridge: Cambridge University Press. 53-79.

LIDDIARD, R. (2005) *Castles in context : power, symbolism and landscape, 1066-1500,* Macclesfield: Windgather Press.

LILLIOS, K. T. & TSAMIS, V. (Eds.) (2010) *Material Mnemonics: everyday memory in Prehistoric Europe,* Oxford: Oxbow Books.

LLOBERA, M. (2001) Building Past Landscape Perception With GIS: Understanding Topographic Prominence, *Journal of Archaeological Science* 28 (9), 1005-14.

LÜNING, J. & VON KAENEL, H.-M. (2006) *Ausgrabungen zur Bandkeramik, Bronze- und Römerzeit in Bad Homburg v.d.H. - Ober-Erlenbach 2001-2002,* Bonn: Habelt.

LÜSCHER, G. (1985) Die Grabhügel in der Muttenzer und Pratteler Hard bei Basel : eine Neubearbeitung, *Basler Zeitschrift für Geschichte und Altertumskunde* 85, 5-84.

LÜSCHER, G. (1986) *Allschwil-Vogelgärten : eine hallstattzeitliche Talsiedlung,* Liestal: Amt für Museum und Archäologie des Kantons Baselland.

LÜSCHER, G. (1989) Die hallstattzeitliche Nekropole von Subingen SO: bemerkungen zum belegungsablauf, *Archäologie des Kantons Solothurn* 6, 101-18.

LÜSCHER, G. (1991) Frühkeltische "Fürstensitze" in der Schweiz, *Archäologie der Schweiz* 14 (1), 68-74.

LÜSCHER, G. (1993) *Unterlunkhofen und die hallstattzeitliche Grabkeramik in der Schweiz,* Basel: Verlag Schweizerische Gesellschaft für Ur- und Frühgeschichte.

LÜSCHER, G. & MÜLLER, F. (1999) Gräber und Kult, in F. MÜLLER, G. KAENEL & G. LÜSCHER (Eds.) *SPM IV Eisenzeit: Die Schweiz vom Paläolithikum bis zum frühen Mittelalter*, Basel: Verlag Schweizerische Gesellschaft für Ur- und Frühgeschichte. 249-82.

MÄDER, A. (2001) *Die spätbronzezeitliche Seeufersiedlung Zürich-Alpenquai 1: Die Metallfunde : Baggerungen von 1916-1919,* Zürich: Baudirektion Kanton Zürich, Hochbauamt, Kantonsarchäologie.

MÄDER, A. (2002) *Die spätbronzezeitlichen und spätlatènezeitlichen Brandstellen und Brandbestattungen in Elgg (Kanton Zürich) : Untersuchungen zu Kremation und Bestattungsbrauchtum,* Zürich: Baudirektion Kanton Zürich.

MAGNY, M. (1992) Holocene lake-level fluctuations in Jura and the northern subalpine ranges, France: regional pattern and climatic implications, *Boreas* 21 (4), 319-34.

MAGNY, M. (1995) *Une histoire du climat, des derniers mammouths au siècle de l'automobile,* Paris: Editions Errance.

MAGNY, M. (2004a) The contribution of palaeoclimatology to the lake-dwellings, in F. MENOTTI (Ed.) *Living on the lake in prehistoric Europe : 150 years of lake-dwelling research*, London: Routledge. 132-43.

MAGNY, M. (2004b) Holocene climate variability as reflected by mid-European lake-level fluctuations and its probable impact on prehistoric human settlements, *Quaternary International* 113 (1), 65-79.

MAGNY, M. (2013a) Orbital, ice-sheet, and possible solar forcing of Holocene lake-level fluctuations in west-central Europe: A comment on Bleicher, *The Holocene* 23 (8), 1202-12.

MAGNY, M. (2013b) Palaeoclimatology and archaeology in the wetlands, in F. MENOTTI & A. O'SULLIVAN (Eds.) *The Oxford Handbook of Wetland Archaeology*, Oxford: Oxford University Press. 585-97.

MAGNY, M., LEROUX, A., BICHET, V., GAUTHIER, E., RICHARD, H. & WALTER-SIMONNET, A.-V. (2013) Climate, vegetation and land use as drivers of Holocene sedimentation: A case study from Lake Saint-Point (Jura Mountains, eastern France), *The Holocene* 23 (1), 137-47.

MAGNY, M., MAISE, C., JACOMET, S. & BURGA, C. A. (1998) Klimaschwankungen im Verlauf der Bronzezeit, in S. HOCHULI, U. NIFFELER & V. RYCHNER (Eds.) *SPM III Bronzezeit: Die Schweiz vom Paläolithikum bis zum frühen Mittelalter*, Basel: Verlag Schweizerische Gesellschaft für Ur- und Frühgeschichte. 135-40.

MAGNY, M. & PEYRON, O. (2008) Variations climatiques et histoire des sociétés à l'Âge du bronze au nord et au sud des Alpes, in J. GUILAINE (Ed.) *Villes, villages, campagnes de l'âge du bronze*, Paris: Editions Errance. 161-76.

MAGNY, M., PEYRON, O., GAUTHIER, É., ROUÈCHE, Y., BORDON, A., BILLAUD, Y., CHAPRON, E., MARGUET, A., PÉTREQUIN, P. & VANNIÈRE, B. (2009) Quantitative reconstruction of climatic variations during the Bronze and early Iron ages based on pollen and lake-level data in the NW Alps, France, *Quaternary International* 200 (1-2), 102-10.

MAIER, F. B. (1986) Die urnenfelderzeitlichen Brandgräber von Möhlin-Niederriburg AG. Grabungsbericht, *Jahrbuch der Schweizerischen Gesellschaft für Ur- und Frühgeschichte* 69, 105-19.

MAINBERGER, M. & MAINBERGER, C. (2010) Grenzland? Zum Naturraum und zu den Anfängen bäuerlicher Kultur zwischen Argen und Bodensee, in I. MATUSCHIK & C. STRAHM (Eds.) *Vernetzungen : Aspekte siedlungsarchäologischer Forschung : Festschrift für Helmut Schlichtherle zum 60. Geburtstag*, Freiburg im Breisgau: Lavori. 331-44.

MAISE, C. (1999) Klima, Umwelt, Landwirtschaft und Ernährung, in F. MÜLLER, G. KAENEL & G. LÜSCHER (Eds.) *SPM IV Eisenzeit: Die Schweiz vom Paläolithikum bis zum frühen Mittelalter*, Basel: Verlag Schweizerische Gesellschaft für Ur- und Frühgeschichte. 93-97.

MAISE, C. & ENDERLE, A. (2000) Stratigrafische Beobachtungen auf der ehemaligen Rheininsel von Bad Säckingen, Kreis Waldshut, *Archäologische Ausgrabungen in Baden-Württemberg* 1999, 52-53.

MALINOWSKI, B. (1922) *Argonauts of the Western Pacific*, London: George Routledge.

MARAZZI, M. (2003) The Mycenaeans in the Western Mediterranean (17th - 13th c. BC), in N. C. STAMPOLIDIS (Ed.) *Sea routes ... from Sidon to Huelva : interconnections in the Mediterranean 16th - 6th c. BC*, Athens: Museum of Cycladic Art. 108-15.

MARCUS, J. (2000) Toward an archaeology of communities, in M. A. CANUTO & J. YAEGER (Eds.) *The Archaeology of communities : a new world perspective*, London: Routledge. 231-42.

MARSHALL, Y. (2000) Transformations of Nuu-chah-nulth Houses, in R. A. JOYCE & S. D. GILLESPIE (Eds.) *Beyond kinship : social and material reproduction in house societies*, Philadelphia: University of Pennsylvania Press. 73-102.

MARTIN, J. (2009) *Die Bronzegefässe in Mecklenburg-Vorpommern, Brandenburg, Berlin, Sachsen-Anhalt, Thüringen und Sachsen*, Prähistorische Bronzefunde 2 / 16, Stuttgart: Franz Steiner.

MATT, C. (2012) Basel BS, Utengasse 15/17 (2011/21), *Jahrbuch Archäologie Schweiz* 95, 167-68.

MATZERATH, S. (2009) Feuerböcke und Mondidole aus Gräbern – Ein Beitrag zum Symbolgut der späten Bronze- und frühen Eisenzeit Mitteleuropas, *Archäologische Informationen* 32 (1 & 2), 165-72.

MATZERATH, S. (2011) „Feuerbock" und „Mondidol" in der späten Urnenfelderzeit. Zur kulturgeschichtlichen Bedeutung eines Symbolträgers und seinen frühesten Belegen in der Beigabensitte, in K. SCHMOTZ (Ed.) *Vorträge des 29. Niederbayerischen Archäologentages*, Rahden, Westf.: Verlag Marie Leidorf. 95-138.

MATZERATH, S. (2012) Religiöse Identität in der späten Bronze- und frühen Eisenzeit – Ein Fallbeispiel, in C. TAPPERT, C. KLATER, J. FRIES-KNOBLACH, P. C. RAMSL, P. TREBSCHE, S. WEFERS & J. WIETHOLD (Eds.) *Wege und Transport. Beiträge zur Sitzung der AG Eisenzeit während der 80. Verbandstagung des West- und Süddeutschen Verbandes für Altertumsforschung e.V. in Nürnberg 2010*: 221-33.

MAUVILLY, M. (2008) L'âge du Bronze, in J.-L. BOISAUBERT, D. BUGNON & M. MAUVILLY (Eds.) *Archéologie et autoroute A1, destins croisés : 25 années de fouilles en terres fribourgeoises, premier bilan (1975-2000)*, Fribourg: Service archéologique de l'Etat de Fribourg. 347-70.

MAUVILLY, M., ANTENEN, I., BROMBACHER, C., GASSMANN, P., GUÉLAT, M., MORINA-CURTY, L., OLIVE, C., PILLONEL, D., RICHOZ, I. & STUDER, J. (1997) Frasses "Praz au Doux" (FR), un site du Hallstatt ancien en bordure de rivière, *Archäologie Schweiz* 20 (3), 112-25.

MAUVILLY, M. & RUFFIEUX, M. (2008) Frasses/Praz au Doux, in J.-L. BOISAUBERT, D. BUGNON & M. MAUVILLY (Eds.) *Archéologie et autoroute A1, destins croisés : 25 années de fouilles en terres fribourgeoises, premier bilan (1975-2000)*, Fribourg: Service archéologique de l'Etat de Fribourg. 204-11.

MAYEWSKI, P. A., ROHLING, E. E., CURT STAGER, J., KARLÉN, W., MAASCH, K. A., DAVID MEEKER, L., MEYERSON, E. A., GASSE, F., VAN KREVELD, S., HOLMGREN, K., LEE-THORP, J., ROSQVIST, G., RACK, F., STAUBWASSER, M., SCHNEIDER, R. R. & STEIG, E. J. (2004) Holocene climate variability, *Quaternary Research* 62 (3), 243-55.

MÉDARD, F. (2011) Switzerland: Neolithic Period, in M. GLEBA & U. MANNERING (Eds.) *Textiles & Textile Production Europe : From Prehistory to AD 400*, Oxford: Oxbow Books. 367-77.

MENOTTI, F. (2001a) *"The missing period" : Middle Bronze Age lake-dwellings in the Alps*, Oxford: Archaeopress.

MENOTTI, F. (2001b) The *Pfahlbauproblem* and the History of Lake-Dwelling Research in the Alps, *Oxford Journal of Archaeology* 20 (4), 319-28.

MENOTTI, F. (2003) Cultural response to environmental change in the Alpine lacustrine regions: the displacement model, *Oxford Journal of Archaeology* 22 (4), 375-96.

MENOTTI, F. (2004a) Displacement, readaptation, and cultural continuity, a lake-dwelling perspective, in F. MENOTTI (Ed.) *Living on the lake in prehistoric Europe : 150 years of lake-dwelling research*, London: Routledge. 207-17.

MENOTTI, F. (2004b) Introduction: the lake-dwelling phenomenon and wetland archaeology, in F. MENOTTI (Ed.) *Living on the lake in prehistoric Europe : 150 years of lake-dwelling research*, London: Routledge. 1-6.

MENOTTI, F. (Ed.) (2004c) *Living on the lake in prehistoric Europe : 150 years of lake-dwelling research*, London: Routledge.

MENOTTI, F. (2009) Climate variations in the Circum-Alpine region and their influence on Neolithic-Bronze Age lacustrine communities: displacement and/or cultural adaptation, in M. BUDJA (Ed.) *Documenta Praehistorica XXXVI*, Ljubljana: Faculty of Art, Univeristy of Ljubljana. 61-66.

MENOTTI, F. (2012) *Wetland Archaeology and Beyond: Theory and Practice,* Oxford: Oxford University Press.

MENOTTI, F. (In Press) The lake-dwelling phenomenon: myth, reality and…archaeology, in F. MENOTTI (Ed.) *The end of the lake-dwellings in the Circum-Alpine region*, Oxford: Oxbow Books.

MENOTTI, F., JENNINGS, B. & GOLLNISCH-MOOS, H. (2014) 'Gifts for the Gods': lake-dwellers' macabre remedies against floods in the central European Bronze Age, *Antiquity* 88 (340), 456-69.

MENOTTI, F. & PRANCKĖNAITĖ, E. (2008) Lake-dwelling building techniques in prehistory: driving wooden piles into lacustrine sediments, *euroREA* 5, 3-7.

MILLER, D. (1982) Structures and strategies: an aspect of the relationship between social hierarchy and cultural change, in I. HODDER (Ed.) *Symbolic and structural archaeology*, Cambridge: Cambridge University Press. 89-98.

MILLER, D. (Ed.) (1998) *Material cultures: why some things matter*, London: UCL Press.

MÖDLINGER, M. (2011) *Herstellung und Verwendung bronzezeitlicher Schwerter Mitteleuropas : eine vertiefende Studie zur mittelbronze- und urnenfelderzeitlichen Bewaffnung und Sozialstruktur,* Bonn: Rudolf Habelt.

MOHEN, J.-P. (1977) Broches à rôtir articulées de l'Age du Bronze, *Antiquités Nationales* 9, 34-39.

MOINAT, P. & DAVID-ELBIALI, M. (2003) *Défunts, bûchers et céramiques : la nécropole de Lausanne-Vidy (VD) et les pratiques funéraires sur le Plateau suisse du XIe au VIIIe s.av.J.-C,* Lausanne: Cahiers d'archéologie romande.

MONAGHAN, J. (1998) The Person, Destiny, and the Construction of Difference in Mesoamerica, *RES: Anthropology and Aesthetics* 33, 137-46.

MONNA, F., JEBRANE, A., GABILLOT, M., LAFFONT, R., SPECHT, M., BOHARD, B., CAMIZULI, E., PETIT, C., CHATEAU, C. & ALIBERT, P. (2013) Morphometry of Middle Bronze Age palstaves. Part II – spatial distribution of shapes in two typological groups, implications for production and exportation, *Journal of Archaeological Science* 40 (1), 507-16.

MOORE, H. (1987) Problems in the analysis of social change: an example from the Marakwet, in I. HODDER (Ed.) *Archaeology as long-term history*, Cambridge: Cambridge University Press. 85-104.

MOORE, T. (2007) Percieving Communities: exchange, landscapes and social networks in the later Iron Age of western Britain, *Oxford Journal of Archaeology* 26 (1), 79-102.

MORAN, E. F. (2000) *Human adaptability: An introduction to ecological anthropology,* Boulder: Westview.

MORGENROTH, U. (1999) Southern Iberia and the Mediterranean Trade-routes, *Oxford Journal of Archaeology* 18 (4), 395-401.

MÖSLEIN, S. (1998/99) Siedlung, Depotfund und Gräberfeld der Urnenfelderzeit auf der Innterrasse am Fusse der Rachelburg bei Flintsbach a. Inn, LKR Rosenheim, *Bericht der Bayerischen Bodendenkmalpflege* 39/40, 331-48.

MÜHLETHALER, H. (1967) Die Ur- und Frühgeschtichlichen funde von Wangen an der Aare, *Jahrbuch des Oberaargaus* 10, 25-46.

MÜLLER, F. (1993) Argumente zu einer Deutung von "Pfahlbaubronzen", *Jahrbuch der Schweizerischen Gesellschaft für Ur- und Frühgeschichte* 76, 71-92.

MÜLLER, F., KAENEL, G. & LÜSCHER, G. (Eds.) (1999) *SPM IV Eisenzeit: Die Schweiz vom Paläolithikum bis zum frühen Mittelalter*, Basel: Verlag Schweizerische Gesellschaft für Ur- und Frühgeschichte.

MÜLLER, F. & KÖNIG, F. E. (1990) *Der Massenfund von der Tiefenau bei Bern : zur Deutung latènezeitlicher Sammelfunde mit Waffen*, Basel: Verlag Schweizerische Gesellschaft für Ur- und Frühgeschichte.

MULLIN, D. (2012) The river has never divided us: Bronze Age metalwork deposition in western Britain, *Oxford Journal of Archaeology* 31 (1), 47-57.

MUNN, N. D. (1986) *The fame of Gawa : a symbolic study of value transformation in a Massim (Papua New Guinea) society*, Cambridge: Cambridge University Press.

NAGLER-ZANIER, C. (1999) *Die hallstattzeitliche Siedlung mit Grabenanlage von Geiselhöring, Niederbayern*, Büchenbach: Verlag Dr. Faustus.

NAGY, G. (1999) *Keramik und Kleinfunde der spätestbronzezeitlichen Siedlung*, Archäologie im Thurgau 6, Frauenfeld: Departement für Erziehung und Kultur des Kantons Thurgau.

NASH BRIGGS, D. (2003) Metals, Salt, and Slaves: Economic Links Between Gaul and Italy From the Eighth to the Late Sixth Centuries BC, *Oxford Journal of Archaeology* 22 (3), 243-59.

NEBELSICK, L. (2000) Rent asunder: ritual violence in Late Bronze Age hoards, in C. F. E. PARE (Ed.) *Metals make the world go round : the supply and circulation of metals in Bronze Age Europe*, Oxford: Oxbow Books. 160-75.

NEEDHAM, S. P. & BOWMAN, S. (2005) Flesh-hooks, technological complexity and the Atlantic Bronze Age feasting complex, *European Journal of Archaeology* 8 (2), 93-136.

NEUSTUPNÝ, E. (1998) Structures and events: the theoretical basis of spatial archaeology, in E. NEUSTUPNÝ (Ed.) *Space in prehistoric Bohemia*, Praha: Institute of Archaeology, Academy of Sciences of the Czech Republic. 9-44.

NICOLAS, I. (2003) Au fil du rasoir: étude des rasoirs métalliques de l'âge du Bronze jusqu'a haut Moyen Age en Suisse, in M. BESSE, L.-I. STAHL GRETSCH & P. CURDY (Eds.) *ConstellaSion. Hommage à Alain Gallay*, Lausanne: Cahiers d'archéologie romande. 273-89.

NYMOEN, P. (2008) Boats for Rivers and Mountains: Sources for New Narratives about River Travel?, *International Journal of Nautical Archaeology* 37 (1), 3-16.

ODNER, K. (1983) Reflection or Autonomy. Thoughts on European Cultural Development, *Norwegian archaeological review* 16, 1-13.

OKA, R. & KUSIMBA, C. (2008) The Archaeology of Trading Systems, Part 1: Towards a New Trade Synthesis, *Journal of Archaeological Research* 16 (4), 339-95.

OSTERWALDER, C. (1982) Oberbipp, Hasenrain, *Jahrbuch des Bernischen Historischen Museums* 61-62, 29.

PALAFITTES (2010) UNESCO World Heritage Candidature "Prehistoric Pile Dwellings around the Alps": Database Palafittes_v3, in PALAFITTES CD *"Pfahlbauten"*, Neuchâtel: Office et Musee d'archeologie Neuchâtel.

PALAFITTES (2011) *Palafittes Guide*; available online at *http://www.palafittes.org/de/pfahlbauten-besuchen/palafittes-guide/index.html.* [accessed 09-07-2014].

PALAVESTRA, A. (2007) Was there an amber route?, in I. GALANAKI, H. TOMAS, Y. GALANAKIS & R. LAFFINEUR (Eds.) *Between the Aegean and Baltic seas : prehistory across borders*, Liège: Université de Liège. 349-56.

PAPE, J. (2000) Die attische Keramik der Heuneburg und der keramische Südimport in der Zone nördlich der Alpen während der Hallstattzeit, in W. KIMMIG & E. BÖHR (Eds.) *Importe und mediterrane Einflüsse auf der Heuneburg*, Mainz am Rhein: Philipp von Zabern. 71-175.

PARE, C. F. E. (1991) Fürstensitze, Celts and the Mediterranean World: Developments in the West Hallstatt Culture in the 6th and 5th Centuries BC, *Proceedings of the Prehistoric Society* 57 (2), 183-202.

PARE, C. F. E. (1992) *Wagons and wagon-graves of the Early Iron Age in Central Europe*, Oxford: Oxford University Committee for Archaeology.

PARE, C. F. E. (1999) Weights and Weighing in Bronze Age Central Europe, in RÖMISCH-GERMANISCHES ZENTRALMUSEUM (MAINZ). KOLLOQUIUM (Ed.) *Eliten in der Bronzezeit*, Bonn: Habelt. 421-514.

PARE, C. F. E. (2013) Weighing, commodification, and money, in H. FOKKENS & A. F. HARDING (Eds.) *The Oxford handbook of the European Bronze Age*, Oxford: Oxford University Press. 508-27.

PARET, O. (1926-28) Neue Funde im Steinhauser Ried bei Schussenried, *Fundberichte aus Schwaben. Neue Folge* 4, 52-58.

PARET, O. (1942) Die Pfahlbauten. Ein Nachruf, *Schriften des Verein für Geschichte des Bodensees* 68, 75-84.

PARKER PEARSON, M. (1999) *The archaeology of death and burial*, Thrupp Stroud: Sutton Publishing.

PARZINGER, H. (1995) The Beginning of La Tène Culture in Central Europe, in J. D. HILL & C. G. CUMBERPATCH (Eds.) *Different Iron Ages : studies on the Iron Age in temperate Europe*, Oxford: Tempvs Reparatvm. 95-110.

PÁSZTHORY, K. (1985) *Der bronzezeitliche Arm- und Beinschmuck in der Schweiz*, Prähistorische Bronzefunde 10 / 3, München: C. H. Beck.

PATZEL, G. (1977) Der zeitliche Ablauf und das Ausmass postglazialer Klimaschwankungen in der Alpen, *Erdwissenschaftliche Forschung* 13, 248-59.

PAYNE, A., CORNEY, M., BURTON, N. & CUNLIFFE, B. W. (2006) *The Wessex hillforts project : extensive survey of hillfort interiors in central southern England*, London: English Heritage.

PEARCE, M. (1995) Exchange Northwards from Peninsular Italy in the First Millenium BC: the Western Po Plain and the Alpine Passes, in J. SWADDLING, P. ROBERTS & S. WALKER (Eds.) *Italy in Europe: economic relations 700 BC - AD 50*, London: British Museum. Department of Greek and Roman Antiquities. 145-57.

PERNET, L. & SCHMID-SIKIMIĆ, B. (2008) Les fers de lances à douilles facettées de la fin de l'age du Brandopferplatz de Wartau-Ochsenberg (Cant. Saint-Gall, Suisse), *Archäologisches Korrespondenzblatt* 38 (3), 365-77.

PÉTREQUIN, P. (1984) *Gens de l'eau, gens de la terre : ethno-archéologie des communautés lacustres,* Paris: Librairie Hachette.

PÉTREQUIN, P. (2011) La circolazione delle grandi asce in pietra verde delle Alpi, nell'Europa tra il VI e il IV millennio a.C., in F. MARZATICO, R. GEBHARD & P. GLEIRSCHER (Eds.) *Le grandi vie delle civiltà : relazioni e scambi fra Mediterraneo e il centro Europa dalla preistoria alla romanità*, Trento: Castello del Buonconsiglio, Monumenti e collezioni provinciali. 79-81.

PÉTREQUIN, P. (2013) Lake-dwellings in the Alpine region, in F. MENOTTI & A. O'SULLIVAN (Eds.) *The Oxford Handbook of Wetland Archaeology*, Oxford: Oxford University Press. 253-67.

PÉTREQUIN, P. & BAILLY, M. (2004) Lake-dwelling research in France: from climate to demography, in F. MENOTTI (Ed.) *Living on the lake in prehistoric Europe : 150 years of lake-dwelling research*, London: Routledge. 36-49.

PÉTREQUIN, P., MAGNY, M. & BAILLY, M. (2005) Habitat lacustre, densité de population et climat - L'example du Jura français, in P. DELLA CASA & M. TRACHSEL (Eds.) *WES'04 - Wetland Economies and Societies*, Zurich: Chronos. 143-68.

PICCOLI, A. & PERONI, R. (1992) Per una ricostruzione della sequenza cronologica dell'isolone del mincio nell'ambito dell'età del bronzo padana, in G. BARTOLI, M. BARTOLI, P. CAVICCHI, F. FEDELI, A. GALIBERTI, S. GELICHI, L. GIANNONI, P. GORINI & M. RICCI (Eds.) *Rassegna di Archaeologia (10): L'Età del Bronzo in Italia nei secoli dal XVI al XIV a.c.*, Firenze: All'Insegna Del Giglio. 295-317.

PILLONEL, D. (2007) *Hauterives-Champréveyres 14: Technologie et usage du bois au Bronze final,* Neuchâtel: Office et musée cantonal d'archéologie de Neuchâtel.

POLLA, A., ANGELINI, I., ARTIOLI, G., BELLINTANI, P. & DORE, A. (2011) Archaeometric Investigation of Early Iron Age Glasses from Bologna, in I. TURBANTI-MEMMI (Ed.) *Proceedings of the 37th International Symposium on Archaeometry*, Berlin: Springer. 139-44.

PONCET SCHMID, M., SCHOPFER, A., NIŢU, C., RYCHNER-FARAGGI, A.-M., NUOFFER, P. & BLOMJOUS, C. (2013) *Les occupations de l'âge du Bronze final: Onnens-Le Moti, La Golette, Beau Site,* Lausanne: Cahiers d'archéologie romande.

POTREBICA, H. (2008) Contacts between Greece and Pannonia in the Early Iron Age - with special concern to the area of Thessalonica, in P. F. BIEHL & Y. Y. RASSAMAKIN (Eds.) *Import and imitation in archaeology*, Langenweissbach: Beier & Beran. 187-212.

POUSAZ, N., ELYAQTINE, M., GUÉLAT, M. & MARCHAND, K. (2000) Delémont JU-En La Pran. De l'âge du Bronze au Moyen Age. Une nécropole du Bronze final dans son environnement archéologique et sédimentaire, *Jahrbuch der Schweizerischen Gesellschaft für Ur- und Frühgeschichte* 83, 79-94.

POUSAZ, N., TAILLARD, P. & SCHENARDI, M. (1994) *Sites protohistoriques à Courfaivre et âge du Bronze dans le Jura,* Porrentruy: Office du patrimoine historique et Société jurassienne d'émulation.

PRIMAS, M. (1970) *Die südschweizerischen Grabfunde der älteren Eisenzeit und ihre Chronologie,* Basel: Birkhäuser.

PRIMAS, M. (1971) Der Beginn der Spätbronzezeit im Mittelland und Jura, in W. DRACK (Ed.) *Ur- und frühgeschichtliche Archäologie der Schweiz III*, Basel: Verlag Schweizerische Gesellschaft für Ur- und Frühgeschichte. 55.

PRIMAS, M. (1977) Beobachtungen zu den spätbronzezeitlichen Siedlungs- und Depotfunden der Schweiz, in K. STÜBER & A. ZÜRCHER (Eds.) *Festschrift Walter Drack zu seinem 60. Geburtstag*, Zürich: Th. Gut & Co. 44-55.

PRIMAS, M. (1986) *Die Sicheln in Mitteleuropa I (Österreich, Schweiz, Süddeutschland)*, Prähistorische Bronzefunde 18 / 2, München: C. H. Beck.

PRIMAS, M. (2004) Wirtschaft und Gessellschaft urnenfelderzeitlicher Seeufersiedlungen - eine Aktualisierung, in B. HÄNSEL (Ed.) *Parerga Praehistorica : Jubiläumsschrift zur Prähistorischen Archäologie : 15 Jahre UPA*, Bonn: R. Habelt. 113-33.

PRIMAS, M. (2008) *Bronzezeit zwischen Elbe und Po : Strukturwandel in Zentraleuropa 2200-800 v. Chr,* Bonn: Verlag Habelt.

PRIMAS, M., DELLA CASA, P. & SCHMID-SIKIMIĆ, B. (1992) *Archäologie zwischen Vierwaldstättersee und Gotthard : Siedlungen und Funde der ur- und frühgeschichtlichen Epochen,* Bonn: Rudolf Habelt.

PRIMAS, M. & PERNICKA, E. (1998) Der Depotfund von Oberwilflingen, *Germania* 76 (1), 25-65.

PRIMAS, M. & SCHMID-SIKIMIĆ, B. (1997) Interaction Across the Alps, in ISTITUTO ITALIANO DI PREISTORIA E PROTOSTORIA (Ed.) *La Valle D'Aosta nel quadro della preistoria e protostoria dell'arco alpino centro-occidentale*, Firenze: Istituto Italiano di Preistoria e Protostoria 455-474.

PRIMAS, M., TAROT, J., MEIER, W., SCHMID-SIKIMIĆ, B. & FANKHAUSER, C. (1989) *Eschenz Insel Werd 4: Die Keramik der Spätbronzezeit,* Zürich: Abt. Ur- und Frühgeschichte der Universität Zürich.

PRÜSSING, P. (1982) *Die Messer im nördlichen Westdeutschland (Schleswig-Holstein, Hamburg und Niedersachsen)*, Prähistorische Bronzefunde 7 / 3, München: C. H. Beck.

PULAK, C. (1998) The Uluburun shipwreck: an overview, *International Journal of Nautical Archaeology* 27 (3), 188-224.

PYDYN, A. (1998) Universal or relative? Social, economic and symbolic values in central Europe in the transition from the Bronze Age to the Iron Age, in D. W. BAILEY (Ed.) *The archaeology of value: essays on prestige and the processes of valuation*, Oxford: Hedges. 97-105.

PYDYN, A. (1999) *Exchange and cultural interactions : a study of long-distance trade and cross-cultural contacts in the Late Bronze Age and Early Iron Age in Central and Eastern Europe,* Oxford: Archaeopress.

PYDYN, A. (2010) Archeologiczne penetracje podwodne strefy przybrżnej Jeziora Powidzkiego, in A. PYDYN (Ed.) *Archeologia Jeziora Powidzkiego*, Toruń: Wydawnictwo Naukowe Uniwersytetu Mikołaja Kopernika. 15-39.

PYDYN, A. & GACKOWSKI, J. (2011) Wetland archaeology of the Late Bronze Age and the Early Iron Age settlements from Poland, in E. PRANCKĖNAITĖ (Ed.) *Wetland settlements of the Baltic. A prehistoric perspective*, Vilnius: Centre of Underwater Archaeology. 123-39.

QUILLFELDT, I. V. (1995) *Die Vollgriffschwerter in Süddeutschland*, Prähistorische Bronzefunde 4 / 11, Stuttgart: Franz Steiner.

RACHOUD-SCHNEIDER, A.-M. (2009) Analyse palynologique des dépôts protohistoriques de Délemont - En La Pran, in N. POUSAZ, M. GUÉLAT, L. FREI PAROZ & V. PIUZ LOUBIER (Eds.) *Delémont - En La Pran 1 (Jura, Suisse). Environnement alluvial et premières installations humaines entre Mésolithique réecent at âge du Bronze*, Porrentruy: Office de la culture : Société jurassienne d'émulation. 91-99.

RAGETH, J. (1976) Die bronzezeitliche Siedlung auf dem Padnal bei Savognin (Oberhalbstein GR), Grabungen 1971 und 1972, *Jahrbuch der Schweizerischen Gesellschaft für Ur- und Frühgeschichte* 59, 123-79.

RAGETH, J. (1986) Die wichtigsten Resultate der Ausgrabungen in der bronzezeitlichen Siedlung auf dem Padnal bei Savognin (Oberhalbstein GR), *Jahrbuch der Schweizerischen Gesellschaft für Ur- und Frühgeschichte* 69, 63-104.

RALSTON, I. (1995) Fortifications and Defence, in M. J. GREEN (Ed.) *The Celtic World*, London: Routledge. 59-81.

RAMSTEIN, M. (2005a) Ipsach - Räberain. Spätbronzezeitliche Siedlungen und römischer Gutshof, *Archäologie im Kanton Bern* 6, 569-614.

RAMSTEIN, M. (2005b) Pieterlen, Vorem Holz 3, *Archäologie im Kanton Bern* 6 (1), 102.

RAMSTEIN, M. (2010) Attiswil, Wybrunne. Fundmaterial einer hallstattzeitlichen Siedlung, *Archäologie Bern* 2010, 199-220.

RAMSTEIN, M. (2012) Kernenried, Oberholz. Gräber der Hallstattzeit, *Archäologie Bern* 2012, 95-134.

RAMSTEIN, M. & CUENI, A. (2005) Koppigen - Usserfeld. Spätbronzezeitliche Gräber, *Archäologie im Kanton Bern* 6 (b), 547-58.

REDFIELD, R., LINTON, R. & HERSKOVITS, M. J. (1936) Memorandum for the study of acculturation, *American Anthropologist* 38 (1), 149-52.

REDKNAP, M. (2006) Lake dwellings in Wales: reflections on legends, historical events and archaeology, in A. HAFNER, U. NIFFELER & U. RUOFF (Eds.) *Die neue Sicht : Unterwasserarchäologie und Geschichtsbild : Akten des 2. Internationalen Kongresses für Unterwasserarchäologie,* Basel: Archäologie Schweiz. 88-91.

REINBOLD, A. L. (1957) Saint-Prex, distr. Morges, VD, *Jahrbuch der Schweizerischen Gesellschaft für Urgeschichte* 46, 103.

REINERTH, H. (1928) *Die Wasserburg Buchau : eine befestigte Inselsiedlung aus der Zeit 100-800 v. Chr,* Augsburg: Benno Filser.

REINERTH, H. (1932) *Das Pfahlbaudorf Sipplingen am Bodensee,* Leipzig: Rosch Verlag.

RENFREW, C. (Ed.) (1973) *The explanation of culture change : models in prehistory,* London: Duckworth.

RENFREW, C. (1975) Trade as Action at a Distance: Questions of Integration and Communication, in J. A. SABLOFF & C. C. LAMBERG-KARLOVSKY (Eds.) *Ancient civilization and trade,* Albuquerque: University of New Mexico Press. 3-59.

RENFREW, C. (1984a) Culture Systems and the Multiplier Effect, in C. RENFREW *Approaches to social archaeology,* Edinburgh: Edinburgh University Press. 258-82.

RENFREW, C. (1984b) The Multiplier Effect in action, in C. RENFREW *Approaches to social archaeology,* Edinburgh: Edinburgh University Press. 283-308.

RENFREW, C. (1986) Varna and the emergence of wealth in prehistoric Europe, in A. APPADURAI (Ed.) *The social life of things : commodities in cultural perspective,* Cambridge: Cambridge University Press. 141-68.

RENFREW, C. (1993) Trade Beyond the Material, in C. J. SCARRE & F. HEALY (Eds.) *Trade and Exchange in Prehistoric Europe,* Oxford: Oxbow Books. 5-16.

RENFREW, C. (2005) Archaeology and commodification: the role of things in societal transformation, in W. M. J. V. BINSBERGEN & P. GESCHIERE (Eds.) *Commodification : Things, Agency, and Identities : (The Social Life of Things Revisited),* Münster: Lit. 85-97.

RENFREW, C. & BAHN, P. G. (2012) *Archaeology : theories, methods and practice,* (6th edition), London: Thames & Hudson.

RENFREW, C. & COOKE, K. L. (Eds.) (1979) *Transformations : mathematical approaches to culture change,* New York: Academic Press.

RENNER, F. B. (1982) *Beiträge zur Gletschergeschichte des Gotthardgebietes und dendroklimatologische Analysen an fossilen Hölzern,* Zürich: Geographisches Institut Universität Zürich.

RIEK, G. (1962) *Der Hohmichele : ein Fürstengrabhügel der späten Hallstattzeit bei der Heuneburg,* Berlin: Walter de Gruyter.

RIGERT, E. (1997) *Die spätbronzezeitliche Siedlung Sursee "Landzunge" bei Mariazell (Kanton Luzern) : Auswertung der Befunde und des Fundmaterials der archäologischen Ausgrabung von 1991,* Basel: Univ.

ŘÍHOVSKÝ, J. (1972) *Das Messer in Mähren und dem Ostalpengebiet,* Prähistorische Bronzefunde 7 / 1, München: Beck.

ŘÍHOVSKÝ, J. (1979) *Die Nadeln in Mähren und im Ostalpengebiet (von der mittleren Bronzezeit bis zur älteren Eisenzeit),* Prähistorische Bronzefunde 13 / 5, München: Beck.

RIND, M. M. (1999) *Der Frauenberg oberhalb Kloster Weltenburg I,* Regensburg: Universitätsverlag Regensburg.

RIVERS, W. H. R. (1910) The genealogical method of anthropological inquiry, *Sociological Review* 3 (1), 1-12.

RIVIÈRE, P. (1995) Houses, places and people: community and continuity in Guiana, in J. CARSTEN & S. HUGH-JONES (Eds.) *About the house : Lévi-Strauss and beyond,* Cambridge: Cambridge University Press. 189-205.

ROBINSON, G. (2013) Re-building memory, identity and place: the long term re-use of prehistoric settlements on the Isles of Scilly, in A. M. CHADWICK & C. D. GIBSON (Eds.) *Memory, myth and long-term landscape inhabitation*, Oxford: Oxbow Books. 146-64.

ROOS-BARRACLOUGH, F., VAN DER KNAAP, W. O., VAN LEEUWEN, J. F. N. & SHOTYK, W. (2004) A Late-glacial and Holocene record of climatic change from a Swiss peat humification profile, *The Holocene* 14 (1), 7-19.

ROYMANS, N. (1991) Late Urnfield Societies in the Northwest European Plain and the expanding networks of Central European Hallstatt Groups, in N. ROYMANS & F. THEUWS (Eds.) *Images of the past : studies on ancient societies in Northwestern Europe*, Amsterdam: Instituut voor Pre- en Protohistorische Archeologie. 9-89.

RUBAT BOREL, F. (2009) Entre Italie et Gaule: le Bronze Final et le Premier âge du Fer dans le Piémont nord-occidental et la Vallée d'Aoste, *Colloque International de l'Association Française pour l'Etude de l'Âge du Fer (A. F. E. A. F.) No. 30*, Dijon: Société archéologique de l'Est. 237-52.

RUCKSTUHL, B. (1989) Hallstattzeitliche Siedlungsgruben aus Neunkich-Tobeläcker (SH), *Jahrbuch der Schweizerischen Gesellschaft für Ur- und Frühgeschichte* 72, 59-98.

RUOFF, U. (1974) *Zur Frage der Kontinuität zwischen Bronze- und Eisenzeit in der Schweiz,* Basel: Schweizerische Gesellschaft für Ur- und Frühgeschichte.

RUOFF, U. (2004) Lake dwelling studies in Switzerland since 'Meilen 1854', in F. MENOTTI (Ed.) *Living on the lake in prehistoric Europe : 150 years of lake-dwelling research*, London: Routledge. 9-21.

RUOFF, U. (2006) 150 Jahre nach der Entdeckung der Pfahlbauten, in A. HAFNER, U. NIFFELER & U. RUOFF (Eds.) *Die neue Sicht : Unterwasserarchäologie und Geschichtsbild : Akten des 2. Internationalen Kongresses für Unterwasserarchäologie*, Basel: Archäologie Schweiz. 14-23.

RYCHNER-FARAGGI, A.-M. (1993) *Hauterive-Champréveyres 9: Métal et parure au Bronze final,* Neuchâtel: Musée cantonal d'archéologie.

RYCHNER, V. (1979) *L'âge du bronze final à Auvernier (Lac de Neuchâtel, Suisse) : typologie et chronologie des anciennes collections conservées en Suisse,* Lausanne: Bibliothèque historique vaudoise.

RYCHNER, V. (1984) La matière première des bronziers lacustres, *Archäologie der Schweiz* 7 (2), 73-78.

RYCHNER, V. (1987) *Auvernier 1968-1975, le mobilier métallique du Bronze final : formes et techniques,* Lausanne: Bibliothèque historique vaudoise.

RYCHNER, V. (1998a) Geschichte und Kulturen der Bronzezeit in der Schweiz, in S. HOCHULI, U. NIFFELER & V. RYCHNER (Eds.) *SPM III Bronzezeit: Die Schweiz vom Paläolithikum bis zum frühen Mittelalter*, Basel: Verlag Schweizerische Gesellschaft für Ur- und Frühgeschichte. 103-32.

RYCHNER, V. (1998b) Spätbronzezeit, in S. HOCHULI, U. NIFFELER & V. RYCHNER (Eds.) *SPM III Bronzezeit: Die Schweiz vom Paläolithikum bis zum frühen Mittelalter*, Basel: Verlag Schweizerische Gesellschaft für Ur- und Frühgeschichte. 70-79.

RYCHNER, V. (2001) Objects "manipulés" des Palafittes de Suisse Occidentale au Bronze Final : une première approche, *Revue archéologique de l'Ouest* supplément no. 9, 217-24.

SAHLINS, M. D. (1974) *Stone age economics,* London: Tavistock.

SALZANI, L. (2009) Rovigo. Notizie preliminari sulle ricerche nel sito dell'età del Bronzo di Grignano Polesine, *Quaderni di archeologia del Veneto* 25, 37-39.

SALZANI, L. & COLONNA, C. (2010) *la Fragilità dell'Urna: I recenti scavi a Narde Necropoli di Frattesina (XII-IX sec. a.C.),* Rovigo: Soprintendenza per i beni archeologici del Veneto.

SANTI, P., RENZULLI, A., ANTONELLI, F. & ALBERTI, A. (2009) Classification and provenance of soapstones and garnet chlorite schist artifacts from Medieval sites of Tuscany (Central Italy): insights into the Tyrrhenian and Adriatic trade, *Journal of Archaeological Science* 36 (11), 2493-501.

SARBACH, H. (1959) Neue mittel- und spätbronzezeitliche funde von Spiez (Berner Oberland), *Jahrbuch des Bernischen Historischen Museums in Bern* 37-38 (1957-1958), 239-48.

SARBACH, H. (1966) Die Wallanlage Grasburg-Schlössli, *Jahrbuch des Bernischen Historischen Museums in Bern* 43 - 44 (1963 - 1964), 461-70.

SAUNDERS, N. J. (1999) Biographies of Brilliance: Pearls, Transformations of Matter and being, c. AD 1492, in C. GOSDEN & Y. MARSHALL (Eds.) *The cultural biography of objects*, World Archaeology Vol. 31.2, London: Routledge. 243-57.

SCHAUER, P. (1971) *Die Schwerter in Süddeutschland, Oesterreich und der Schweiz I : (Griffplatten-, Griffangel- und Griffzungenschwerter)*, Prähistorische Bronzefunde 4 / 2, München: Beck.

SCHAUER, P. (1995) Stand und Aufgaben der Urnenfelderforschung in Süddeutschland, in RÖMISCH-GERMANISCHES ZENTRALMUSEUM MAINZ (Ed.) *Beiträge zur Urnenfelderzeit nördlich und südlich der Alpen*, Bonn: Rudolf Habelt. 121-99.

SCHIBLER, J., BREITENLECHNER, E., DESCHLER-ERB, S., GOLDENBERG, G., HANKE, K., HIEBEL, G., PLOGMANN, H. H., NICOLUSSI, K., MARTI-GRÄDEL, E., PICHLER, S., SCHMIDL, A., SCHWARZ, S., STOPP, B. & OEGGL, K. (2011) Miners and mining in the Late Bronze Age: a multidisciplinary study from Austria, *Antiquity* 85 (330), 1259-78.

SCHIBLER, J. & CHAIX, L. (1995) Wirtschaftliche Entwicklung aufgrund archäozoologischer Daten, in W. E. STÖCKLI, U. NIFFELER & E. GROSS-KLEE (Eds.) *SPM II Neolithikum: Die Schweiz vom Paläolithikum bis zum frühen Mittelalter*, Basel: Verlag Schweizerische Gesellschaft für Ur- und Frühgeschichte. 97-118.

SCHIFFER, M. B. (1996) *Formation processes of the archaeological record,* Salt Lake City: University of Utah Press.

SCHINDLER, C. (1971) Geologie von Zürich und ihre Beziehung zu Seespiegelschwankungen, *Vierteljahrsschrift der Naturforschenden Gesellschaft in Zürich* 116 (2), 285-315.

SCHLICHTHERLE, H. (1995) Bemerkungen zur Siedlungsstruktur der Feuchtbodensiedlungen im Südwestdeutschen Alpenvorland, in A. ASPES (Ed.) *Settlement patterns between the Alps and the Black Sea 5th to 2nd Millennium B.C.*, Verona: Museo Civico di Storia Naturale di Verona. 251-59.

SCHLICHTHERLE, H. (1997) Pfahlbauten rund um die Alpen, in H. SCHLICHTHERLE (Ed.) *Pfahlbauten rund um die Alpen*, Stuttgart: Theiss. 7-15.

SCHLICHTHERLE, H. (2002) Prähistorische Siedlungen, Bohlenwege und Fischfanganlagen. Fortschritte der archäologischen Federseeforschung, *Denkmalpflege in Baden-Württemberg* 31, 115-21.

SCHLICHTHERLE, H. (2004) Lake dwellings in south west Germany: history of research and contemporary perspectives, in F. MENOTTI (Ed.) *Living on the lake in prehistoric Europe : 150 years of lake-dwelling research*, London: Routledge. 22-35.

SCHLICHTHERLE, H. (2009) Eine neue Siedlungskammer im westlichen Federseeried und ihre Bedeutung für das Verständnis neolithischer Siedelsysteme, in J. BIEL, J. HEILIGMANN & D. KRAUSSE (Eds.) *Landesarchäologie: Festschrift für Dieter Planck zum 65. Geburtstag*, Stuttgart: Forschungen und Berichte zur Vor- und Frühgeschichte in Baden-Württemberg. 61-86.

SCHLICHTHERLE, H. & STROBEL, M. (Eds.) (1999) *Archaeology and Protection of Nature in the Federsee Bog*, Stuttgart: Landesdenkmalamt Baden-Württemberg.

SCHMID-SIKIMIĆ, B. (1995) Wo sind die Männer geblieben? Bemerkungen zur geschlechtsspezifischen Ausstatting hallstattzeitlicher Gräber, in B. SCHMID-SIKIMIĆ, P. DELLA CASA & M. PRIMAS (Eds.) *Trans Europam : Beiträge zur Bronze- und Eisenzeit zwischen Atlantik und Altai : Festschrift für Margarita Primas*, Bonn: Rudolf Habelt. 169-89.

SCHMID-SIKIMIĆ, B. (1996) *Der Arm- und Beinschmuck der Hallstattzeit in der Schweiz : mit einem Anhang der Gürtelhaken und Gürtelgehänge der Hallstattzeit im Schweizerischen Mittelland, Jura und Wallis*, Prähistorische Bronzefunde 10 / 5, Stuttgart: Franz Steiner Verlag.

SCHMIDHEINY, M. (2006) *Zürich-Mozartstrasse (ZH) : die frühbronzezeitliche Besiedlung,* Zürich / Egg: FO-publishing.

SCHNEKENBURGER, G. (2002) *Über die Alpen : Menschen Wege Waren,* Stuttgart: Theiss.

SCHÖBEL, G. (1992) Die Pfahlbauten von Unteruhldingen, *Plattform* 1, 9-23.

SCHÖBEL, G. (1996) Die Spätbronzezeit am nordwestlichen Bodensee. Taucharchäologische Untersuchungen in Hagnau und Unteruhldingen 1982-1989, in G. SCHÖBEL (Ed.) *Siedlungsarchäologie im Alpenvorland IV*, Stuttgart: Konrad Theiss Verlag. 9-202.

SCHWAB, H. (1961) Oberburg, *Jahrbuch des Bernischen Historischen Museums in Bern* 39-40 (1959-1960), 335.

SCHWAB, H. (1982) La necropole de l'age du bronze a Vuadens/Le Briez, *histoire et archéologie: les dossiers* 62 (April), 36-41.

SCHWEIZERISCHES LANDESMUSEUM (2004) *Die Pfahlbauer : 150 Objekte erzählen 150 Geschichten : Begleitband zur Ausstellung im Schweizerischen Landesmuseum Zürich,* Zürich: Schweizerisches Landesmuseum.

SEIFERT, M. (1996) Der archäologische Befund von Zug-Sumpf, in REGIERUNGSRAT DES KANTONS ZUG (Ed.) *Die Dorfgeschichte,* Zug: Kantonales Museum für Urgeschichte Zug. 1-197.

SEIFERT, M. (1997) *Die Funde der Grabungen 1952-54,* Zug: Kantonales Museum für Urgeschichte Zug.

SHANKS, M. (1998) The life of an artifact in an interpretive archaeology, *Fennoscandia Archaeologica* 15, 15-30.

SHANKS, M. (2001) Culture/Archaeology: The Dispersion of a Discipline and its Objects, in I. HODDER (Ed.) *Archaeological Theory Today,* Cambridge: Polity. 284-305.

SHANKS, M. & TILLEY, C. Y. (1992) *Re-constructing archaeology : theory and practice,* (2nd edition), Cambridge: Cambridge University Press.

SHARPLES, N. M. (2007) Building communities and creating identities in the first millenium B.C, in C. HASELGROVE & R. POPE (Eds.) *The earlier Iron Age in Britain and the near continent,* Oxford: Oxbow Books. 174-84.

SHARPLES, N. M. (2010) *Social relations in later prehistory : Wessex in the first millennium BC,* Oxford: Oxford University Press.

SHEFTON, B. B. (2000) On the material in its northern setting, in W. KIMMIG (Ed.) *Importe und mediterrane Einflüsse auf der Heuneburg,* Mainz am Rhein: Philipp von Zabern. 27-41.

SHENNAN, S. J. (1982) Exchange and ranking: the role of amber in the earlier bronze age of Europe, in C. RENFREW & S. SHENNAN (Eds.) *Ranking, resource, and exchange : aspects of the archaeology of early European society,* Cambridge: Cambridge University Press. 33-45.

SHENNAN, S. J. (Ed.) (2009) *Pattern and process in cultural evolution,* Berkeley: University of California Press.

SHERIDAN, A. & DAVIS, M. (1998) The Welsh 'Jet Set' in Prehistory: a Case of Keeping Up with the Joneses?, in A. GIBSON & A. BURL (Eds.) *Prehistoric ritual and religion,* Stroud: Sutton Publishing. 148-62.

SHERIDAN, A. & DAVIS, M. (2002) Investigating jet and jet-like artefacts from Prehistoric Scotland: the National Museums of Scotland project, *Antiquity* 76 (293), 812-25.

SHERRATT, A. (1993) What would a Bronze Age World System look like?, *European Journal of Archaeology* 1 (2), 1-57.

SHERRATT, A. (1996) Why Wessex? The Avon Route and River Transport in Later British Prehistory, *Oxford Journal of Archaeology* 15 (2), 211-34.

SHERRATT, A. (1998) The Human Geography of Europe: A Prehistoric Perspective, in R. A. BUTLIN & R. A. DODGSHON (Eds.) *An historical geography of Europe*, Oxford: Clarendon Press. 1-25.

SHERRATT, S. (2010) Greeks and Phoenicians: Perceptions of Trade and Traders in the Early First Millennium BC, in A. A. BAUER & A. S. AGBE-DAVIES (Eds.) *Social Archaeologies of Trade and Exchange: Exploring Relationships among People, Places, and Things*, California: West Cost Press. 119-42.

SHERRATT, S. & SHERRATT, A. (1993) The Growth of the Mediterranean Economy in the Early First Millennium B.C., *World archaeology* 24 (3), 361-78.

SIEDLUNGSARCHÄOLOGIE IM ALPENVORLAND XI (Ed.) (2009) *Die früh- und mittelbronzezeitliche "Siedlung Forschner" im Federseemoor. Befunde und Dendrochronologie*, Stuttgart: Konrad Theiss.

SIEVERS, S. (1982) *Die mitteleuropäischen Hallstattdolche*, Prähistorische Bronzefunde 6 / 6, München: C. H. Beck.

SIEVERS, S., DRESCHER, H. & ROCHNA, O. (1984) *Die Kleinfunde der Heuneburg : die Funde aus den Grabungen von 1950-1979,* Mainz/Rh: Philipp von Zabern.

SIMMEL, G. (1978) *The Philosophy of Money,* London: Routledge.

SKEATES, R. (1995) Animate objects: a biography of prehistoric 'axe-amulets' in the central Mediterranean region, *Proceedings of the Prehistoric Society* 61, 279-301.

SKEATES, R. (2009) Trade and Interaction, in B. W. CUNLIFFE, C. GOSDEN & R. A. JOYCE (Eds.) *The Oxford handbook of archaeology*, Oxford: Oxford University Press. 555-78.

SNODGRASS, A. M. (1980) Iron and Early Metallurgy in the Mediterranean, in T. A. WERTIME & J. D. MUHLY (Eds.) *The coming of the age of iron*, New Haven: Yale University Press. 335-74.

SOMMERFELD, C. (1994) *Gerätegeld Sichel : Studien zur monetären Struktur bronzezeitlicher Horte im nördlichen Mitteleuropa,* Berlin: Walter de Gruyter.

SØRENSEN, M. L. S. (1987) Material order and cultural classification: the role of bronze objects in the transition from Bronze Age to Iron Age in Scandinavia, in I. HODDER (Ed.) *The Archaeology of contextual meanings*, Cambridge: Cambridge University Press. 90-101.

SPECK, J. (1955) Ausgrabungen in der spätbronzezeitlichen Ufersiedlung Zug-Sumpf, in W. U. GUYAN (Ed.) *Das Pfahlbauproblem*, Basel: Birkhäuser. 275-334.

SPECK, J. (1981a) Frühes Eisen in den Ufersiedlungen der Spätbronzezeit, *Helvetia Archaeologica* 45/48, 265-71.

SPECK, J. (1981b) Pfahlbauten: Dichtung oder Wahrheit? Ein Querschnitt durch 125 Jahre Forschungsgeschichte, *Helvetia Archaeologica* 45/48, 98-138.

SPECK, J. (1981c) Schloss und Schlüssel zur späten Pfahlbauzeit, *Helvetia Archaeologica* 45/48, 230-41.

SPINDLER, K. (1996) *Die frühen Kelten,* Stuttgart: Philipp Reclam jun.

SPINDLER, K. (2001) *The Man in the Ice: The Preserved Body of a Neolithic Man Reveals the Secrets of the Stone Age,* London: Phoenix.

SPRIGGS, M. (2008) Ethnographic parallels and the denial of history, *World archaeology* 40 (4), 538 - 52.

SPROCKHOFF, E. (1951) Pfahlbaubronzen in der Südzone des Nordischen Kreises während der jüngeren Bronzezeit, *Archaeologica Geographica* 2 (3/4), 120-28.

SPROCKHOFF, E. (1966) Ein Geschenk aus dem Norden, in R. DEGEN, W. DRACK & R. WYSS (Eds.) *Helvetia antiqua : Festschrift Emil Vogt : Beiträge zur Prähistorie und Archäologie der Schweiz,* Zürich: Conzett und Huber. 101-10.

STAHL, C. (2006) *Mitteleuropäische Bernsteinfunde von der Frühbronze- bis zur Frühlatènezeit : ihre Verbreitung, Formgebung, Zeitstellung und Herkunft,* Dettelbach: J.H. Röll.

STAMPOLIDIS, N. C. (Ed.) (2003) *Sea routes ... from Sidon to Huelva : interconnections in the Mediterranean 16th - 6th c.BC,* Athens: Museum of Cycladic Art.

STARY, P. F. (1995) Rohstoffe im früheisenzeitlichen Nord-Süd-Handel, *Münstersche Beiträge zur antiken Handelgeschichte* 14 (1), 82-108.

STAUFFER-ISENRING, L. & KAUFMANN, B. (1983) *Die Siedlungsreste von Scuol-Munt Baselgia (Unterengadin GR) : ein Beitrag zur inneralpinen Bronze- und Eisenzeit,* Basel: Verlag Schweizerische Gesellschaft für Ur- und Frühgeschichte Basel.

STEIN, F. (1979) *Katalog der vorgeschichtlichen Hortfunde in Süddeutschland,* Bonn: Habelt.

STEIN, G. J. (2002) From Passive Periphery to Active Agents: Emerging Perspectives in the Archaeology of Interregional Interaction, *American Anthropologist* 104 (3), 903-16.

STEINHAUSER-ZIMMERMANN, R. A. (1989) *Der Montlingerberg im Kanton St. Gallen (Schweiz) : Funde und Grabungen von 1898 bis 1960,* Buchs: Amt für Kulturpflege des Kantons St. Gallen.

STEINHAUSER-ZIMMERMANN, R. A. (2002) Früher Handel mit Luxusgütern auf dem Montlingerberg im St. Galler Rheintal, in G. SCHNEKENBURGER (Ed.) *Über die Alpen : Menschen - Wege - Waren,* Stuttgart: Theiss. 169-74.

STEINHAUSER, R. A. & PRIMAS, M. (1987) Der Bernsteinfund vom Montlingerberg (Kt. St. Gallen, Schweiz), *Germania* 65, 203-14.

STÖCKLI, W. E. (2000) Die Besiedlungsgeschichte der Baarburg (Gemeinde Baar, Kanton Zug). Unter besonderer Berücksichtigung der Resultate der Prospektion mit einem Metallsuchgerät im Jahre 1997, *Jahrbuch der Schweizerischen Gesellschaft für Ur- und Frühgeschichte* 83, 7-24.

STRAHM, C. (1997) Chronologie der Pfahlbauten, in H. SCHLICHTHERLE (Ed.) *Pfahlbauten rund um die Alpen,* Stuttgart: Theiss. 124-26.

STRATHERN, M. (1988) *The gender of the gift : problems with women and problems with society in Melanesia,* Berkeley: University of California Press.

STRATHERN, M. (1991) One man and many men, in M. GODELIER & M. STRATHERN (Eds.) *Big men and great men : personifications of power in Melanesia*, Cambridge: Cambridge University Press. 197-214.

STROBEL, P. (1874) Intorno all'origine delle terramare, *Archivio per l'Antropologia e l'Etnologia* IV, 1-19.

SULLIVAN, A. P. (1978) Inference and Evidence in Archaeology: A Discussion of the Conceptual Problems, in M. B. SCHIFFER (Ed.) *Advances in Archaeological Method and Theory*, Vol. 1, New York: Academic Press. 183-222.

SULLIVAN, L. H. (1896) The tall office building artistically considered, *Lippincott's Magazine* 1896 (March), 403-09.

SUTER, P. J., JACOMET, S., RICHTER, B., SCHIBLER, J. & SCHUBERT, P. (1987) *Zürich "Kleiner Hafner" : Tauchgrabungen 1981-1984,* Zürich: Fotorotar AG.

SUTER, P. J. & SCHLICHTHERLE, H. (2009) *Pfahlbauten : UNESCO Welterbe-Kandidatur "Prähistorische Pfahlbauten rund um die Alpen",* Bern: Palafittes, Archäologischer Dienst des Kantons Bern.

SZABÓ, G. & SZÓNÓKY, M. (2002) Experimental data on the trade of raw materials in Europe during the Late Bronze Age, in E. JEREM & K. T. BIRÓ (Eds.) *Archaeometry 98 : proceedings of the 31st symposium*, Oxford: Archaeopress. 267-72.

TACKENBERG, K. (1971) *Die jüngere Bronzezeit in Nordwestdeutschland,* Hildesheim: Lax.

TEHRANI, J. J., COLLARD, M. & SHENNAN, S. J. (2010) The cophylogeny of populations and cultures: reconstructing the evolution of Iranian tribal craft traditions using trees and jungles, *Philosophical Transactions of the Royal Society of London (B) on Cultural and Linguistic Diversity* 365 (1559), 3865-74.

TERŽAN, B. (2004) L'aristocrazia femminile nella prima età del Ferro, in F. MARZATICO & P. GLEIRSCHER (Eds.) *Guerrieri, principi ed eroi fra il Danubio e il Po dalla Preistoria all'Alto Medioevo*, Trento: Castello del Buonconsiglio. 221-29.

TERŽAN, B., MIHOVILIĆ, K. & HÄNSEL, B. (1999) Eine protourbane Siedlung der älteren Bronzezeit im istrischen Karst, *Praehistorische Zeitschrift* 74, 154-93.

TEXETERA (2011) *Palafittes Guide*; available online at *http://www.texetera.ch/deutsch/referenzen/outdoor/palafittes-guide.* [accessed 09-07-2014].

THOMAS, J. (2013) Mounds, memories and myths: ancient monuments and place in the Leicestershire landscape, in A. M. CHADWICK & C. D. GIBSON (Eds.) *Memory, myth and long-term landscape inhabitation*, Oxford: Oxbow Books. 76-98.

THOMAS, N. (1991) *Entangled objects : exchange, material culture, and colonialism in the Pacific,* Cambridge (Mass.): Harvard University Press.

THRANE, H. (1975) *Europaeiske forbindelser : bidrag til studiet af fremmede forbindelser i Danmarks yngre broncealder (periode IV-V),* København: Nationalmuseet.

THURSTON, T. (2009) Unity and Diversity in the European Iron Age: Out of the Mists, Some Clarity?, *Journal of Archaeological Research* 17 (4), 347-423.

TILLEY, C. Y. (1982) Social formation, social structures and social change, in I. HODDER (Ed.) *Symbolic and structural archaeology*, Cambridge: Cambridge University Press. 26-38.

TILLEY, C. Y. (1996) *An ethnography of the Neolithic: early prehistoric societies in southern Scandinavia,* Cambridge: Cambridge University Press.

TILLEY, C. Y. (2010) *Interpreting Lanscapes: Geologies, Topographies, Identities,* Walnut Creek (California): Left Coast Press.

TOMEDI, G. (2002) Zur Emblematik der späten Bronzezeit und der frühen Eisenzeit im alpinen Raum, in L. ZEMMER-PLANK (Ed.) *Kult der Vorzeit in den Alpen : Opfergaben - Opferplätze - Opferbrauchtum*, Bozen: Athesia. 1211-35.

TORBRÜGGE, W. (1959) *Vor- und Frühgeschichte in Stadt und Landkreis Rosenheim,* Rosenheim

TORBRÜGGE, W. (1965) *Die Hallstattzeit in der Oberpfalz,* Kallmünz/Opf.: Lassleben.

TORBRÜGGE, W. (1972) Vor- und frühgeschichtliche Flußfunde. Zur Ordnung und Bestimmung einer Denkmälergruppe, *Bericht der Römisch-Germanischen Kommission* 51-52 (1970-1971), 1-145.

TRACHSEL, M. (2004) *Untersuchungen zur relativen und absoluten Chronologie der Hallstattzeit,* Bonn: Rudolf Habelt.

TRIFKOVIĆ, V. (2005) *Construction of space in early Holocene Iron Gates*, unpublished thesis for D.Phil, Archaeology, (University of Oxford).

TRIGGER, B. G. (2004) Cross-Cultural Comparison and Archaeological Theory, in L. MESKELL & R. W. PREUCEL (Eds.) *A companion to social archaeology*, Oxford: Blackwell. 43-65.

TRINGHAM, R. (2000) The Continuous House. A view from the deep past, in R. A. JOYCE & S. D. GILLESPIE (Eds.) *Beyond kinship : social and material reproduction in house societies*, Philadelphia: University of Pennsylvania Press. 115-34.

TSCHUMI, O. (1934) Beiträge zur Siedlungsgeschichte des Kantons Bern. Nr. 11, *Jahrbuch des Bernischen Historischen Museums in Bern* 13 (1933), 66-73.

TSCHUMI, O. (1935) Verschiedene Ausgrabungen, *Jahrbuch des Bernischen Historischen Museums in Bern* 15, 71-75.

TSCHUMI, O. (1937) Die Ausgrabungen der bronzezeitlichen Höhensiedlung und -Festung "Bürg" bei Faulensee, Gemeinde Spiez, *Jahrbuch des Bernischen Historischen Museums in Bern* 16 (1936), 51-52.

TSCHUMI, O. (1938) *Die Ur- und Frühgeschichte des Simmentals,* Bern: Haupt.

TSCHUMI, O. (1953) *Urgeschichte des Kantons Bern (alter Kantonsteil) : Einführung und Fundstatistik bis 1950,* Bern / Stuttgart: Huber.

UNZ, C. (1973) Die spätbronzezeitliche Keramik in Südwestdeutschland, in der Schweiz und in Ostfrankreich, *Prähistorische Zeitschrift* 48, 1-124.

URBAN, G. (2010) Objects, Social Relations, and Cultural Motion, in A. A. BAUER & A. S. AGBE-DAVIES (Eds.) *Social Archaeologies of Trade and Exchange: Exploring Relationships among People, Places, and Things*, California: West Coast Press. 207-25.

VAGNETTI, L. (1999) Mycenaean pottery in the central Mediterranean: imports and local production in their context, in J. P. CRIELAARD, V. STISSI & G. J. VAN WIJNGAARDEN (Eds.) *The complex past of pottery : production, circulation and consumption of Mycenaen and Greek pottery (sixteenth to early fifth centuries BC) : proceedings of the ARCHON international conference*, Amsterdam: J. C. Gieben. 137-61.

VAN DYKE, R. M. & ALCOCK, S. E. (2003) Archaeologies of Memory: An Introduction, in R. M. VAN DYKE & S. E. ALCOCK (Eds.) *Archaeologies of memory*, Oxford: Blackwell. 1-13.

VAN GEEL, B., BUURMAN, J. & WATERBOLK, H. T. (1996) Archaeological and palaeoecological indications of an abrupt climate change in The Netherlands, and evidence for climatological teleconnections around 2650 BP, *Journal of Quaternary Science* 11 (6), 451-60.

VAN GEEL, B. & MAGNY, M. (2002) Mise en évidence d'un forçage solaire du climat á partir de données paléoécologiques et archéologiques: la transition Subboréal-Subatlantique, in H. RICHARD & A. VIGNOT (Eds.) *Équilibres et ruptures dans les écosystèmes durant les 20 derniers millénaires en Europe de l'Ouest*, Besançon: Presses Universitaires Fromc-Comtoises. 107-22.

VAN WILLIGEN, S. (2011) 3.48. Chiave, in F. MARZATICO, R. GEBHARD & P. GLEIRSCHER (Eds.) *Le grandi vie delle civiltà : relazioni e scambi fra Mediterraneo e il centro Europa dalla preistoria alla romanità*, Trento: Castello del Buonconsiglio, Monumenti e collezioni provinciali. 476.

VENCLOVÁ, N. (1983) Prehistoric Eye Beads in Central Europe, *Journal of Glass Studies* 25, 11-17.

VIANELLO, A. (2005) *Late Bronze Age Mycenaean and Italic products in the West Mediterranean : a social and economic analysis,* Oxford: Archaeopress.

VIGNEAU, H. & BOISAUBERT, J.-L. (2008) Châbles/Les Biolleyres 1, in J.-L. BOISAUBERT, D. BUGNON & M. MAUVILLY (Eds.) *Archéologie et autoroute A1, destins croisés : 25 années de fouilles en terres fribourgeoises, premier bilan (1975-2000)*, Fribourg: Service archéologique de l'Etat de Fribourg. 277-89.

VIOLLIER, D., SULZBERGER, K., SCHERER, P., EMANUEL, SCHLAGINHAUFEN, O., HESCHELER, K. & NEUWEILER, E. (1924) *Pfahlbauten, zehnter Bericht*, Mitteilungen der Antiquarischen Gesellschaft in Zürich, Zürich: Leemann.

VITAL, J. (1992) Du IXe au VIIe siècle av. J.-C. dans le Jura méridional: scénario d'évolution culturelle, in G. KAENEL & P. CURDY (Eds.) *L'âge du Fer dans le Jura : actes du 15e colloque de l'Association française pour l'étude sur l'âge du Fer*, Lausanne: Bibliothèque historique vaudoise. 163-80.

VITAL, J. (1993) *Habitats et sociétés du Bronze final au Premier Age du Fer dans le Jura : les occupations protohistoriques et néolithiques du Pré de la Cour à Montagnieu (Ain),* Paris: CNRS Editions.

VITAL, J. & VORUZ, J.-L. (1984) *L'habitat protohistorique de Bavois-en-Raillon (Vaud),* Lausanne: Bibliothèque historique vaudoise.

VOGT, E. (1931) Die ältesten Schlüssel, *Germania* 15 (1), 142-45.

VOGT, E. (1951) Das steinzeitliche Uferdorf Egolzwil 3 (Kt. Luzern). Bericht über die Ausgrabung 1950, *Zuschrift für Schweizerische Archäologie und Kunstgeschichte* 12, 193-219.

VOGT, E. (1952) Der Zierstil der späten Pfahlbaubronzen, *Zeitschrift für Schweizerische Archäologie und Kunstgeschichte* 4, 193-206.

VOGT, E. & GUYAN, W. U. (1977) *Schriften zum Neolithikum : Chronologie und Pfahlbaufrage,* Frauenfeld: Huber.

VON FREEDEN, U. & VON SCHNURBEIN, S. (2002) *Spuren der Jahrtausende : Archäologie und Geschichte in Deutschland,* Stuttgart: Theiss.

VORLAUF, D. (1997) *Die etruskischen Bronzeschnabelkannen : eine Untersuchung anhand der technologisch-typologischen Methode,* Espelkamp: Verlag Marie Leidorf.

WAGNER, R. (1991) The fractal person, in M. GODELIER & M. STRATHERN (Eds.) *Big men and great men : personifications of power in Melanesia*, Cambridge: Cambridge University Press. 159-73.

WALSH, K. (2014) *The archaeology of Mediterranean landscapes : human-environment interaction from the Neolithic to the Roman period,* Cambridge: Cambridge University Press.

WEIDMANN, T. (1982) Keramische Gussformen aus der spätbronzezeitlichen Seerandsiedlung Zug "Sumpf", *Jahrbuch der Schweizerischen Gesellschaft für Ur- und Frühgeschichte* 65, 69-81.

WEIDMANN, T. (1983) Ein reicher Ringfund der Spätbronzezeit aus Sursee, *Helvetia Archaeologica* 55/56 (1), 179-92.

WEINER, A. B. (1992) *Inalienable possessions : the paradox of keeping-while-giving,* Berkeley: University of California Press.

WELLS, P. S. (1989) Intensification, Entrepreneurship, and Cognitive Change in the Bronze-Iron Age Transition, in M. L. S. SØRENSEN & R. THOMAS (Eds.) *The Bronze Age-Iron Age transition in Europe : aspects of continuity and change in European societies, c. 1200 to 500 B.C,* Vol. 1, Oxford: British Archaeological Reports (483). 173-83.

WELLS, P. S. (2007) Boundaries and identity in Early Iron Age Europe, in C. HASELGROVE & R. POPE (Eds.) *The earlier Iron Age in Britain and the near continent,* Oxford: Oxbow Books. 390-99.

WENZLER, J. K. (2001) *Die vorgeschichtliche Höhensiedlung Spiez-'Bürg', Kanton Bern : eine Auswertung unter besonderer Berücksichtigung der bronzezeitlichen Gefäßkeramik,* unpublished thesis for PhD in Alte Geschichte, Archäologie, (Freiburg im Breisgau).

WHEATLEY, D. (1995) Cumulative viewshed analysis: a GIS-based method for investigating intervisibility, and its archaeological application, in G. R. LOCK & Z. STANČIČ (Eds.) *Archaeology and geographical information systems : a European perspective,* London: Taylor and Francis. 171-86.

WHEATLEY, D. & GILLINGS, M. (2002) *Spatial technology and archaeology : the archaeological applications of GIS,* London: Taylor & Francis.

WHITLEY, J. (2002) Objects with Attitude: Biographical Facts and Fallacies in the Study of Late Bronze Age and Early Iron Age Warrior Graves, *Cambridge Archaeological Journal* 12 (02), 217-32.

WHITTAKER, H. (Ed.) (2008) *The Aegean Bronze Age in relation to the wider European context : papers from a session at the eleventh annual meeting of the European Association of Archaeologists, Cork, 5-11 September 2005*, Oxford: Archaeopress.

WHITTLE, A. (2003) *The archaeology of people : dimensions of Neolithic life,* London: Routledge.

WIEDMER-STERN, J. (1909) Die archäologische Abteilung, *Jahresbericht des Historischen Museums in Bern* 1909, 7-20.

WIEMANN, P., KÜHN, M., HEITZ-WENIGER, A., STOPP, B., JENNINGS, B., RENTZEL, P. & MENOTTI, F. (2012) Zurich-Alpenquai: A Multidisciplinary Approach to the Chronological Development of a Late Bronze Age Lakeside Settlement in the Northern Circum-Alpine Region, *Journal of Wetland Archaeology* 12, 58-85.

WIEMANN, P. & SCHERER, T. (2008) Freienbach SZ-Hurden Rosshorn: Ur- und frühgeschichtliche Wege und Brücken über den Zürichsee, *Jahrbuch der Archäologie Schweiz* 91, 7-38.

WIEMANN, P. & SCHERER, T. (2011) Furt, Weg, Steg, Brücke, Seedamm. Vor- und frühgeschichtliche Querungen des Zürichsees (Schweiz), in BAYERISCHE GESELLSCHAFT FÜR UNTERWASSERARCHÄOLOGIE (Ed.) *Archäologie der Brücken*, Regensburg: Pustet. 16-22.

WIENER, M. H. (1991) The nature and control of Minoan foreign trade, in N. H. GALE (Ed.) *Bronze Age Trade in the Mediterranean*, Göteborg: Paul Åström. 325-50.

WINGHART, S. (1998) Produktion, Verarbeitung und Distribution - Zur Rolle spätbronzezeitlicher Eliten im Alpenvorland, in B. HÄNSEL (Ed.) *Mensch und Umwelt in der Bronzezeit Europas*, Kiel: Oetker-Voges Verlag. 261-63.

WINGHART, S. (2000) Mining, processing and distribution of bronze: reflections on the organisation of metal supply between the northern Alps and the Danube region, in C. F. E. PARE (Ed.) *Metals make the world go round : the supply and circulation of metals in Bronze Age Europe*, Oxford: Oxbow Books. 151-59.

WINTER, L. (2008) From Diffusion to Interaction: connections between the Nordic area and Valcamonica during the First Millennium BC, in H. WHITTAKER (Ed.) *The Aegean Bronze Age in relation to the wider European context : papers from a session at the eleventh annual meeting of the European Association of Archaeologists, Cork, 5-11 September 2005*, Oxford: Archaeopress. 35-55.

WOODMAN, P. E. (2000) Beyond significant patterning, towards past intentions: the location of Orcadian chambered tombs, in C. E. BUCK, V. CUMMINGS, C. HENLEY, S. MILLS & S. TRICK (Eds.) *Proceedings of the UK chapter of Computer Applications and Quantitative Methods in Archaeology 1999*, Oxford: Archaeopress. 91-105.

WYSS, R. (1955) Funde aus der alten Zihl und ihre Deutung, *Germania* 33, 349-55.

WYSS, R. (1972) *Bronzezeitliches Töpferhandwerk*, Bern, Haupt.

WYSS, R. (1981) Archäologische Zeugnisse der Gaesaten, *Zeitschrift für Schweizerische Archäologie und Kunstgeschichte* 38 (4), 227-38.

WYSS, R. (1983) *Die jungsteinzeitlichen Bauerndörfer von Egolzwil 4 im Wauwilermoos,* Zürich: Schweizerisches Landesmuseum.

WYSS, R. (1990) Ein Netzbeutel zur Thematik des Fernhandels, in M. HÖNEISEN (Ed.) *Die ersten Bauern : Pfahlbaufunde Europas,* Vol. 1, Zürich: Schweizerisches Landesmuseum. 131-33.

ZANINI, A. & MARTINELLI, N. (2005) New data on the absolute chronology of the Late Bronze Age in central Italy, in R. LAFFINEUR (Ed.) *L'âge du bronze en Europe et en Méditerranée : sessions générales et posters / The bronze age in Europe and the Mediterranean : general sessions and posters. Actes du XIVème Congrès UISPP,* Oxford: Archaeopress. 147-55.

ZOLLER, H. (1977) Alter und Ausmass Postglazialer Klimaschwankungen in den Schweizer Alpen, in B. FRENZEL (Ed.) *Dendrochronologie und postglaziale Klimaschwankungen in Europa : Verhandlungen des Sympsoiums über die Dendrochronologie des Postglazials, Grundlagen und Ergebnisse,* Weisbaden: Franz Steiner Verlag. 271-81.